THE GREAT RISK SHIFT

The Great Risk Shift

The Assault on
American Jobs, Families,
Health Care, and Retirement
And How You Can Fight Back

Jacob S. Hacker

OXFORD
UNIVERSITY PRESS

2006

OXFORD
UNIVERSITY PRESS

Oxford University Press, Inc., publishes works that
further Oxford University's objective of excellence
in research, scholarship, and education.

Oxford   New York
Auckland   Cape Town   Dar es Salaam   Hong Kong   Karachi
Kuala Lumpur   Madrid   Melbourne   Mexico City   Nairobi
New Delhi   Shanghai   Taipei   Toronto

With offices in
Argentina   Austria   Brazil   Chile   Czech Republic   France   Greece
Guatemala   Hungary   Italy   Japan   Poland   Portugal   Singapore
South Korea   Switzerland   Thailand   Turkey   Ukraine   Vietnam

Copyright © 2006 by Jacob S. Hacker

Published by Oxford University Press, Inc.
198 Madison Avenue, New York, NY 10016
www.oup.com

Oxford is a registered trademark of Oxford University Press

Library of Congress Cataloging-in-Publication Data
Hacker, Jacob S.
The great risk shift : The assault on American jobs, families, health care, and
retirement and how you can fight back / Jacob S. Hacker.
p . cm.
ISBN-13: 978-0-19-517950-7
ISBN-10: 0-19-517950-1
1. Economic security—United States
2. United States—Economic conditions.
3. United States—Social policy.
I. Title.
HD7125.H24 2006
330.973—dc22
2006015484

9 8 7 6 5 4 3 2 1
Printed in the United States of America
on acid-free paper

To my mother and father

Contents

Preface

THE GREAT RISK SHIFT tells a story that more and more of us are coming to know and yet few of us still fully comprehend—the story of growing economic insecurity in the United States. The story is elusive for many reasons: It is so starkly at odds with our nation's evident prosperity. It reaches across so many different areas of our lives—our jobs, our families, our retirement, our health care. And it's a story we have heard only in terms of single issues: how we are more at risk of job layoffs than we once were, or how we are increasingly responsible for our own retirement, or how Health Savings Accounts might make us sole providers for our own health care. But while we know something larger is going on, we have no common language and few reliable indicators for linking these fragmented pieces together and understanding why they make us feel so insecure.

I wrote this book to change that. Using new evidence that unlocks the puzzle of growing insecurity, I show how more and more economic risk has been offloaded by government and corporations onto the increasingly fragile balance sheets of workers and their families. This fundamental transformation, which I call the "Great Risk Shift," has affected Americans of every walk of life, class standing, and political persuasion. It connects the insecurities of the new workplace, the strains facing modern families, the rising uncertainties of retirement, and the growing gaps in American health insurance. It is at the root of Americans' rising anxiety about their economic standing and future. And it is at the heart of the biggest debates over domestic policy that now dominate our polarized politics.

The Great Risk Shift is not just an economic change; it is also an ideological change. For decades, Americans and their government were committed to a powerful set of ideals—never wholly achieved, never without internal tension—that combined a commitment to economic security with a faith in economic opportunity. Animating this vision was a conviction that a strong economy and society hinged on basic financial security, on the guarantee that those who worked hard and did right by their families had a true safety net when disaster struck. Social Security, Medicare, private health insurance, traditional guaranteed pensions—all sent the same reassuring message: someone is watching out for you, *all of us are watching out for you*, when things go bad.

Today, the message is starkly different: *You are on your own.* Private employment-based health plans and pensions have eroded, or been radically transformed, to shift more and more risk onto workers' shoulders. Government programs of economic security have been cut, restructured, or simply allowed to grow ever more threadbare. Millions of Americans lack health insurance. Millions more lack guaranteed retirement benefits. Our jobs and our families are less and less financially secure.

And yet what do our political leaders tell us? They tell us we need to take "ownership" of our economic future, giving up the security of insurance in favor of individualized private accounts that leave us at the mercy of market instabilities precisely when we most need stability. They tell us that millions of middle-class Americans who are declaring bankruptcy or losing their houses are failing to take "personal responsibility" for their lives. They tell us the economy is "strong and getting stronger," when for most of us it has only grown more uncertain and insecure. Or they tell us, with a fatalism that scarcely befits a nation built on optimism and hope, that there is nothing that can be done. Our economy is insecure. Deal with it.

It is indeed time to deal with it. But the solution is not to shift more and more risk onto Americans' already burdened shoulders. I wrote this book because there is a real alternative to the Great Risk Shift, a vision that I call an "insurance and opportunity society." An insurance and opportunity society is based on a simple but powerful notion: We are most capable of fully participating in our economy and our society, most capable of taking risks and looking toward our future, when we have a basic foundation of financial security. Economic security is not opposed to economic opportunity; it is its cornerstone. And restoring a measure of economic security in the United States today is the key to transforming the nation's great wealth and productivity into an engine for broad-based prosperity and opportunity in an ever more uncertain economic world.

To see the future, however, we must first understand the past. For more than a decade, I have been studying the history and structure of America's distinctive framework of economic security: how it came into being, why it differs from what is found in other nations, what its strengths and weaknesses are, and how it can be made stronger. I have surveyed the experience of other nations and delved into our own conflicted history. I have amassed statistics and stories that show how our system of economic protection works, and why it sometimes works so poorly. I have talked with experts and everyday people about where we have come from and where me might yet go. And I have been shocked by how swiftly our framework of economic security is crumbling in the face of changing realities and fierce but largely misdirected criticism. If we do not make the investments necessary to build an insurance and opportunity society today, we will face far higher costs and far greater social dislocation in the years to come.

An insurance and opportunity society does not mean clinging stubbornly to institutions of the past when they no longer work. It does not mean insuring Americans against every contingency or ignoring the need for responsibility and thrift. What it calls on us

to do—all of us—is to reconstruct our framework of economic security on a new and stronger foundation for the twenty-first century,
so that every person stirred by the promise of this great nation can
have the confidence to reach for and achieve the American Dream.

THE GREAT RISK SHIFT

Introduction

On the Edge

ANDREA CASE PAUSES on the other end of the line to compliment her nine-year-old son, Jack, who is proudly displaying a handful of fish that he has dredged from the river that runs behind their suburban New Jersey home. Besides overseeing Jack's impromptu fishing expedition, Andrea is pushing her preschool-aged daughter on the swing, the phone against her ear. It's a now-common scene of modern middle-class motherhood: the multitasking mom managing two kids and an animated conversation at the same time. Yet Andrea's life isn't as tranquil as it seems, and the person on the other line isn't her husband or babysitter or friend. It's a researcher asking her about her recent experience with economic insecurity. And that researcher, competing with clamoring kids and gasping fish for Andrea Case's divided attention, is me.

I have called Andrea in response to an e-mail that she wrote me in January 2004, just after I published an op-ed for the *New York Times* arguing that American families were becoming more economically insecure. The op-ed was titled "Call It the Family Risk Factor," and what was perhaps most notable about the piece was the large line chart that appeared alongside the text (reprinted on the next page, in updated form, as figure 1). The chart, taking up a good chunk of the *Times* op-ed page, showed the post-1970s trajectory of an abstruse economic statistic: the volatility of American family incomes.[1]

Volatility is an accepted measure of the riskiness of stocks. Rather than showing the level of a stock's return, it shows how uncertain, or risky, those returns are likely to be. And what the skyrocketing line on the chart made clear, even to those unversed in statistics, is that the volatility of family incomes has gone up—way, way up. Americans have gotten richer in the last thirty years (though neither as quickly nor as evenly as commonly believed), but they have also faced rapidly growing economic insecurity. Family incomes now rise and fall ever more sharply. In fact, over the past generation the economic *instability* of American families has actually risen much faster than economic *inequality*—the growing gap between rich and poor that is often taken as a defining feature of the contemporary U.S. economy.

Figure 1: The Rising Volatility of American Family Incomes, 1974–2002

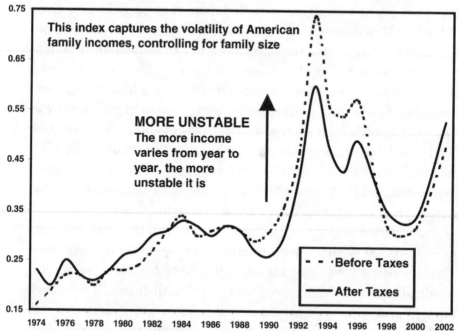

Source: *Panel Study of Income Dynamics, University of Michigan; Cross-National Equivalent File, Cornell University.*

I had hoped for some response to my op-ed. But writing about complex economic trends (with a graph, no less), I didn't have high hopes. I was wrong: The letters and e-mails poured in. Experts on pension plans wrote to tell me about the risks and challenges that retirement savings accounts like 401(k)s presented. Health policy specialists shared horror stories about the medically uninsured. Economists, including a Nobel laureate, inquired about my evidence.

But most gratifying—and troubling—were the responses from nonexperts who just wanted to share their experiences and views. There was Robert, who had tried to set up a health clinic for the working poor but then succumbed to an unexpected sickness and ended up living "four and a half years of sheer hell" trying to gain assistance from America's "safety net." There was Elizabeth, a well-educated consultant who said she "felt responsible for herself" but feared what would happen if either she or her husband were laid off, because, with two kids and unstable incomes, they hadn't been able to "save to the extent that we have a good safety net." There was the Yale undergraduate whose middle-class but chronically ill parents couldn't find a company that would even sell them a health care policy. There were tales of lost jobs and lost income, unexpected setbacks and unwelcome hardships. And then there was the graceful yet angry e-mail of Andrea Case.

"I am in one of the families of which you speak," Andrea's note began. Then she proceeded to explain how her husband, a computer engineer, and she had been slammed by the exploding tech bubble. They had watched for months as her husband's firm sank, both fearing his job would go down with it at any time. The family's earnings plummeted, but the bills just kept coming: the mortgage payments for their new house, the tuition for the Montessori school they'd enrolled their son in because he had learning problems, statements for the gas, electric, telephone, car, and on and on. In the space of a few months they had gone from taking their lives—and smooth upward path—for granted to worrying about paying the utilities. Their income dropped by more than a third. Andrea went from sleeping soundly to lying awake asking herself tough questions. Should they pull their son from the school? Sell the house?

Should Andrea go back to work—and if so, full time? What about health care? Her husband had eventually jumped to a lower-paying job, but under its stingy health plan, the family had to pay nearly $10,000 in health premiums and out-of-pocket medical costs.

Their freefall stopped when her husband found another position with better benefits, though even lower pay. Yet Andrea still did not feel secure, and she didn't know where to turn. "Who is the candidate for people like me?" her e-mail closed.

> Where is the AARP for families? I feel like we need the equivalent of the Million Mom March to let candidates know that parents with young children are hurting. How can busy, overwhelmed parents be educated and motivated? How can we have our voice heard above those of huge PACs and corporations? I know this is nearly a rant, but I am angry and frustrated and don't know where to turn to be effective in getting the leadership this country needs.

WHEN I FINALLY CATCH UP WITH ANDREA on the phone almost two years later, she is still angry but mostly resigned. She has gone back to work, doing two part-time jobs for extra money—a stint at Barnes and Noble for "incredibly low pay" and no benefits, and a Saturday job at her son's Montessori school. But despite having a master's degree from Harvard, she knows she's off the "career track for a while." Her husband's hours and income have improved, but the family is still stretched thin. Their lives changed in an instant, but the road back has been slow. The recovery still isn't complete.

To Andrea, the shift now stands as a painful marker in her life, a branching point in her hopes and outlook. "Up until then," she explains, speaking of the plummet in her husband's earnings, "everything exceeded our expectations." Out of college, they were riding the upward tide of the tech economy. Their combined income was high enough to allow them to move out of a Manhattan apartment near Battery Park, just a few blocks from the World Trade Center, into a three-bedroom, two-bath home on a cul-de-sac in suburban New Jersey—nothing as spectacular as the big homes with granite kitchens nearby, but grand compared with their old apartment. It also allowed Andrea to leave work to have kids. Then, the stock-market bubble burst, the 9/11 attacks occurred, her husband's firm started shedding workers, his pay dropped sharply. Everything seemed to come undone at once, and the low seemed all the lower because the high had been so high.

The low seemed lower, too, because their situation was at odds with everything they'd been told: Here they were, college-educated, frugal, responsible—and suddenly facing a very different life than they'd had or thought they'd have. In an instant everything had changed. It was as if their old life had been swept away by a hurricane.

ECONOMIC RISK is a lot like a hurricane. Hurricanes strike powerfully and suddenly. They rip apart what they touch: property, landscape, and lives. They are common enough to affect many, yet rare enough still to shock. And although they can be prepared for, they cannot be prevented. Some people will inevitably suffer and require help; others will be spared. Recovery is inevitably traumatic and slow. And so it is with families whose lives have been touched by economic risk. What happens in an instant may change a life forever.

The comparison is not just metaphorical: For more than half a century, Americans responded to economic risk as if it were a natural disaster largely beyond the control or responsibility of those it struck.[2] In the wake of the Great Depression in the 1930s, which left a "third of the nation," in FDR's famous telling, "ill-housed, ill-clad, ill-nourished," political and business leaders put in place new institutions designed to spread broadly the burden of key economic risks, including the risk of poverty in retirement, the risk of unemployment and disability, and the risk of widowhood due to the premature death of a breadwinner.[3] These public and private institutions did not let the individual off the hook; they required contributions and work and proof of eligibility. But they were based on an ideal known as "social insurance"—the notion that certain risks can be effectively dealt with only through institutions that spread their costs across rich and poor, healthy and sick, able-bodied and disabled, young and old.

Today, however, the social fabric that bound us together in good times and bad is unraveling. Over the last generation, we have witnessed a massive transfer of economic risk from broad structures of insurance, including those sponsored by the corporate sector as well as by government, onto the fragile balance sheets of American families. This transformation, which I call the "Great Risk Shift," is the defining feature of the contemporary American economy—as important as the shift from agriculture to industry a century ago. It has fundamentally reshaped Americans' relationships to their government, their employers, and each other. Andrea Case's parents never enjoyed the same economic highs that she did, but they had higher expectations of security: a stable middle-class income, a guaranteed pension, good health insurance coverage, greater economic security for their kids. One by one, the Great Risk Shift has dashed these expectations, transforming the economic circumstances of American families from the bottom of the economic ladder to its highest rungs.

One crucial point must be understood from the start: This dramatic transformation isn't a natural occurrence—a financial hurricane beyond human control. Sweeping changes in the global and domestic economy have helped propel it, but America's corporate and political leaders could have responded to these powerful forces by reinforcing the floodwalls that protect families from economic risk. Instead, in the name of personal responsibility, many of these leaders are busy tearing the floodwalls down. Proponents of these changes speak of a nirvana of individual economic management—a society of empowered "owners," in which Americans are free to choose. What these advocates are helping to create, however, is very different: a harsh new world of economic insecurity, in which far too many Americans are free to lose.

ECONOMIC INSECURITY isn't just a problem of the poor and uneducated, as most of us assume. Increasingly, it affects people like Andrea Case: educated, upper-middle-class Americans—men and women who thought that by staying in school, by buying a home, by investing in their 401(k)s, they had bought the ticket to upward mobility and economic stability. Insecurity today reaches across the income spectrum, across the racial divide, across lines of geography and gender. It speaks to the common "us" rather than to the insular, marginalized "them."

To understand the change, we must first understand what is changing. America's distinctive framework of economic protection grew out of specific political struggles and a unique set of values and beliefs. Less expansive than some hoped, more expansive than others desired, it was a curious and sometimes contradictory amalgam of goals and institutions. By the early 1970s, it worked tolerably well in insulating most middle-class Americans from the major financial risks of a dynamic capitalist economy. Today, however, it is falling apart under the weight of political attack and economic change, its conflicting elements falling in on each other, its gaps and traps growing by the day.

It is common to say that the United States does little to provide economic security compared with other rich capitalist democracies. Whether because of a deeply embedded mistrust of government, a constitutional structure that makes big policy reforms hard to achieve, the weakness of the American labor movement, or the depth of American ethnic divisions, the United States has provided infertile soil for the comprehensive welfare states that now dominate the economic landscape of most affluent countries. This is true, but it is only half the story. The United States does spend less on government benefits as a share of its economy, but it also relies more—far more—on private workplace benefits, such as health care and retirement pensions. Indeed, when these private benefits are factored into the mix, the U.S. framework of economic security is *not* smaller than the average system in other rich democracies; it is actually slightly larger.[4] With the help of hundreds of billions in tax breaks, American employers serve as the United States' unique mini-welfare states—the first line of defense for millions of workers buffeted by the winds of economic change.

The problem is that these mini-welfare states are coming undone, and in the process, risk is shifting back onto workers and their families. Employers want out of the social contract forged in the more stable economy of the past. And because they do not need to answer to the broader public that depends on the jerry-rigged systems of security they provide, employers are getting what they want. Meanwhile, America's framework of government support is also strained. Patently inadequate to deal with families' growing risks, it is nonetheless attacked for costing and doing too much—by critics who claim that the ideal of insurance is both outmoded and harmful to economic growth and advancement.

As private and public support erodes, workers and their families must bear a greater burden. This is the essence of the Great Risk Shift. Through the cutback and restructuring of workplace benefits, employers are seeking to offload more and more of the risk once pooled under their auspices. Facing fiscal constraints and political opposition, public social programs have eroded even as the demands on them have risen. And if critics have their way, these programs will erode even further. The next frontier in the Great Risk Shift is the transformation of existing programs—Medicare and Social Security chief among them—from guaranteed benefits defined by law to individualized private accounts that leave workers and families shouldering more and more of the risks that these programs once covered.

The Great Risk Shift might be less worrisome if work and family were stable sources of security themselves. Unfortunately, they are not. Beneath the rosy economic talk, the job market has grown markedly more uncertain and unstable, especially for those who were once best protected from its vagaries. The family, once a refuge from economic risk, is creating new risks of its own. With families needing two earners to maintain a middle-class standard of living, families' economic calculus has changed in ways that accentuate many of the risks they face. At the same time, families are making greater, and more risky, investments in their futures—in buying a home, in gaining new skills, in raising well-educated children—and they are paying the price when those investments fail.

THE GOAL OF THIS BOOK is to explain why the Great Risk Shift has played out, and how it can be countered. I start by demonstrating how dramatic the rise in insecurity is and dissecting one of its overarching causes, what I call "The Personal Responsibility Crusade"—a political drive to shift a growing amount of economic risk from government and the corporate sector onto ordinary Americans in the name of enhanced individual responsibility and control. Thanks in part to this crusade, even middle-class families are facing greater insecurity in the workplace, in the balancing of work and family, in planning for retirement, and in obtaining and paying for health care.

The shift of risk within these areas—how it has happened, who and what is behind it, and where it leaves us today—is the heart of my story. Work, family, and public and private benefits have all grown more risky at roughly the same time, which is one reason why the weakening of these traditional sources of security has proved so sweeping and so difficult to address. To take in the full scope of the Great Risk Shift, however, requires considering these transformations one by one: the new world of work, the increasingly risk-bound family, and America's enfeebled public-private framework of health insurance and retirement pensions, in which Americans have invested so much money, faith, and hope. The failures here are not small or fleeting. They are enormous and endemic—and the solutions proposed by the Personal Responsibility Crusade will only make them immeasurably worse.

These deep and worsening problems call for bold solutions. What we need are new ways of allowing families to save and insure against some of the most potent risks to their income, coupled with new ideas for revitalizing American social insurance and providing economic opportunity to all. An "insurance and opportunity society" would emphasize work and responsibility. But it would also provide real protection when families fall from the ladder of economic advancement, encouraging families to look to the future rather than fear the present. The old canard that ensuring security always hurts the economy turns out to be cruelly false. Economic security is vital to economic opportunity, and economic insecurity is one of the greatest barriers between American families and the American Dream.

1

The New Economic Insecurity

I WAS BORN in a small college town in Oregon in the early 1970s—just before the oil shocks, stagflation, and upheaval of the decade. I remember gas lines snaking around the block near my family's rented home, and my mother's dismay as prices in the supermarket, like unemployment, just kept rising. Underlying the surface calm was a growing unease—a sense that the nation was unsettled. My first real political memory was the Iranian hostage crisis; the first election I remember was Reagan's rout of Carter in 1980. What I didn't realize as I rode my red Raleigh bike through the quiet streets of my neighborhood was that a larger shift was also occurring in the wider world. An era was ending. A thirty-year period of shared prosperity in the United States was giving way to a new age of insecurity.

Today, the Internet, newspapers, and the airwaves are filled with debates over American national security. Yet a different kind of security threat, the kind many of us got our first taste of in the seventies, is looming larger and larger in the American consciousness. It's a threat that strikes middle-class families like Andrea Case's, workers recently laid off from well-paying jobs in high-tech, parents struggling under the costs of a child's unexpected health problems—in short, our next-door neighbors, our friends, the people we cross paths with everyday. The threat level started rising around the time of my youth, slowly eroding the confidence of middle-class Americans that they'd have stable jobs, generous benefits, and smooth upward mobility, and that their children would enjoy greater economic security than they'd enjoyed. But who killed economic security and why remains a mystery that we have only just begun to plumb.

We all know something about rising *inequality* in the United States, the growing space between the rungs of America's economic ladder. We hear about the soaring incomes of princely executives who garner hundreds of millions in compensation even as workers at the middle and bottom fall farther and farther behind. Yet we have heard much less about rising *insecurity*, the growing risk of slipping from the economic ladder itself. Perhaps that's because the stories here seem more random—blue-collar workers laid off after long years of service, college-educated middle managers whose upward trajectories have been abruptly halted, working families thrown off balance by catastrophic expenses, middle-class parents who find that health and retirement plans are shifting more costs and uncertainties onto them. It's easy to find the common thread when the subject is hardening divisions between two Americas— one marked by deprivation, the other by excess. It's harder to find it in stories of loss and anxiety whose common element is not constancy or stability, but sudden and often unexpected change.

Inequality and insecurity are deeply interwoven, but they are not the same. Inequality has indeed risen sharply. Between 1979 and 2003 the average income of the richest Americans more than doubled after adjusting for inflation, while that of middle-class Americans increased by only around 15 percent.[1] Nonetheless, it is possible to look at rising inequality and still paint a positive picture. After all, Americans at all points on the income ladder have gotten richer—just not at equal rates—and during this same period, our economy has expanded handsomely. A rising tide may not be lifting all boats as well as it did in the 1950s and 1960s, but it is lifting them nonetheless.

But another tide has been rising in the United States since my youth—the rising tide of economic risk. Americans may be richer than they were in the 1970s, but they are also facing much greater economic insecurity. And this insecurity is increasingly plunging ordinary middle-class families into a sea of economic turmoil.

Consider some of the alarming facts. Personal bankruptcy has gone from a rare occurrence to a routine one, with the number of households filing for bankruptcy rising from fewer than 290,000 in 1980 to more than two million in 2005.[2] The bankrupt are pretty much like other Americans before they file: slightly better educated, more likely to be married and have children, roughly as likely to have had a good job, and modestly less likely to own a home.[3] They are not the persistently poor, the downtrodden looking for relief. They are refugees of the middle class, frequently wondering how they fell so far so fast.

Americans are also losing their homes at record rates. Since the early 1970s, the mortgage foreclosure rate has increased fivefold.[4] From 2001 to 2005 an average of one in every sixty households with a mortgage fell into foreclosure a year—a legal process that begins when homeowners default on their mortgages and can end with homes being auctioned to the highest bidder in local courthouses.[5] David Lamberger, a Michigan resident who has worked in the auto industry most of his life, can testify to just how shattering the process can be. David and his wife, Mary, purchased their two-story home in the metro Detroit area as an investment in the future for themselves and their four children. When David lost his job at an auto parts maker, he declared bankruptcy to delay foreclosure on the house. But the money he made working at a used-car lot hasn't been sufficient to keep them afloat, and now he's on the verge of losing his family's modest home.[6] For David and scores of other ordinary homeowners, the American Dream has mutated into what former U.S. Comptroller of the Currency Julie L. Williams calls "the American nightmare."[7]

Meanwhile, the number of Americans who lack health insurance has increased with little interruption over the last twenty-five years as corporations have cut back on workplace coverage for employees and their dependents. Over a two-year period, more than 80 million adults and children—one out of three nonelderly Americans, 85 percent of them working or the kids of working parents—spend some time without the protection against ruinous health costs that insurance offers.[8] They are people like Mark Herrara, a union carpenter who went out on his own to become an independent contractor. Health insurance wasn't a priority when Herrara was using all his resources to get his business off the ground. Or at least it wasn't until he woke up one morning with a massive headache. Reluctant to go to the hospital for fear of the costs, he finally relented only to discover that he had suffered two strokes and his brain was bleeding. Ineligible for Medicaid, his bills now outstrip his pay several times over. "I've got a $225,000 debt and yeah, if I come into any money, well, the first people I got to pay back is for this medical coverage," says Herrara.[9]

At the same time that the financial threats associated with our jobs, our homes, and our health care have all increased, corporations have raced away from the promise of guaranteed benefits in retirement. Twenty-five years ago, 83 percent of medium and large firms offered traditional "defined-benefit" pensions that provided a predetermined monthly benefit for the remainder of a worker's life. Today, the share is below a third.[10] Instead, companies that offer pensions provide "defined-contribution" plans, such as the 401(k), in which returns are neither predictable nor assured. Defined-contribution pensions can earn big returns, but they also can mean big risks: the risk of stock market downturns, the risk of inadequate savings, the risk of outliving one's account balances. Between 1989 and 1998— a decade in which 401(k) coverage exploded and the stock market boomed—the share of families whose pension savings allowed them to replace at least half of their prior income in retirement actually declined, as old-style guaranteed pensions rapidly became a thing of the past. [11]

Perhaps most alarming of all, American family incomes are now on a frightening roller coaster, rising and falling much more sharply from year to year than they did thirty years ago. Indeed, the *instability* of American families' incomes has risen substantially faster than the *inequality* of families' incomes. In other words, while the gaps between the rungs on the ladder of the American economy have increased, what has increased even more quickly is how far people slip down the ladder when they lose their financial footing.

And this rising insecurity does not come with any obvious silver linings. The chance that families will see their income plummet has risen. The chance that they will experience long-term movement up the income ladder has not. For average families, the economic roller coaster takes them up and down. It doesn't leave them any higher than when they started. As David Lamberger, the Michigan man who is in the process of losing his house, puts it, "There have been years I made $80,000, and there have been years I made $28,000. . . . Sometimes we're able to pay bills and get by, but then stuff from the slow times never goes away. You can't catch up, and it comes back to haunt you."[12]

What's more, while these up-and-down swings are more severe for workers like David Lamberger who lack a college education, the pace by which instability has increased since the 1970s has been almost exactly the same for workers who've received a college degree as it has been for those who never earned a high school diploma. Educated professionals may comfort themselves with the thought that they are more financially stable than the check-out clerk who never finished high school. But compared with educated professionals in the past, they are experiencing much greater income swings—swings in fact comparable to those experienced by less-educated workers in the 1970s.

And while national income and wealth have indeed grown handsomely during the era in which insecurity has risen, the economic standing of the American middle class has increased only modestly. The incomes of middle-class families aren't much higher today than they were in the 1970s—and they are much more at risk.

Americans may be willing to turn a blind eye to growing inequality, confident in the belief that their own standard of living is still rising. But economic insecurity strikes at the very heart of the American Dream. It is a fixed American belief that people who work hard, make good choices, and do right by their families can buy themselves permanent membership in the middle class. The rising tide of economic risk swamps these expectations, leaving individuals who have worked hard to reach their present heights facing uncertainty about whether they can keep from falling. Economic inequality may stir up our envy as we ogle the BMWs and

McMansions of our richer neighbors, but the prospect of economic insecurity—of being laid off, or losing health coverage, or having a serious illness befall a family member—stirs up our anxiety. And anxiety, as we shall see, is just what millions of middle-class Americans increasingly feel.

America's Hidden Insecurity

All this is likely to come as a surprise to those who follow current economic debate. Yes, stories of economic hardship appear in the news. Yes, complaints about particular economic problems, from low savings to high gas prices, are ubiquitous. But the general tone of economic discussion today is decidedly sunny. Americans, we are told, are richer than they have ever been—and not just at the top of the economic ladder. Most working Americans, analysts claim with certainty, are far surpassing their parents' incomes. Back in the fifties and sixties, the optimists point out, owning a new kitchen appliance or installing one's children in a thin-walled bedroom in a Levittown Cape Cod was the height of middle-class luxury. Now, those same middle-income families have DVD players, air conditioners, a cell phone, a bedroom for each family member, and a second car—amenities that only the very rich in the mid-twentieth century could afford.[13]

Not only are middle-income Americans enjoying riches beyond the imagination of citizens of any nation or time, according to this familiar account, they are also living in an age of virtually unparalleled growth. Productivity is rising handily. The economy is humming along. And even as growth rises, inflation and unemployment remain low.[14] In late 2005, the *Wall Street Journal* headlined an online news story about the economy: "The Miracle Continues."[15]

There's just one problem: Americans don't believe the miracle exists. In poll after poll in recent years, Americans have heaped scorn on the happy talk and the sunny statistics. They have said that the country is on the wrong economic track. They have said that they expect the economy to get worse, not better. They have said that their own financial situation is weakening. And they have said that leaders on both sides of the partisan aisle are failing to address their most fundamental economic concerns.

In exit polls taken as Americans left the voting booth in 2004, for instance, less than a quarter of middle-class voters said that the job situation in their community had improved in the previous four years, and less than a third said their own family's financial situation had improved.[16] Forecasts of the election that crunched just the economic numbers predicted the incumbent president, George W. Bush, would win in a landslide.[17] But on Election Day he squeaked through with the smallest popular vote margin for a winning incumbent president since 1828. Since then, public ratings of the economy have dropped even farther, as have Bush's approval numbers. Today, for all the happy talk, a majority of Americans say that the economy is worsening, that it's a bad time to find a good job, and that economic conditions are "fair" or "poor," rather than "excellent" or even "good." As a Gallup Poll report noted in March 2006, "Americans continue to resist giving the nation's economy positive ratings, regardless of what so-called 'hard' economic indicators may show."[18]

Commentators have offered plenty of reasons to explain—or, more accurately, explain away—Americans' continuing grumpiness. According to the curmudgeonly columnist Robert Samuelson, the United States has become a land of whiners: "Americans have developed perfectionist standards. We expect total prosperity and are disappointed by anything less. There should be no doubts or deficiencies."[19] Others have pointed to the negativity of the news media as the culprit, or Americans' growing unease about the war in Iraq.[20] But perhaps the most popular explanation is that voters have simply not woken up and smelled the economic coffee. Fully four years since the recession of 2001, Americans, we are told, are still gripped by an outdated and irrational pessimism that blinds them to the bountiful riches of the Miracle Economy.

It is high time to embrace a simpler thesis: Americans don't think the economy is all that good because, as far as they're concerned, it's not. And the main reason why it's not that good is that Americans' economic lives are becoming more insecure even though the basic statistics are strong. In March 2004, for example, unemployment and inflation were both low. Yet roughly half of Americans agreed that "America no longer has the same economic security it has had in the past," while another fifth thought the statement could be true down the road. By contrast, just 27 percent believed that their economic complaints merely reflected the normal downside of the business cycle.[21]

This is not the first time that there has been a disconnect between basic economic statistics and what Americans say they are experiencing. Back in the mid-1990s, a similar—and similarly puzzling—process played out: Voters were far more negative about the economy than most statistics suggested they should be. In 1982, amid a severe recession that had pushed the unemployment rate up to nearly 10 percent, a poll by the private business research firm ISR found that only 12 percent of workers were "frequently concerned about being laid off." Yet in 1996, with the unemployment rate hovering around 5 percent—half what it was when the 1982 poll was done—the percentage of workers who said they were frequently concerned was 46 percent. Even in 2005, with the unemployment rate again at only 5 percent, the number of Americans worried that they would lose their jobs was still about three times as high as it was during the steep economic downturn of 1982 (see figure 1.1).[22]

Americans, it seems, just don't get what the pundits are crowing about. And that's because the statistics that pundits love to cite don't capture what most Americans feel: a sense of ever-increasing financial risk.

The Risk Factor

Pundits fixate on the current state of the economy: Is GDP growth accelerating or slowing? Is the job market expanding or contracting? Is the stock market rising or falling? These are important questions, but they are about the short-term waves of our economy—the movement on the surface, rather than the fundamental changes

Figure 1.1: A Growing Perception of Job Insecurity

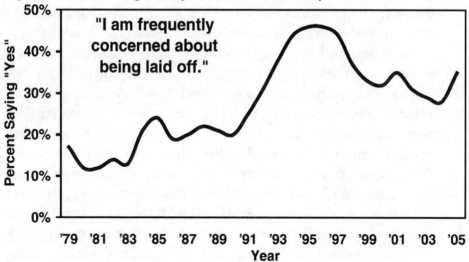

Source: *Proprietary data courtesy of ISR; for general information,*
see www.isrinsight.com.

below. The Great Risk Shift isn't a wave—it's a rising tide that has increased the level of economic insecurity for nearly all Americans, in good times as well as bad.

Everyone knows what risk is when they experience it. When we first get behind the wheel of a car, or traverse the edge of a perilous cliff, we feel the butterflies in our stomach, the lightheadness of fear. But conceptually, risk is not so easy to grasp. It turns all our conventional frames of reference on their head. We are used to thinking about averages, rather than about ranges; about what happens, rather than what could happen; about events at one point, rather than evolution over time—in sum, about levels, rather than dynamics.

Yet risk—the possibility of multiple outcomes, whether good or bad—is all about dynamics. Sophisticated investors in the stock market (the fearless surfers on the waves of risk) recognize this when they talk about the *volatility* of a stock as well as its return. If a stock has higher volatility, its price undergoes more substantial up and down shifts over time. These fluctuations in its price, or return, mean that the stock embodies greater risk for the investor, which is why savvy traders only snap up high-volatility stocks when they have high returns as well. Much of our increasingly sophisticated appreciation of risk comes from the efforts of economic players who deal with risk day in and day out to come up with new measures and new models for judging its magnitude and effects.

Risk is at the heart of some of capitalism's greatest successes. The entrepreneurs who financed the nation's first railroad tracks, prospected for oil, and bet on the success of microchips reaped outsized profits. Risk has also been the source of untold misery. For every story of a successful financial or business risk taken, there is one in which individuals lose their shirts. Risk is the reason companies go bankrupt, workers end up on the streets, and, at the extreme, financial markets crash. Seeing risk and understanding it, finding ways to quantify and share and manage it, gaining from its upsides while minimizing its downsides—these constitute some of the greatest achievements of the last two centuries. But while societies have the ability to master risk—to pool it across many people or address its root causes—societies also create risks: the risks of a dynamic investment market, the risks of interruption of earnings that arise in a division-of-labor economy in which people trade their work for pay, and, of course, the risks to health and the environment that modern production and consumption can pose.[23]

Economic insecurity lies on the dark side of risk. Although the term is rarely defined, *economic insecurity* can be understood as a psychological response to the possibility of hardship-causing economic loss. The psychology of insecurity is crucial, for it motivates many of our personal and social responses to risk—responses that can be either positive (buying insurance, building up private savings, forming a family) or negative (suffering anxiety, withdrawing from social life, postponing investments in the future because of fear of loss). Yet a feeling of insecurity is not enough to say someone is insecure. Insecurity requires real risk that threatens real hardship. We know that Americans think they are insecure. What I will show is that they have good reason to think so—that, like the investor who buys a highly volatile stock, Americans are facing much greater risk of substantial economic loss. The Great Risk

Shift is the story of how a myriad of risks that were once managed and pooled by government and private corporations have been shifted onto workers and their families—and how this has created both real hardship for millions and growing anxiety for millions more.

Risk turns out to be a lot harder to capture precisely with people than with stocks. To know what the volatility of a stock is, we need only follow the ticker for a while (with the familiar caveat that past performance is no guarantee of future performance). To know what the volatility of families' economic standing is, however, we need to trace a representative set of families over time, preferably long periods of time. We need to follow these families through all the normal and abnormal events of life: births, deaths, relocations, the formation and destruction of families, and so on. We need, in short, to look at the economy the way people actually live it—as a moving picture, rather than an isolated snapshot.

That's not, however, what economic statistics typically do. Consider the growing body of research on inequality in the United States. We know the gap between the rich and the rest has grown dramatically over the last thirty years, reaching levels not seen since before the late 1930s. The spoils of our system are now so unevenly divided that we must reach back to the Robber Barons of the 1890s and Gatsbys of the 1920s for a similar comparison to today's gap between middle-income Americans and the super-rich. In 2003, the richest 1 percent of U.S. households averaged over $800,000 in annual income, or more than eighteen times the average for middle-income households. A quarter century ago, the richest 1 percent raked in less than twelve times as much as the middle class.[24]

Yet as arresting as this fact is, it's based on annual surveys that reach different people every year. These surveys can tell us how many people are rich and how many are poor, and how big the gap between the two is. But they cannot tell us whether the same people are rich or poor from year to year, or whether movement up (or down) the income ladder is greater or smaller than it used to be. We all know we'll never be as rich as Bill Gates. But can we depend, as our parents once did, on maintaining—or, even better, steadily augmenting—our income and standard of living? And how many people are experiencing the wild fluctuations in income (fluctuations that resemble some of our most volatile stocks) that David Lamberger's family has seen?

To answer these sorts of questions, we need to do more than take annual snapshots of income. We need to survey the same people over many years, following them even as they experience death, birth, marriage, pay raises, pay cuts, new jobs, lost jobs, relocations, and all the other events, good and bad, that mark the passage from childhood into old age. We need to see Mark Herrara ensconced in his union job as a carpenter as well as Mark Herrara, independent contractor, as he returns from the hospital, hundreds of thousands of dollars in debt. These kinds of surveys are called "panel surveys," and compared with the usual approach—contacting a different random group of people for each survey—they are exceedingly difficult to carry out. Surveyors must stay in contact with respondents (and their descendants) over long periods of time while periodically adding new respondents to keep the survey representative of a changing population.

Given the difficulties, it's perhaps understandable that no official economic statistic tries to assess directly the dynamics of family income. Curious citizens who spend a few hours on the websites of the Commerce Department or Census Bureau will come away with a wealth of snapshots of the financial health of American families—from annual wages and income to the gap between rich and poor. But they will search fruitlessly for even the most basic information about how the economic status of American families changes over time, much less about what causes these shifts. If they extend their search beyond official statistics, they will do better, but not much better. Many studies of income dynamics have been done. Yet when I began my research, nobody had looked at the simple question of whether the up-and-down swing of family incomes— the volatility of the American family stock, if you will—had risen or fallen over the last generation.

The answer can be found in the Panel Study of Income Dynamics (PSID)—a nationally representative survey that has been tracking thousands of families from year to year since the late 1960s. Nearly forty years into its operation, the survey has included more than 65,000 people, some of whom have been answering questions for their entire adult lives, others of whom have been in the survey since their birth. As a result, the PSID is uniquely well suited to examining how and why incomes rise and fall over time.

And what becomes immediately clear is that family incomes rise and fall a lot—far more than one would suspect just looking at static income-distribution figures. To take just one simple measure, during a ten-year period, Americans aged twenty-five to sixty-one have less than a fourth the income in the year they're poorest, on average, as they do in the year they're richest.[25] Over ten years, in other words, an average Betty who had $60,000 in her best year would have less than $15,000 in her worst. This striking disparity, it turns out, is a dramatic increase from even the relatively recent past: In the 1970s, as figure 1.2 shows, the low was just shy of 50

Figure 1.2: The Rising Ratio of Low-to-High Family Incomes over 10-Year Periods

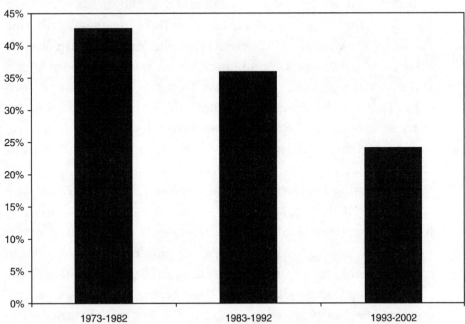

Source: Panel Study of Income Dynamics; Cross National Equivalent File. These are the average ratios of low-to-high family income over 10 years; the analysis follows household heads, with top and bottom 1 percent of observations trimmed.

percent below the high—meaning our average Betty would have around $30,000 in her worst year, rather than less than $15,000.

These up-and-down swings are what get missed when we use annual snapshots to look at the distribution of American family income. There are not just the well off and the poor. There are Americans who are doing well one year and poorly the next—and vice versa. In fact, a surprisingly big chunk of the income inequality that we see across families at any point in time is due to transitory shifts of family income, rather than to permanent differences across families.

This is a point that the Miracle Economy crowd loves: Sure, inequality is growing, they say, but mobility is alive and well, making any comparison of income groups misleading. The fact that Betty could make $20,000 one year and more than $60,000 in another just shows that the American Dream remains strong for those willing to pull themselves up by their own bootstraps.

But this conclusion is as wrongheaded as the image of a frozen class structure that is sometimes taken from income-distribution statistics. Upward mobility is real. Men like Mark Herrara do start their own businesses; David Lamberger does get his dream house. But upward mobility is usually not dramatic, and there is no evidence that it has increased substantially in the contemporary era of rising inequality.[26] Recently, the *Economist* magazine, no foe of American-style capitalism, reported that "a growing body of evidence suggests that the meritocratic ideal is in trouble in America. Income inequality is growing to levels not seen since the Gilded Age, around the 1880s. But social mobility is not increasing at anything like the same pace: would-be Horatio Algers are finding it no easier to climb from rags to riches, while the children of the privileged have a greater chance of staying at the top of the social heap."[27]

The evidence shows, moreover, that income mobility across generations is actually lower in the United States than in other affluent nations. According to recent studies, there is more social mobility in European nations such as Sweden than in the United States, and in fact only South Africa and Britain have as little mobility across generations.[28]

Plus, there's an even more glaring oversight of paeans to social mobility: What goes up also goes down. As we saw with David Lamberger, volatility of income can mean making $80,000 one year and freefalling to $28,000 the next—and the year of the freefall could be the year one loses not only one's job but also the family home.

The difference between these two scenarios is profound, because both research and common sense suggest that downward mobility is far more painful than upward mobility is pleasurable. In fact, in the 1970s, the psychologists Amos Tversky and Daniel Kahneman gave a name to this bias: "loss aversion."[29] Most people, it turns out, aren't just highly risk-averse—they prefer a bird in the hand to even a very good chance of two in the bush. They are also far more cautious when it comes to bad outcomes than when it comes to good outcomes of exactly the same magnitude. *The search for economic security is, in large part, a reflection of a basic human desire for protection against losing what one already has.*

Anybody who has watched the differing responses of a toddler to the pleasure of receiving a new toy and the pain of having one taken away knows about loss aversion. Yet it is something of a puzzle why adults behave like toddlers when it comes to things they own. After all, in classic economic theory, goods are simply tickets to enhanced welfare, and we should have no special attachment to things we already possess if other items could deliver welfare just as effectively. Aside from the "diminishing marginal utility" of income (the fact that every dollar buys slightly less happiness or well-being, making us value a $100 gain modestly less than we lament a $100 loss), people should, according to standard theory, value losses and gains in roughly equal terms.

Experiments show that few actual people think this way. Even when given a trivial item, we suddenly become willing to pay a much higher price to retain it than we were willing to shell out to buy it. (One clever study involved giving college students mugs and pencils—seemingly trivial items—and finding that they insisted on selling their gift for much more than they'd earlier said they would pay for it.) Researchers call this the "endowment effect," and it helps explain myriad features of the economic world that are otherwise inexplicable: why, for example, wages don't generally fall during recessions; why stocks have historically had to pay much higher returns than bonds to entice people to take on the increased risk of loss—and why insurance against economic injury remains the most popular and extensive of all the activities that modern governments engage in. (In 2001, for example, spending by public and private social programs like Medicare, Social Security, workplace retirement pensions, and unemployment insurance represented a quarter of our economy.)[30]

The endowment effect is surprisingly strong. Americans are famously opportunity-loving. But when asked in 2005 whether they were "more concerned with the opportunity to make money in the future, or the stability of knowing that your present sources of income are protected," 62 percent favored stability and just 29 percent favored opportunity.[31] In 1996 the Panel Study of Income Dynamics asked participants a similar question. Which would you choose: your present job with your current income for life, or a new job that offered a fifty-fifty chance of doubling your income and a fifty-fifty chance of cutting your income by a third?

On paper, the deal was pretty good. If John was making $30,000 and won the gamble, he'd have $60,000—a comparative fortune. If he lost the gamble, he'd make $20,000—not great, but not terrible compared with what he had. If John didn't worry at all about risk, the choice would be easy: Since he has a fifty-fifty chance of ending up with $60,000 and a fifty-fifty chance of ending up with $20,000, the rational position would be to treat the gamble as offering $40,000 (the average of the two salaries)—an amount a third higher than his present income.

Few people who were asked whether they'd take the gamble were rational in this fashion: Only 35 percent said they would roll the dice. Lowering the potential income loss budged some of the cautious, but surprisingly few. More than a third of respondents said they wouldn't accept even the most generous deal that the survey presented (which promised, on average, an almost 50 percent income increase). People like to gamble, but not, it seems, when they think that their long-term economic security is on the line.

Loss aversion is a well-known phenomenon in behavioral economics —the study of how people actually reason about economic choices. But the implications of loss aversion for our understanding of the ups and downs of economic life are often missed. What loss aversion means is that drops in income, even when later compensated for by equal or even larger gains, are intensely psychologically difficult. (Perhaps that's why a recent cross-national study finds that the best predictor of the self-reported happiness of a nation's citizenry isn't national income, but the extent of economic security.)[32] Upward mobility is nice; downward mobility is devastating, especially since it's on the downward trips that jobs, houses, savings, and the other things gained on the way up often get lost.

The Economic Roller Coaster

Judged on these terms, what my evidence shows is troubling, to say the least. When I started out, I expected to see a modest rise in instability. But I was positively thunderstruck by what I found: Instability of before-tax family incomes had skyrocketed. *At its peak in the mid-1990s, income instability was almost five times as great as it was in the early 1970s.* And while it dropped during the boom of the late 1990s, it never fell below twice its starting level, and it shot up again in recent years (my data end in 2002) to three times what it was in the early 1970s. The rise is less pronounced when taxes are taken into account, but it's still dramatic.[33] Moreover, while instability and inequality have both risen substantially, instability has actually risen faster and farther than inequality. The gap between Bill Gates and Joe Citizen is a lot larger than it used to be, but it's actually grown less quickly than the gap between Joe Citizen in a good year and Joe Citizen in a bad year.

Isn't this just a problem of the less educated, the workers who've fallen farthest behind in our skills-based economy? The answer is no. Volatility is indeed higher for less educated Americans than for more educated Americans—slightly more than twice as high.[34] (It is also higher for blacks and Hispanics than for whites, and for women than for men.) Yet, surprisingly, volatility has risen by roughly the same amount across all these groups over the last generation. During the 1980s, people with less formal education experienced a large rise in volatility, while those with more formal education saw a modest rise. During the 1990s, however, the situation was reversed: Educated workers saw the instability of their income rise more, and by the end of the decade, as figure 1.3 shows, the overall instability of their income had increased by almost as much from the 1970s baseline. The story of the 1990s is the generalization of the income instability that once afflicted mostly the less educated and disadvantaged. Increasingly, more educated workers are riding the economic roller coaster once reserved for the working poor.

This suggests that growing economic instability cannot easily be chalked up to poor personal choices. It might be argued that workers without a college degree could have gotten additional education (although this would leave open the question of who exactly

Figure 1.3: Instability Rise at Both High and Low Education Levels

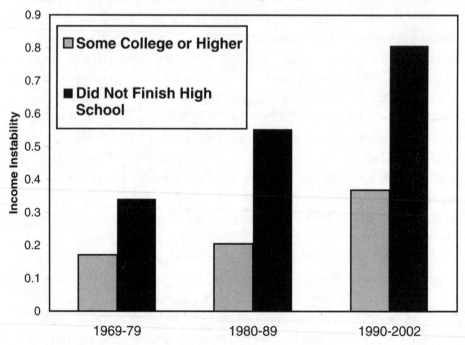

Source: Panel Study of Income Dynamics.

would fill the millions of jobs that require little advanced train-ing or skills). But how can we say that about workers who did stay in school and yet still experience high levels of volatility? The forces that have created the new economic roller coaster—growing workplace insecurity, the new risks of the contemporary family, and the erosion of stable social benefits—have swept through the lives of almost every American. Prudent choices can reduce but not eliminate exposure to the growing level of eco-nomic risk. Indeed, many of the choices that expose Americans to risk—from going to school to seeking a better job to building a family—are precisely the ones that most greatly benefit families and society as a whole. Families can give up many of these risks only by giving up on the American Dream.

A major clue on this point is found in the Panel Study of Income Dynamic's questions about risk mentioned earlier, questions that mea-sure the extent to which people are risk-seeking or risk-avoiding. If much of the volatility in income that we see in the PSID was caused by voluntary choices, then we would expect that people who are more worried about risk would be less likely to experience large income swings. After all, if you want to avoid risk and you have the power to do so, you are unlikely to put yourself in a position where your income is highly unstable. If you are risk-averse, you won't choose to go back to graduate school when you can continue working at the local bank, and you won't leave your cushy corpo-rate job for that one-in-a-million opportunity to get your own busi-ness off the ground.

Yet the PSID data reveal few consistent relationships between how risk tolerant someone is and how unstable their income is.[35] The risk tolerance of someone in the PSID turns out to be a ter-rible predictor of their income experience. People who are highly risk-seeking experience wild income swings, but so too do people who are highly risk-averse—which is not at all what one would expect if income volatility were mostly voluntary. It's as if a cau-tious grandmother and reckless teenager were each equally likely to take up bungee jumping, a sure sign that something other than unfettered free choice is at work.

Maybe so, but couldn't family breakup be driving the results? If a family divorces, for example, does one family become two, each with a lower income? The answer is yes, divorce does cause some instability in my measure, but that's because divorce is a real risk to family incomes. The analysis looks at how unstable people's incomes are, and family changes (birth, death, marriage, divorce, separation, and the like) are an important cause of income instability. Lest it be thought that rising divorce rates are the main reason for the rise in income instability, however, it's worth pointing out that the U.S. divorce rate actually peaked in the early 1980s and fell in the 1990s—precisely when economic instability climbed.[36]

How can we make sure that we aren't confusing instability with income growth? If Americans are getting richer and richer, wouldn't that show up as greater income variance? The answer is no. (The premise of the question is also wrong—most Americans are not flying into the income stratosphere.) Just as with the volatility of a stock, the volatility of family incomes is meant to capture how much income bounces around its overall growth path. If the income of a family rises smoothly, then it's not counted as unstable. It has to swing, not just climb.[37]

Drop Zone

Still, it's hard to think about income instability in the same way we think about stock volatility. When most of us contemplate the financial risks in our lives, we don't worry about the up-and-down movement of our finances around some long-term path, even though that's technically what financial risk is. We think about downside risks, about drops in our income—and understandably so: We are loss averse, in major part, because losing what we have can require wrenching adjustments. We have to cut back, to go without, to adjust our expectations, to rethink our lives. When losses are catastrophic, people have to confront what the anthropologist Katherine Newman calls "falling from grace"—to contend "not only with financial hardship, but also with the psychological, social, and practical consequences" of losing our proper place.[38]

We can get a better sense of these "falls from grace" by looking specifically at *drops* in family income. About half of all families in the PSID experience a drop in real income over a two-year period, and the number has remained fairly steady. Yet families that experience an income drop fall much farther than they used to. In the early 1970s the typical income loss was a bit more than 25 percent of prior income; by the late 1990s it was around 40 percent.[39] For a family earning $42,000 (the median income for U.S. households in 1999), a 40 percent loss would mean an income drop of almost $17,000. And remember, this is the *median* drop: Half of families whose incomes dropped experienced even larger declines.

Figure 1.4 uses somewhat fancier statistics to show what the chance of experiencing a 50 percent or greater family income drop is for an average person each year. The probability of a 50 percent or greater drop for an average person was just 7 percent in the

Figure 1.4: Americans' Chance of a 50 Percent or Greater Income Drop

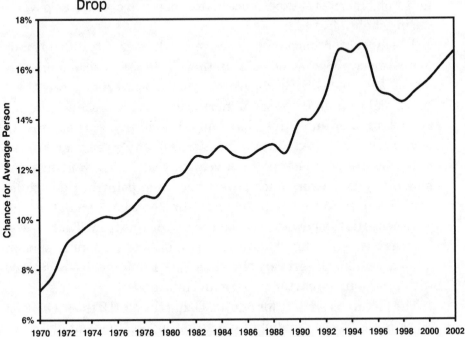

Source: Panel Study of Income Dynamics. Results are from a logistic regression predicting drops in household-size-adjusted family income among individuals aged 25–61.

1970s. It's risen dramatically since, and while (like income volatil- ity) it fell in the strong economy of the 1990s, it has recently spiked to record levels.[40] There is nothing extraordinary about "falling from grace." You can be perfectly average—with an average in- come, an average-sized family, an average likelihood of losing your job or becoming disabled—and you're still two-and-a-half times as likely to see your income plummet as an average person was thirty years ago.

The most dramatic consequence of "falling from grace" is poverty— subsistence at a level below the federal poverty line (for 2006, an annual income of slightly less than $10,000 for an individual and about twice that for a family of four).[41] Our conventional view of poverty envisions a distinct group—"the poor," "the truly disad- vantaged," "the underclass"—whose experience of deprivation lasts for years, and perhaps even extends across generations. Yet long- term poverty, though real and worrisome, is rarer than we think. Most of the poor at any moment are not poor for long. Less than a tenth of Americans experience five consecutive years of poverty during their adult life.[42]

The flipside of this picture, however, is that poverty afflicts many more Americans at some point in their lives than is commonly be- lieved. Take the U.S. child poverty rate of 20 percent—a rate three times higher than the norm in northern Europe. Most people look at this number and think that "only" one in five kids experience poverty in the United States. That's true in any given year, but the kids who are poor change from year to year. If we want to know how many kids experience poverty at some point in their child- hood, we need to count up the total number who spend at least a year beneath the poverty line by the age of eighteen. The answer, it turns out, is shocking: More than *half* of American kids spend at least a year in poverty by the time they're eighteen—compared with less than a quarter of German children.[43]

The picture is similar for adults. Using the PSID, the sociologist Mark Rank has calculated that a stunning 58.5 percent of Ameri- cans will spend at least a year in poverty between the ages of twenty and seventy-five.[44] I have asked Rank whether this striking result somehow hinges on including cash-poor college students in the calculations, and he has assured me it does not. Indeed, even if *everyone* younger than twenty-five is excluded from the calculations, the chance of experiencing poverty by the age of seventy-five is still almost 50 percent.

Worse, the chance of spending at least a year in poverty has increased substantially since the late 1960s, even for workers in their peak earning years. People who were in their forties in the 1970s had around a 13 percent chance of experiencing at least a year in poverty during their forties. By the 1990s, people in their forties had more than a 36 percent chance of ending up in poverty—an almost threefold rise.[45]

These numbers illuminate the hidden side of the Miracle Economy: the growing economic insecurity faced by ordinary workers and their families. And unlike other possible measures, these statistics are as direct and comprehensive as they come. They tell us by exactly how much the roller coaster goes up and down, looking at every source of a family's income, from friends to employers to government. Rates of bankruptcy or home foreclosure (which have both increased dramatically in the last generation) might go up because financial meltdowns have lost their stigma or because people are making foolish choices about spending and debt. But nobody files for a major income drop or spends their way into a highly unstable income. Income instability is the DNA of economic insecurity, its basic building block.

Income instability is the building block of insecurity, but it is not the whole. Indeed, as dramatic and troubling as the trends we have examined are, they vastly *understate* the true depth of the problem. The up-and-down movement of income among working-age Americans is a powerful indicator of the economic risks faced by families today. Yet economic insecurity is also driven by the rising threat to families' financial well-being posed by budget-busting expenses like catastrophic medical costs, as well as by the massively increased risk that retirement has come to represent, as more and more of the responsibility of planning for the post-work years has shifted onto Americans and their families. When we take in this larger picture, we see an economy not merely changed but fundamentally transformed.

What's Going On?

Over the years as I've revisited the old neighborhood where I once rode my bike, it looks essentially unchanged—a city in amber. The supermarket is still there. Close by, other neighborhoods have sprouted large new homes amid long stretches of green. The surface is tranquil, even improved. The old gas station where I remember gas-crisis lines is gone; a microbrewery has moved in nearby. But beneath the calm facade is a growing canker. Families whose lawns remain manicured fear not being able to meet their next mortgage payment. Having seen their salaries drop once, if not more than once, they question their ability to hang on.

The Great Risk Shift is a classic murder mystery: Who killed economic security in the United States? The potential culprits are many, the motives murky, the evidence often circumstantial. Yet much of this book is devoted to pinning the suspects and explaining their role in the crime. The answer is not as neat or simple as some murder mysteries, but then again we are talking about momentous shifts in our economy, our society, and our nation's social policies. A change as big as the Great Risk Shift does not usually stem from a single grand cause.

The mystery, it turns out, is not just *why* Americans have come to face greater economic risk. There are straightforward reasons why workers and their families experience heightened financial instability in today's economy and society. The big puzzle is why political and corporate leaders have been so slow to respond. In fact, the puzzle is even deeper than that. Political and corporate leaders haven't simply failed to respond; they've actually piled on new risks even as Americans have become increasingly less secure.

To answer this puzzle requires not further statistical inquiries but a historical journey into the rise and decline of an ideal—the ideal of insurance. This is our next subject: America's sweeping ideological transformation away from an all-in-the-same-boat philosophy of shared risk toward a go-it-alone vision of personal responsibility.

2

Risking It All

"Who's Afraid of Personal Responsibility?" That was the rhetorical title of a recent law-review article by Richard Kaplan, a law professor at the University of Illinois.[1] The article concerned Health Savings Accounts (HSAs), tax-free individual accounts that are now being hotly promoted by financial institutions, medical insurers, and free-market policy advocates to allow people to save money so that they can pay their routine health care expenses directly, rather than through traditional group insurance.

The idea behind HSAs is that you should save for most of your health care expenses on your own, paying them out of pocket just as patients did in the days before group health insurance. Insurance would be only for the truly catastrophic costs—the costs that exceed $5,000 or $10,000 a year. In return for taking on this hefty risk, you get a tax-free investment account that is under your control. You can use it however you wish for medical care; you can even pass it on to your heirs or surviving spouse when you die. As the Treasury Department brochure for HSAs reads: "You own and you control the money in your HSA. Decisions on how to spend the money are made by you without relying on a third party or a health insurer. You will also decide what types of investments to make with the money in the account in order to make it grow."[2]

Felix Meschke, a thirty-two-year-old professor at the University of Minnesota, is one of more than 3 million Americans who heard about HSAs and bit.[3] On January 1, 2006, just before President Bush called for $156 billion over ten years in expanded support for Health Savings Accounts in his State of the Union Address, Meschke signed up his family for an HSA.[4] In doing so, Meschke was taking personal responsibility for his family's health care. Less than two weeks later, he found himself in an emergency room, deciding whether or not to hospitalize his eleven-month-old son, whose ear infection had developed into a high fever and wracking cough. Thankfully, his son recovered after a night in the hospital, but the family was left with a whopping bill, a bill that under an old-style insurance plan would have been fully covered. Now the Meschkes alone would be responsible for the entire amount—whether or not they could afford to pay.

Although only a tiny fraction of employers now offer HSAs, almost half of businesses say they are considering them, and more than a quarter are expected to offer them in 2006.[5] And Health Savings Accounts are only the latest volley in an ongoing transformation of our health plans, retirement pensions, and other insurance benefits. Human resource directors everywhere are scrambling to meet the new realities, politicians in Washington are feverishly debating the course that public programs should take, and individuals are only just beginning to feel the full effects. For more than two decades, our nation has been undergoing a fundamental revolution in its approach to widely distributed economic risks. Yet so sweeping, steady, and subterranean has this transformation been that few of us stop to consider how dramatically our experiences and assumptions have changed.

A generation ago, if we had been offered a retirement plan by our employer, it would have been a traditional guaranteed pension that looked much like Social Security. Today, those of us who are lucky enough to receive a pension are almost universally enrolled in individual account plans like 401(k)s. A generation ago, had we been offered a workplace health plan, it would have provided Blue Cross–style coverage, with most of the cost paid directly by our employer. Today, only around half (56.4 percent) of workers employed more than twenty hours a week receive health coverage (down from more than 70 percent in 1980), and old-style coverage with no-money-down care and free choice of physicians has become virtually nonexistent.[6] Instead, if we find ourselves among the fortunate half of workers receiving coverage, our plan is likely to have one noticeable trait: It places a good chunk of medical costs onto our own financial shoulders, in the form of deductibles, co-payments, co-insurance, and employee-paid premiums. And a generation ago, nobody in Washington talked about turning Medicare into a system of competing private health plans or transforming employer-provided health insurance into a system of individual Health Savings Accounts, much less about privatizing Social Security—at least if they wanted their careers to continue.

Today, however, Washington is abuzz with discussions of Social Security privatization, Medicare reform, Health Savings Accounts, and scores of exotic new tax breaks to encourage families to set up private accounts to deal with economic risks on their own. What all these discussions have in common is the mantra of individual control and personal responsibility. Cutbacks in Medicaid are defended on the grounds that greater contributions by low-income families will, in the words of one Republican congressman, "encourage personal responsibility."[7] The 2005 bankruptcy bill, which greatly tightened the nation's rules for filing personal bankruptcy, was signed by President George W. Bush with the explanation: "America is a nation of personal responsibility where people are expected to meet their obligations."[8] In his unsuccessful battle for Social Security privatization, Bush reached for an even loftier goal—an "ownership society." As the Cato Institute, a libertarian think tank, explains, an ownership society "values responsibility, liberty and property. Individuals are empowered by freeing them from dependence on government handouts and making them owners instead, in control of their own lives and destinies. In the ownership society, patients control their own health care, parents control their own children's education, and workers control their retirement savings."[9]

What has changed? In a word, ideology. Over the past two decades, the corporate and government policies that once provided a basic foundation of economic security for American workers and their families have run headlong into a collection of beliefs, institutions, and advocates that I call the "Personal Responsibility Crusade." The core assertion embodied in the Personal Responsibility Crusade is that Americans are best off dealing with economic risks on their own, without the overweening interference or expense of wider systems of risk sharing. Insurance, by protecting us from the full consequences of our choices, takes away our incentives to be economically productive and personally prudent. Or, as former Republican Congressman Dick Armey—the ex-economist who was House Speaker Newt Gingrich's right-hand man—summed up the credo in 1995: "Social responsibility is a euphemism for individual *irresponsibility*."[10]

Janis Joplin once sang, "Freedom is just another word for nothing left to lose." The Personal Responsibility crusade offers a new twist: "*Insurance* is just another word for nothing left to lose." And to leaders of the Crusade, the solution is as straightforward as the problem: Insurance should be limited; individuals should bear the full weight of both responsibility and risk—all to promote wise consumer choices and enhanced self-reliance. As one leading Senate advocate of Health Savings Accounts explains, "I believe it is necessary to get the consumer back involved in their health-care decisions. . . . [Insurance] buffers people from the true cost of health care."[11] The director of President Bush's National Economic Council states: "Health care is expensive because the vast majority of Americans consume it as if it were free. . . . To control health care costs, we must give consumers an incentive to spend money wisely."[12] Arkansas's Republican governor puts the point more bluntly: "One of the reasons we have a health care crisis is because, as a consumer, I don't have that much skin in the game."[13]

The Personal Responsibility Crusade is all about putting more "skin in the game"—making people more responsible for the management and finance of the major economic risks they face. More skin means we reap the rewards when the game goes well. More skin also means we bear the losses when the game goes badly.

The Personal Responsibility Crusade is not a momentary response to the recent gains of antigovernment politicians. It is a movement that has been building steam for years, refining its arguments and strategies for challenging the very notion of shared risk. Its ideas are institutionalized in think tanks, embedded in our tax code, and increasingly, part of our most established social programs. Its intellectual and organizational leaders are the primary force pressing for plans to further transform American social protections—most notably, Social Security. Its adherents are not coy about their larger goals, though they generally don't trumpet them in public. In early 2005, when President Bush was beginning his ill-fated campaign to privatize Social Security, a top White House aide wrote to his boss Karl Rove (with excessive hubris, it turns out): "For the first time in six decades, the Social Security battle is one we can win—and in doing so, we can help transform the political and philosophical landscape of the country. We have it within our grasp to move away from dependency on government and toward giving greater power and responsibility to individuals."[14]

How did economic risk become a matter of individual rather than shared responsibility? Why, at the same time that Americans are becoming more insecure, is more and more risk and responsibility being shifted onto them? What is at stake in the personal responsibility debate, for us and for American society? Who stands to win, and who is likely to lose, if the personal responsibility vision is fulfilled? And what will the brave new world of individually managed risks look like? In order to understand the full scope of the transformation—and thus the distance we've come—we must travel back to the beginning: 1935, the year of Social Security's birth, and the moment when a powerful new ideal of insurance was planted in America's famously individualistic soil.

The Birth of American Social Insurance

It was spring 1935, and Edwin Witte was worried. The mild-mannered University of Wisconsin professor had come to the nation's capital in 1934 at the request of Labor Secretary Frances Perkins. Cautious and self-effacing, Witte was no firebrand. But his charge was ambitious, even radical—to assist with the development of what was being called the Economic Security Act, the greatest break yet with the federal government's historically hands-off policy toward victims of economic misfortune. The scope of the effort was dauntingly broad, "embracing," Witte later wrote, "all measures to promote recovery and to develop a more stable economic system, as well as assistance to the victims of insecurity and maladjustment"— including health insurance, unemployment insurance, and old-age protections.[15]

By early 1935, however, Witte was far from certain the effort would succeed. "Practically all of the letters which the member of Congress received on the economic security bill," he lamented, "were critical or hostile"—leaving the "net impression . . . that there was serious opposition to the bill and no real support."[16] Worse, a private insurance consultant successfully lobbied the Senate to amend the bill so that those corporations that operated private retirement plans for their workers could opt out of the proposed federal retirement system and not pay the required taxes. Witte knew that this provision was a poison pill that could kill the entire retirement program, preventing it from spreading risks broadly across all workers.

Witte's pessimism, of course, proved unwarranted. The bill, renamed the "Social Security Act," passed in the summer of 1935. At the eleventh hour, Congress dropped the proposal to let companies with private pensions opt out of public old-age insurance. The threat of an old-age program with warring public and private components had been averted.

Nonetheless, the new retirement program (which soon appropriated the label "Social Security" all for itself) was scarcely the crown jewel of U.S. social policy it would later become. True, it was the only fully national program in the 1935 legislation. Yet only half of workers were initially covered, benefits were meager (and failed to rise until after World War II), and nearly all blacks were excluded (due to the exemption of domestic and agricultural workers from coverage—a provision sought by southern conservatives). Moreover, a program for health insurance did not make it into the bill. Though Roosevelt considered the idea, the opposition of the

AMA helped convince him to put it aside, creating the opening for the predominantly private insurance system of health insurance that the United States has today.[17]

And while the Social Security Act was more ambitious than what most business leaders and Republicans wanted, it was a disappointment to many on the Left, who had called for more fundamental restructuring of the economy and more extensive redistribution of wealth. The act aimed to stabilize capitalism, not stab it. It was about giving workers "a floor of protection," rather than a luxurious carpet of wealth. In describing the act a year after its passage, Witte noted with unconcealed pride that "only in a very minor degree did [the Social Security Act] modify the distribution of wealth and it does not alter at all the fundamentals of our capitalistic and individualist economy."[18]

The breakthrough of 1935 was momentous all the same, for Social Security embodied a bold new imperative of government action: *insurance*. The word rings familiar today, but it once had a radical air. Insurance was an affirmation of free will over fate. If not an effort to stay the hand of God, it was an attempt to soften his blow. And it rested on modern statistics and actuarial science— which were being employed with increasing sophistication by America's growing network of insurance companies in the 1930s. Witte, in fact, packed the technical working group that was developing the Economic Security Act with private insurance experts willing to deploy the intelligence of insurance on behalf of the nation's economic future.

The intelligence of insurance became genius when insurance principles were coupled with the power of the state to require participation and ensure adequate and affordable coverage. "Social insurance," as it was called, transformed individual misfortunes into common problems. It made the inevitable dislocations of capitalist society risks that could be managed and redistributed, rather than blows of fate that could only be feared and suffered. The "insurance" in social insurance came from the power of aggregation: Risks that could devastate an individual or community could be managed if they were spread across many individuals and many communities. The "social" in social insurance came from the principle of shared fate, the reassurance that "we're all in this together." All insurance pools risks. Only social insurance pools risks on terms that enable the poor as well as the rich, the aged as well as the young, the ill as well as the healthy to afford protection. The crafters of the Economic Security Act believed that insurance had to be available and within the means of those who needed insurance most.

At the heart of this belief was a simple conviction: broadly distributed threats to economic well-being—sickness, injury, disability, unemployment, penurious old age—were not the responsibility of individuals alone. They were a widespread and often unavoidable feature of an interdependent industrial society. And because they were, the cost of these risks should be distributed widely across the citizenry, not concentrated on those unlucky enough to experience them—a goal made possible by the unique power of government to compel participation and require contributions. Government could pool the risks of millions of citizens. It could guarantee that even workers of limited means were able to afford basic protection. And it could require that everyone contributed to this common pool throughout their lives, rather than waiting until they fell on hard times or disaster struck, when—for all but the richest—it would be too late.

Today, critics of Social Security often describe it as "outmoded"—a program built for a very different set of circumstances. But the ideal of insurance wasn't meant to deal with the calamity of the Depression; it was meant to provide a secure foundation for economic activity and advancement for decades to come. The architects of the Social Security Act contrasted insurance for working Americans with relief for those who were already destitute. Relief was reactive, demeaning, inevitably stingy. Insurance was proactive, uplifting, generous. Relief was backward looking; insurance was forward looking. By creating a basic floor of protection, it allowed Americans to seize on economic opportunities they might otherwise view with anxiety and fear.

The wealthy had long taken basic economic security of this sort for granted, in part because of longstanding protections for businesses and entrepreneurs whose investments went sour.[19] Social insurance extended economic security to those least capable of obtaining it on their own—namely, those with modest means or a high probability of needing assistance. FDR put it best in a 1938 address commemorating the third anniversary of the Social Security Act: "We must face the fact that in this country we have a rich man's security and a poor man's security and that the Government owes equal obligations to both. National security is not a half and half matter: it is all or none."[20]

Insuring America

In the three decades after Roosevelt's 1938 speech, what he had called the "frontier of insecurity" shrunk dramatically.[21] A massively expanded Social Security program, disability insurance, Medicare and Medicaid to provide health insurance to the elderly and the poor—all expressed a commitment to protect Americans against the "hazards and vicissitudes" of modern industrial life.[22]

Nor was government the only force pushing back the borders of American insecurity. Pressed on by an aggressive labor movement and flush with profits in an ascendant economy, corporate America also got into the act. Employers built extensive guaranteed pension plans on top of Social Security; they offered private health insurance as an alternative to public protections. The result was a vast system of private security—subsidized by the tax code and regulated by the government—that shielded millions from uncertainty and fear. When this private system was factored into the mix, many better-off and unionized Americans received insurance benefits that were as large, or larger, than those enjoyed by the citizens of such left-leaning European nations as Sweden.[23]

Indeed, the Social Security Act turned out to be a huge boon for private benefits. Life insurance flourished. Retirement pension plans grew more extensive and generous, particularly for highly paid workers. Even corporations that had fought the old-age insurance legislation, or argued that employers with private pensions should be exempted from it, came to recognize the substantial benefits of building their retirement plans on top of Social Security. The private pension consultant who had lobbied most actively for letting employers that operated private retirement plans opt out of Social Security later exclaimed: "It was the greatest mistake of my life. Business is booming as never before."[24]

Americans were also gaining private health insurance coverage at a record pace. Spurred in part by wartime wage controls that exempted workplace fringe benefits, private insurance coverage expanded to reach more than half of Americans in 1950.[25] Most of that coverage, moreover, came through Blue Cross, a nationwide network of hospital-run health plans. Blue Cross plans certainly weren't public programs, but they weren't really commercial insurance, either. Instead of sorting people by their expected cost and charging rates based on these risk categories, the Blues offered insurance to all enrollees at roughly the same premium. With the help of special enabling legislation that was enacted in most states, Blue Cross plans also aspired to enroll lower-income citizens as well as the highly paid. A 1939 press release declared: "The [Blue Cross] plans are a form of social insurance under nongovernmental auspices, not merely a form of private insurance under non-profit auspices."[26]

"Social insurance under nongovernmental auspices" seems an odd rallying cry for a private health plan. But it nicely indicates the extent to which the original vision of Social Security was picked up, and reworked, in the decades after the act's passage. Employers and insurers and, soon, labor unions all saw their own advantages in backing private benefits that pooled risks broadly, though never as broadly as government would have. These actors also demanded, successfully, that the federal tax code generously subsidize these benefits, and they defended them on terms remarkably similar to those that had been used to justify the Social Security Act itself. In the process, they created a unique public-private system of insurance that, for a few brief decades, united government and corporations in pursuit of a common goal—economic security.

Picture Perfect

In the robust economy that followed World War II, many large employers embraced their invigorated role in ensuring economic security with true enthusiasm. Here, in the eyes of corporate leaders, was a distinctive American response to the problems that other nations had addressed through government programs. In 1965 the National Association of Manufacturers announced: "Private employee benefit plans with their inherent flexibility to adapt to the almost infinite requirements of employees and employers should be encouraged to grow and prosper within a favorable government policy and climate."[27] And for three decades after World War II, grow they did.

Consider the giant photo manufacturer Eastman Kodak, always on the forefront of these developments. Based in Rochester, New York, where it once employed a stunning fifth of the city's workforce, "Big Yellow"—as its employees called it—was a pioneer in benevolent welfare capitalism. The benefits offered by Kodak surpass even today's nostalgic accounts of corporate generosity in the 1950s: company housing, in-house health programs, production planning to minimize layoffs, profit-sharing, even jobless benefits paid out of Kodak's own private fund for the unemployed.[28] Kodak *was* its employees' security.

Kodak did not keep its business model to itself, either. Kodak's treasurer, Marion Folsom, served on the advisory committee that helped design Social Security and was secretary of the Department of Health, Education, and Welfare during the Eisenhower Administration. Folsom, a southerner by birth who had served in the army during World War I and seemed to be involved in every major political debate over Social Security from 1935 until his death in 1968, was a tireless proselytizer for generous private benefits within corporate circles. In the 1940s Folsom helped Kodak initiate one of the nation's first pension plans that built on top of the nascent Social Security program by offering supplemental retirement benefits. In 1953 Kodak adopted the first medical plan for workers in manufacturing, and it created a health plan for retirees a year later.

Company leaders credited this private welfare system for Kodak's low turnover, high worker morale, and impenetrability to unions. Yet they also saw this system as a model for the *nation's* approach to economic insecurity. Looking back from the vantage point of the late 1960s, Folsom saw it only as a matter of time before the direction of Kodak was the direction of the country: "[W]e have made considerable progress in the last 50 years in protecting people against the major economic hazards of life. . . . We've still got a few gaps, but on the whole, we're making pretty good progress. . . . In other words, the two systems [private and public] are working together. Now we've got to extend the voluntary plans to cover these people that are not now covered, most in small unstable companies."[29]

Looking at the American economy of the late 1960s, one could be forgiven for thinking—as Folsom clearly did—that America's unique public-private system of insurance was on the verge of achieving something close to universal economic security. And yet that system was about to be hit with a series of shocks as cumulatively profound as those that had prompted the development of social insurance in the United States. What would emerge would be a very different vision of the role of insurance in American society.

The Attack on Insurance

Social insurance always had its share of critics. Yet rarely did those critics repudiate the ideal of insurance itself. Instead, they argued that the private sector could fill the need without the costly interventions of an overbearing federal government. By the 1960s many erstwhile foes of public social insurance did not even go this far. They merely insisted that government should not do too much to crowd out private protections. As Social Security expanded in the 1960s, the U.S. Chamber of Commerce meekly stated, "Social Security should be continued . . . at a reasonable level. Our only fear is that if Social Security grows too large, it will overtake everything else."[30] When Medicare and Medicaid were created in 1965, it looked as if protection against economic insecurity—once denounced as a fearsome Bolshevist plot—had come to be seen as American as apple pie.

Looks, however, can be deceiving. For even as moderate Republicans like Folsom were offering effusive praise for America's public-private partnership, a new guard of critics was waiting in the wings. And this new guard had a new line of attack as well: Insurance was grossly inefficient.

At the heart of this attack was a previously obscure insurance concept known as *moral hazard.* The essence of moral hazard is simple: Protecting people against risks reduces the care people exercise in avoiding those risks. If we have health insurance, according to the logic of moral hazard, we won't take good care of ourselves. If we have coverage for medical costs, we'll spend more on health care. If we are guaranteed Social Security, we'll save less for retirement.

For centuries, insurers have recognized that insuring people against losses that are at least partially under their control gives people less reason to prevent such losses—and, indeed, can even prompt wholly induced or fraudulent claims (as in the classic example of the man who burns down his own home to collect on homeowners' insurance).[31] Moral hazard is an inevitable result of the economic incentives that insurance creates, and all insurers have to design their policies and monitor their payouts to prevent it from becoming too serious a problem. But in the new critique of insurance, moral hazard wasn't just a technical issue that insurers had to address. It was a glaring flaw with insurance itself—and especially with government insurance protections.

The wellspring of this new critique was not the political arena, at least not at first. It was economics. In the 1960s Kenneth Arrow (who would win the Nobel Prize in Economics in 1972) authored a pioneering analysis of the role of insurance in medical care, in which he argued that insurance was a rational and positive response to the inherent uncertainties of the medical field.[32] Arrow, a rigorous, wide-ranging scholar who was also known for his personal generosity and for refusing to engage in ideological squabbling, saw the message of his work as supporting government efforts to encourage broad insurance coverage. "The welfare case for insurance of all sorts is overwhelming," he wrote. "It follows that the government should undertake insurance where the market, for whatever reason, has failed to emerge."[33]

By the 1970s, however, many economists who, like Arrow, subscribed to the tenets of "neoclassical" economics were arguing quite the opposite: that government involvement in insurance could be a huge drag on a dynamic, efficient economy. The first volley came from a freshly minted University of Virginia PhD, Mark Pauly, who launched a no-holds-barred broadside against Arrow's enthusiastic endorsement of government insurance—in what would become "the single most influential article in the health economics literature."[34] Insurance didn't naturally make the medical market work better, Pauly argued. Indeed, it likely made it work worse. The reason was moral hazard, a problem that Pauly insisted had little to do with "moral perfidy" and everything to do with "rational economic behavior." If someone had insurance against medical costs, they consumed excessive care, driving up premiums. They might recognize this fact, even deplore it. But the incentives were clear: Get as much health care as possible, costs be damned. The result, said Pauly, wielding the sharpest rhetorical sword in his profession's arsenal, was "inefficiency."[35] And the only way that moral hazard could be countered, Pauly's critique implied, was by eliminating government involvement in insurance—or at the very least making sure insurance was designed properly.

"Designed properly," in the new efficiency critique of insurance, had two meanings, both of which struck at the heart of the argument for broad-based social insurance. "Designed properly" meant, first, that insurers had to charge subscribers in close accordance with their expected probability of requiring help, something private insurers only halfheartedly did, and government insurance virtually never did. Because they were known risks, people who had preexisting conditions, such as a heart murmur or diabetes, would be asked to pay more or even be denied health insurance. People at greater risk of disability would need to pay more for disability insurance. Otherwise, by this line of logic, insurance would unfairly subsidize high-risk groups, increasing costs for the healthy and prudent, and for society as a whole.

"Designed properly" meant, second, that insurance had to aggressively monitor policyholders' behavior to make sure they didn't engage in insurance-induced opportunism—faking their conditions, or spending excessively on insured services, or doing anything that increased their exposure to risk. If some people with life insurance were routinely going skydiving, companies needed to write such people out of their contracts. If some people with health insurance were going to the doctor whenever they had the sniffles, such people had to be discouraged from overutilizing services—or excluded from coverage. At best, such moral hazard was costly to the insurer. At worst, by encouraging people to take excessive risks, it could worsen the very problems that insurance was meant to solve, further impairing efficiency. Like the child who sees his bicycle helmet as an invitation to ride in rush-hour traffic, insurance could turn people into risk-seeking opportunists, blind to the true costs of their reckless actions.

Of course, this critique—that insurance didn't charge premiums in close accordance with expected risk or aggressively monitor policyholders' behavior—was directly at odds with the conception of insurance that had emerged out of the New Deal. Social insurance (even when under "private auspices," as the proponents of Blue Cross health plans described their mission) was *supposed* to provide subsidized coverage to high-risk groups and those who couldn't easily purchase commercial policies. Social insurance was *supposed* to protect beneficiaries from the intrusive and stigmatizing interventions into private conduct that had been so characteristic of assistance policies in the past. But, according to the new science of moral hazard, these convictions were destined for history's dustbin. The appropriate standard, this perspective insisted, was not whether insurance created broad risk pools or provided economic security. It was *efficiency*, and to the critics, social insurance was anything but efficient.

The most influential of these critics was the most improbable of tenured radicals, Harvard economist Martin Feldstein. Balding, diminutive, and bespectacled, with an unassuming demeanor and amused smile, Feldstein looked every bit as threatening to the established economic consensus as a Chihuahua to a Doberman. The Doberman, however, didn't stand a chance. Feldstein was prolific. He was a skilled teacher, commanding huge audiences in his introductory economics course, which he turned into a running pitch for neoclassical economics and its then-unconventional prescriptions. I remember taking his course as a student in the early 1990s, surrounded by hundreds of young, smart, impressionable freshmen in the grand wood pews of Sanders Theatre. The stained-glass windows gave the auditorium the feel of a church, and it was of sorts—the church of neoclassical economics. Our bible was Adam Smith's *Wealth of Nations*; our catechism the laws of supply and demand; our spiritual leader an unexceptional-looking professor in a drab gray suit whose high forehead glowed angelically under the theater lights.

Feldstein also had the ears of influential politicians. Rising stars in the invigorated conservative movement may not have read or understood his hundreds of articles, but they did understand that Feldstein was providing a sophisticated and credible version of what they were arguing: government was too big, too overbearing, too inefficient. A Feldstein article had two parts, now familiar after years of repetition by disciples and emulators. First, find a well-meaning law, regulation, or program that was designed to protect workers and their families from harm by indemnifying them against certain risks. Second, show that by reducing the costs of these risks, the law, regulation, or program created perverse incentives, making the problem it was meant to solve worse, or at least not much better. For example, Feldstein attacked both unemployment insurance and Social Security on the grounds that they encouraged the very thing they were supposed to prevent— namely, time out of the workforce and inadequate retirement income.[36] The Feldstein one-two punch was always backed up with impressive economic techniques and delivered with an air of regret rather than anger. "You may not like the truth," was Punch 1. "But you cannot deny it," was Punch 2.

Over the course of the 1970s, Feldstein churned out a series of highly technical but hugely influential studies showing that Americans, because of tax breaks and public programs, were excessively insured against health costs and other financial risks. Not only were all existing policies inefficient, Feldstein argued, the taxes used to support them were a huge drain on the economy, drastically reducing the incentives of higher-income Americans to work and invest. (In his classes, Feldstein liked to describe the three U.S. tax rates as "high," "higher," and "highest.") When Ronald Reagan was elected in 1980, he tapped the forty-one-year-old economist to head the White House's Council of Economic Advisers.

The straightforward prescription of all these attacks was that government should dramatically cut back its role in insuring Americans against economic losses. Moral hazard, this growing body of criticism hammered home, was a greater problem than insecurity— and indeed, the critics suggested, one of insecurity's main causes.

The Personal Responsibility Crusade

Politically influential critics of government did not take long to pick up the moral hazard mantra. The notion, after all, resonated deeply with longstanding elements of American political thought: the emphasis on individual self-reliance, the celebration of private markets, and the abiding concern about overweening government power. Implicit in the concept, too, was another potent theme that was gaining ground in the 1970s—a demand for individual self-restraint as the central means of dealing with crime, poverty, and other social ills, which were increasingly blamed on "permissive" government policies. Perhaps most important, moral hazard provided a pragmatic rationale for policy ideas that conservatives had once advocated on idealistic grounds. As moral hazard moved from economic circles into political debate, it thus quickly became an all-purpose critique not just of poorly designed insurance but of the perverse economic effects of government in general.

Efficiency was the lodestar of this new critique, and its most effective weapon. In the past, critics of an activist state had taken on government in broad philosophical tones. Now, they argued that government, whatever its intentions, was a *practical* failure because it impaired economic efficiency.[37] Government was not only incapable of providing economic security, in other words; it actually hurt it by harming the economy. Reagan, perhaps the most successful political figure to ride the antitax, antigovernment wave of the late 1970s, summed up the sentiment in his 1981 inaugural address: "In this present crisis, government is not the solution to our problem; government *is* the problem."[38]

This was—and is—the central message of the Personal Responsibility Crusade: Government should get out of the way and let people succeed or fail on their own. Government insurance upsets the natural working of a free society. It takes from the most energetic individuals and enterprises in society to subsidize those who are a costly drag on a vibrant economy. "Government insurance," in the words of one critic, "taxes the most productive activities to redistribute to the most risky"—one reason why "the government that governs least, governs best."[39] In the early 1980s, conservative scholar Charles Murray coined a simple syllogism to explain why good-intentioned programs inevitably went bad: "Any social transfer increases the net value of being in the condition that prompted the transfer."[40] In other words, helping people just creates more people who need help—moral hazard with a vengeance.

Thus, by the 1980s, the circle was complete. Insurance had been justified as a way of aiding the unfortunate—now it was criticized as a way of coddling the irresponsible. Insurance had been understood as a partial solution to social problems like unemployment and poverty in old age—now it was condemned as worsening the very problems it was meant to solve. Insurance had been seen as a cushion against the sharp edges of a dynamic capitalist economy—now it was disparaged as an impediment to economic efficiency. When economists used the term "moral hazard," they focused on incentives rather than morality. But in the rhetoric of the Personal Responsibility Crusade, morality was never far beneath the surface. "What moral hazard means," according to James K. Glassman, a resident fellow of the conservative American Enterprise Institute (and a leading advocate of Social Security privatization), "is that, if you cushion the consequences of bad behavior, then you encourage that bad behavior."[41]

Statements like these might suggest that the language of moral hazard resonated only on the fringes of conservative thought. Yet nothing could be further from the truth. The concept was powerful precisely because its core message—personal responsibility, self-reliance, individual discipline, private probity—resonated so strongly with so many Americans at a time when concern about the cost and economic impact of existing programs was rising. And yet, while millions of Americans happily repeated the mantra of responsibility, the message of moral hazard was, underneath it all, fundamentally in conflict with many Americans' strongest beliefs about fate, security, and justice. For as enduring as the faith in rugged individualism was, and continues to be, Americans had also come to accept and expect a substantial role for government and corporations in shielding workers from the major economic risks they faced. As soon would become clear, the message of moral hazard was directly in conflict with that role.

From Insurance to Insecurity

The role of corporations was the first to change. Beginning in the late 1970s, American business began to abandon and restructure private benefits to move risks and costs from their balance sheets onto families' bottom lines. The days of the benevolent corporation that *was* its employees' security, as "Big Yellow" once was, were over. Private health insurance declined steadily, as corporations imposed deductibles and dropped coverage, and the health insurance market fragmented into smaller and smaller risk pools.

Meanwhile, personal responsibility—and risk—was also on the rise in the area of retirement pensions. Workers who had traditional guaranteed pension plans held onto them, but new workers weren't given the option, and old-style plans weren't expanded. Instead, new workers whose employers provided a plan were offered 401(k)s and other defined-contribution plans that allowed them to save for their retirement but didn't provide any promise that the benefits would be sufficient for them to finance their old age. Workers had to put away their own money for their own retirement, and they had to manage the money capably themselves. If they didn't—if they failed to take advantage of 401(k) plans or made poor investment decisions or didn't plan their finances carefully enough—that was their problem, not a corporate concern.

To be sure, advocates of personal responsibility weren't directly responsible for these changes, which were driven by business concerns about competitiveness and a sense that workplace benefits no longer delivered the big rewards that companies like Kodak had once celebrated. But proponents of personal responsibility did abet the shift in a variety of ways. One way was by developing attractive new tax breaks to encourage individualized benefit plans that could compete with old-style health and pension benefits. In 1981, for example, the Reagan Administration authorized the first 401(k) retirement plans under the terms of a little-noticed 1978 law. Reagan also pushed for massively expanded Individual Retirement Accounts (IRAs) as an alternative to both Social Security and traditional pensions. The floodgates quickly opened to a growing assortment of costly new tax breaks for IRAs, 401(k)s, education savings plans, health care accounts, and other account-style plans that, conservative supporters hoped, would not only reduce Americans' dependence on government programs but also bolster enthusiasm for new and expanded private options.

Conservative backers of individualized private options had plenty of reasons to support new tax-subsidized accounts. Such accounts were, after all, generous all-purpose savings and inheritance-planning devices for the wealthy and highly paid. If you made good money, IRAs and 401(k)s not only let you pass on much more to your children but also allowed you to enjoy more goodies yourself in your golden years. If that wasn't enough to get conservatives on board, encouraging people to save for their own health care and retirement in tax-free accounts also undermined government programs by reducing tax revenues. And yet it was not lost on many of the most fervent backers of individualized private plans that tax-free accounts had another important salutary effect as well: having individuals manage their own risk created a powerful alternative to the existing public-private system of security. In strategy sessions, advocates went so far as to call private retirement and savings accounts a "parallel system"—parallel in the sense that it could operate alongside existing programs, gradually fostering a new constituency for private-sector alternatives and transforming popular conceptions of government's role in safeguarding security.[42] These strategists understood that America's system of economic security hadn't been built in a day, and it wouldn't be torn down in a day either. It had to be steadily undermined until—battered by hostile private-sector interests and an increasingly unsympathetic public, all but the poorest segments of which looked to the private sector, not government, for security—it would finally succumb.

This strategic rationale had been laid out as early as 1985 by a prominent conservative policy expert, Stuart Butler of the Heritage Foundation, who was at the center of the intellectual development of conservative proposals for social policy reform throughout the 1980s and 1990s. British by birth, Butler was what might have been called, in his native country, a Red Tory—a conservative free-market enthusiast who nonetheless believed that government could and should play a positive role in people's lives, albeit an indirect one. What made Butler a behind-the-scenes player in nearly every major policy drive launched under the personal responsibility banner—the Waldo, if you will, of the conservative attack on the welfare state— was the unusual savvy with which he married political and policy analysis. A keen student of Margaret Thatcher, Butler believed that the only way to cut back government's role in providing economic security was to offer voters an attractive alternative vision of government's role that was rooted in the self-interest of powerful private actors. The route to victory, Butler argued, wasn't hectoring citizens or futilely chopping away at the margins of existing programs. It was to encourage the private sector—or, more precisely, affluent consumers and private benefit providers—to take matters into its own hands, creating a robust alternative to public programs that would not just benefit influential private actors but also create the institutional means to put the government out of the insurance business down the line.[43]

I had the chance to speak with Butler as I was writing this book, and he was quite candid about the long-term conservative strategy:

> In general, an element of all of these [conservative policy approaches] is to create a parallel system based on more legitimate principles. In the process, you change people's view of risk—you get people to think differently. . . . You could just say, "Accept risk, walk it off." But what we say is "Let's essentially privatize the risk management for health or retirement." You give people other vehicles to manage the risk of living too long or being sick. You wean people gradually off of social-insurance risk management into private risk management without making them fearful about it. You have got to do it in steps and have some government protection, at least at the beginning.[44]

The target of the Personal Responsibility Crusade therefore increasingly shifted from the means (government) to the end (insurance). Rather than calling for the *elimination* of government's role, conservatives demanded that this role shift from providing shared insurance against economic misfortune toward providing individual accounts that people could use to provide for themselves and their families. Yes, these accounts would be sponsored by government. Yes, they would be subsidized by taxpayers. Yes, they would be regulated; indeed, they would sometimes be mandatory. But they would shift risk onto individuals, and this made them consistent with personal responsibility. It also didn't hurt that they could be sold as tax cuts, and that most of their benefits went to upper-income taxpayers, who tend to be reliable Republican voters.

Perhaps most important, advocates of private accounts believed that they would ultimately transform how Americans viewed government and each other. By encouraging Americans to rely on themselves, tax-favored accounts would also make people more deeply invested in the market, more distrustful of direct government programs, more reluctant to join broader risk pools—and more likely to vote for conservative politicians. Shifting from public insurance to publicly encouraged ownership, in the triumphant declaration of James Glassman, will "shift the entire foundation of our domestic politics. Today's Entitlement Age, based on New Deal assumptions . . . will fade."[45] In the new conservative playbook, accounts wouldn't just strike at the heart of the insurance state; they would also peel off voters for a new conservative governing coalition.

This larger political goal is described most grandiosely by Grover Norquist, the bearded antigovernment crusader who heads Americans for Tax Reform and helps coordinate the conservative movement through weekly meetings of an informal network of activists, organizers, and D.C. insiders known as the Leave Us Alone Coalition. New and expanded investment accounts lavishly subsidized through the tax code, Norquist insists, will "change the national psyche: increasing the political constituency for lower taxes, stronger property rights, and greater personal responsibility and self-reliance."[46] Shortly before Bush's reelection in 2004, Norquist, who famously said that government should be shrunk until it can be "drowned in the bathtub," gleefully predicted, "Four more years of more and bigger individual retirement accounts, health savings accounts, Retirement Savings Accounts, and Lifetime Savings Accounts means four more years of more Republicans and fewer Democrats."[47]

The embrace of government-subsidized accounts in pursuit of the Personal Responsibility Crusade adds a paradoxical twist to Reagan's famous credo. To the personal responsibility crusaders, government is the problem, but government is also the solution. For only government can tear Americans away from their dependence on public and private institutions of risk sharing and teach them to appreciate the age-old virtues of individual responsibility and personal thrift.

Who's Afraid of Personal Responsibility?

To pursue their attack on insurance, adherents of the Personal Responsibility Crusade have largely adopted strategies of stealth, seeking to transform existing arrangements beneath the radar screen of public awareness. Rather than tear existing arrangements out by the roots, advocates of personal responsibility have mostly worked to chip away at America's public-private framework of economic security, all the while blocking effort to deal with the growing economic risks that American families face. To see their success thus requires looking for more than dramatic policy upheavals. It requires understanding why, in an era in which more and more risk and responsibility is shifting onto the shoulders of ordinary Americans, there is so little political discussion of the crucial role of insurance in ensuring the vibrancy and humanity of a dynamic capitalist economy.

The main motive for conservatives' strategies of stealth has been simple political pragmatism. Conservatives learned the hard way that for all the natural appeal of the rhetoric of personal responsibility, frontal assaults on existing programs are a nonstarter with most of the American public. Americans believe strongly that people should pull themselves up by their own bootstraps; but they also believe that people should be protected when they are buffeted by the winds of economic fortune.[48] Conservatives gained traction when they talked about the debilitating effects of government programs and taxes in general terms. Their wheels skidded, though, when they singled out specific programs of insurance for cutbacks, restructuring, or all-out dismantling—and so they focused on changing the *form* of insurance, rather than eliminating protections altogether.

In the ideology that guides the Personal Responsibility Crusade, the abandonment of insurance is liberating. Freed from the shackles of old-style risk protections, we can plan for our own future, make our own decisions about how much risk to bear in the market, and enjoy the financial rewards of our newfound freedom as we alone wish. Freed from the specter of moral hazard, our government will be able to scale back its commitment to insurance protections that invite immoral opportunism and subsidize high-risk groups. The state will not wither away, but its role will be limited to providing people with the means—from private accounts to individual vouchers—to cope with economic risk largely on their own.

Picture our liberated worker. A hardworking professional, he takes time each morning to check the level of his IRA, rebalance the portfolio in his 401(k), see if his medical spending is depleting his Health Savings Account, and make sure the Education Savings Account he set up for his kids is accumulating enough for sixteen or more years of private schooling for his twin daughters. If he were to lose his job, he would draw on his Temporary Unemployment Savings Account—which, of course, he's diligently contributed to, knowing full well the risks that all professionals face in today's hyperdynamic, free-agent economy. If he were somehow disabled, he could draw on his Disability Savings Account, as well as the tax-advantaged private disability coverage that he purchased on his own and religiously renews each year.

His wife is staying home to care for their two new children, courtesy of a Caregivers' Account in which the couple socked away money from their first day out of college. Soon, they will draw on the Caregivers' Account to pay for a full-time nanny so his wife can go back to her own professional job. Ever resourceful, he has not only bought a standard life insurance policy but also set up a Long-Term Health Savings Account, which will cover his and his wife's expenses if they ever need nursing home care—and, like all the other accounts, can be passed on to the kids if they don't use the money by their deaths. He often finds himself shaking his head when he hears about young workers who have passed up all these extravagantly subsidized options. To each his own, he shrugs. He is certainly not going to bail them out when they find themselves out of a job or in need of round-the-clock care. And when his kids are older, he will tell them what he has learned from a life of hard work and prudent saving: The entitlement age is over.

Now let's return to our real worker, Felix Meschke, the University of Minnesota professor we met earlier. After signing up for a Health Savings Account, Meschke had been hit with hefty bills for his eleven-month-old son's hospitalization—and a painful reminder about the limits of personal control in health care for even the most educated and informed consumer with plenty of "skin in the game." On the University of Minnesota's website, the HSA's description reads: "you make decisions about how you spend your health care dollars."[49] But in the emergency room, faced with a decision on whether or not to hospitalize their son as his ear infection worsened, the Meschkes did not feel much in control. "I realized that I neither had the bargaining power nor mental capacity," confided Meschke, who teaches courses in financial management and investment. "If you're negotiating a car, you can always say, 'I'll walk off the lot.' If your one-year-old kid has an IV in his arm, you don't have the same situation."[50]

Which of these two pictures of the new world of personal responsibility awaits us? Are we on the verge of a nirvana of empowered owners freed from the harmful consequences of moral hazard, or a harsher reality of increasingly widespread economic risk and insecurity? The Personal Responsibility Crusade says the first. The changes taking place in the United States today suggest the second.

3

Risky Jobs

JEFF MARTINELLI might be considered lucky. He grew up in poverty, sometimes going hungry as a child. Even today, he remembers with shame his family relying on welfare checks to get by and hauling groceries home through the snow on a tiny cart because his parents didn't have a car. Perhaps these hardships help explain why Jeff skipped college to go straight to work to earn a living. But then again, the work was good: a factory job with high pay and generous benefits, a direct route to middle-class life. Then, in 2001, when he was fifty, the bottom fell out of Jeff's American Dream. He was laid off, and despite his factory experience, he couldn't find work. Eventually, he scavenged a new job—in pest control—but he now makes less than half what he used to. A sunny man, Jeff looks on the bright side: "At least I have a job. Some of the guys I worked with have still not found anything. A couple of guys lost their houses."[1]

Teresa Geerling might well lose her house. In 2003 she saw her relatively well-paying job for American Airlines eliminated. Like Jeff, she was lucky enough to find a new job—a night shift at a local hospital as a nurse's aide. In the new job, however, she must pay $200 a month if she wants insurance coverage, a significant dip into her earnings, which are now $2 less an hour than what she made at the airline. And unlike her old job, her new one doesn't offer a guaranteed pension plan, only the option of a 401(k). Teresa is taking classes to become a medical assistant—a better job than a nurse's aide, but one that will still leave her more precarious than in the past. It would be different if her husband's job was secure, but he has his own worries about the future: He's been told his job as a baggage handler is about to be cut as well. Forced to refinance their home, they now think they may not be able to hold onto it at all.[2]

In comparison with Jeff and Teresa, Mark McClellan initially rose higher. He had it all: a big house in the nicest part of town, a swimming pool, a new Jeep. His wife didn't even have to work. "I was right in the middle of middle-class America, and I knew it and I loved it," he said. But when his management job at Kaiser Aluminum in Washington State was eliminated after the company filed for bankruptcy, he fell right out of the middle. Now, his savings depleted, he looks for work and dreams about opening a carwash. But most of his time—and money—goes to caring for his wife, who has a rare brain disease. Because he's no longer employed, it costs him almost $11,000 a year to buy basic health insurance, and he shells out another $6,000 for the medicine she needs to live. He cares for her on his own. "Am I scared just a little bit?" Mark asks. "Yeah, I am."[3]

Mark is not alone. Though his plight is stark, he feels what millions of workers feel: *fear*. But this fear isn't the fear that we typically think of when we talk about "job insecurity"—the fear of losing a job during an economic downturn and then having to tread water until the economy picks up. Nor does this fear affect only low-wage workers in dead-end jobs, as we too often assume. The new workplace insecurity is different from these familiar portrayals: broader, more insidious, and often more damaging to workers' morale than the boom-and-bust layoffs of the past. It is driven by the growing recognition that no worker, no matter how educated, no matter how well trained, is free of the risk of sudden and large economic losses—when the economy is racing along as well as when it is struggling. Indeed, in America's new knowledge and service economy, with its huge and shifting differentials in pay and benefits, the skills in which we invest our time, our money, and our passion are both more necessary to economic success and more fragile as guarantees of economic security than ever before.

Hidden behind America's low official unemployment rate is a rising specter of workplace insecurity. According to the official statistics, the share of workers out of work has fallen in recent years. Yet the rate of involuntary job loss in the American workplace has actually been rising—and is now roughly as high as it was during the recession of the early 1980s, *the worst economic downturn since the Great Depression*. No less important, these job losses come with growing risks. Workers now invest more in education to earn a middle-class living, and yet these costly investments are no guarantee of a high, stable, or upward-sloping path. While the numbers of those displaced from employment has grown, the prospect of gaining new jobs with relatively similar pay and benefits has fallen. Moreover, growing sectors of the economy—especially the service sector, with its mass of low-wage and part-time jobs, the majority of them occupied by women—feature persistently low wages, little or no job security, and few if any benefits. All these forces have dramatically reshaped the expectations and experiences of a workforce that once operated under the assumption that employees could smoothly progress up the income ladder and move between jobs without enduring declines in their pay or benefits.

Job security isn't the same as job stability. Workers have always lost and gained jobs, and the length of time that workers typically spend employed by a given firm does not seem to have dropped much in the last generation.[4] What job security means, most fundamentally, is freedom from fear—the fear that a job will disappear entirely, the fear that specific investments in work will be lost, and the fear that losing a job will mean losing other things of value: health care, retirement security, and the income needed to maintain a middle-class standard of living. American workers today are not free from fear—far from it. And their reasons for fear are real and growing.

The New Work Contract

We've heard much about how the American economy has changed and why. Global trade has increased, exposing once-sheltered jobs to international economic pressure. Cross-border financial flows have exploded, encouraging companies to shift their operations—and jobs—from nation to nation to maximize return. Short-term investment behavior driven by an emphasis on stock value has replaced the more slow-moving cash flows of the past, giving companies less room for error and less cushion against losses. Manufacturing, with its mass of stable, blue-collar jobs, has been in steep decline, while an increasing share of employment is in knowledge and service industries marked by large differentials in pay and benefits and, often, limited job security.

Still, we know surprisingly little about the sum of these changes for American workers. Economists endlessly debate whether job stability has declined. Analysts argue about whether polls showing that workers are fearful of losing their jobs reflect real strains or exaggerated fears. Books and articles take one side and then the other in the dispute over whether the new American worker is liberated or alienated, a free agent or a fall guy. The end result is often confusion rather than clarification—even though the basic contours of what has happened turn out to be abundantly clear.

The one aspect of the new American workplace that everyone seems to agree on is inequality: Highly educated workers are pulling farther and farther ahead; less educated workers are falling farther and farther behind. There is much truth to this assertion, but it is badly incomplete. Only a small slice of the American workforce is truly excelling in the new world of work (one study finds that only the top 10 percent of earners received wage gains as large as the overall growth of U.S. productivity between 1966 and 2001).[5] What's more, inequality is rising *among* skilled workers as well as *between* the skilled and unskilled, and the previously most insulated white-collar workers are actually the ones who have seen the greatest erosion of their workplace preeminence over the past thirty years.

Inequality is real and rising, but looking at the changing economic landscape through its prism occludes as much as it reveals. If we look at the landscape through the prism of risk instead, we see that the most fundamental transformation felt by most workers is much simpler and more profound: the loss of the belief that jobs provide a stable path to or guaranteed place in the American middle class—the loss, in a nutshell, of workplace security. And at the heart of this loss is the new American work contract.

The greatest change in the relationship between workers and their employers is the transformation of the bargain that once governed their mutually beneficial but inherently uneasy relationship. The old contract—never enjoyed by all workers and almost always implicit, yet still a powerful private standard whose influence belied its less-than-complete reach—said that workers and employers shared the risk of uncertainty in the market as well as the gains of productivity from skills and innovation.

The shared gains we know much about, because the three decades after World War II are now widely recognized to have been a period of equalizing incomes and rapidly rising median wages. The shared risks we know less about, because they were less visible, hidden in the private practices of workers, unions, and employers. On the worker side, shared risks meant a certain degree of loyalty to the firm, a certain degree of commitment to the pay and welfare of fellow employees, a certain degree of restraint in demanding benefit and pay increases when times were good so that the fallout would be less painful when times were bad. On the employer side, shared risks meant an emphasis on the development of workers' skills, the provision of generous workplace benefits like health care and pensions, and the buffering of workers from the risks of fluctuating demand. The bargain held because it worked for both parties—workers received job security, guaranteed benefits, and good pay; employers got loyal, productive workers who invested in skills specific to their jobs and didn't jump ship when times were tough.

Who killed the old contract? Was its death inevitable because of competitive pressures? Or was it an inside job, driven by changing corporate strategies or the desire of high-pay workers to go it alone? The answer unquestionably is both—but the specific form that the new contract took was most certainly not inevitable.

The competitive pressures on corporations have indeed intensified. Compared with the early postwar period, firms today face greater volatility in sales, employment, and profits, implying, as one recent analysis concludes, that "Americans now find their paychecks tied to increasingly rocky corporate ships."[6] The old competitive order in which the same companies consistently topped the economic pecking order is gone (indeed, companies rose and fell out of the Fortune 500 four times more quickly in 1990 than in 1970). Gene Sperling, former economic adviser to Bill Clinton, has called this new era "the dynamism economy," one characterized by an acceleration of the "creative destruction" of innovation and restructuring that the great economist Joseph Schumpeter identified as the defining element of the market economy.[7]

But if the rise of the dynamism economy was largely driven by outside forces on companies, the corporate response was formulated in a particular context—the antigovernment era of the late 1970s and early 1980s, when organized labor and the ideal of insurance were both on the wane. Corporations and workers were thus left to forge a new bargain on their own, and not surprisingly, corporations usually had the upper hand.

The essence of the new contract was the idea that workers should be constantly pitted against what economists call the "spot market" for labor—the amount that they could command at a particular moment given particular skills and the particular contours of the economy at that time. Companies acknowledged that workers might jump ship if another better-paying job came calling. But that was the price to pay for the larger change they sought: shifting the major risks of skill obsolescence, unexpected benefit costs, and business fluctuations from corporations onto workers.

The old contract was about *shared fate*—workers and their companies rose and fell together. The new contract was about *individual gain*—workers and companies stayed together when it was beneficial to both, and only so long as it was beneficial to both. Consider the following not-atypical corporate statements of the new contract (these are from an employee memo penned by the CEO of General Electric during the mid-1980s): "The only job security is a successful business" and "If loyalty means that this company will ignore poor performance, then loyalty is off the table." At the telephone giant AT&T, executives described the change in terms eerily similar to those used by critics of the welfare state. From a system based on the ideals of a "fair day's pay, a secure future, and an opportunity to rise through the ranks," AT&T had moved to a system that "encouraged entrepreneurship, individual responsibility, and accountability."[8]

This change didn't mean a shift in pay or benefits per se. Workers who were highly valued outside the firm might do even better under the new system than the old. What it meant was a shift in risk. "If the traditional, lifetime employment relationship was like a marriage," University of Pennsylvania management expert Peter Cappelli says, "then the new employment relationship is like a lifetime of divorces and remarriages."[9] As with real marriages, some emerge from the "divorce" better off than they were before—they might even initiate it. Others fare less well. What they have to offer isn't valued at the moment; they've given their all and can't take what they've given with them; they find themselves forced to compete with younger "suitors" with attributes more highly sought after than theirs. In addition, the "marriage" itself is not based on equality in the first place. Companies have the upper hand in deciding what the terms are, meaning that break-ups usually favor them more than their erstwhile partners.

A seemingly mundane example can illustrate the profound difference between the old and new contracts. Taxicab drivers once were basically in-house employees of cab companies: The cabs were owned by the companies, which handled insurance and fuel, and cabbies split what they took in with the companies. Today, most cabbies lease their cabs from the companies, often paying more than a hundred dollars a day for the use of the licensed cab. They're responsible for fuel, and they have to buy insurance. In return, of course, they keep all their fares and tips—which can be very good or very bad. If they have a good day, they come away with a reasonable living. If they have a bad day, they end up losing money. The old world of the hit TV show *Taxi* is gone. Cabbies don't hang out at the company when business is slow. They work more hours, driving twelve or fourteen or sixteen hours a day, just to break even.

The example at first seems quite removed from the white-collar world of AT&T or GE. But the idea is the same: The risk is on workers, not shared between companies and workers. Workers might do better in this system, or they might not. But that's not the point. The point is that they face far more uncertainty and risk.

Is the new contract good or bad for workers? The answer is obviously good for some (those who are highly prized on the spot market at any moment) and bad for others (those who are not). The new contract is one of the reasons for rising inequality, especially the huge gains at the very top. Virtually all workers, however, are facing much greater insecurity as a result of the new contract, and the burden is being borne almost entirely by workers and their families on their own, rather than with the help of corporate or government measures that might pool and manage these growing risks.

Good Jobs Gone for Good

As the experiences of Jeff Martinelli, Teresa Geerling, and Mark McClellan remind us, the uncertainties of the new world of work are never clearer than when work disappears. The unemployed, like the poor, have always been with us. Yet the nature of unemployment has dramatically shifted from its pattern in the immediate decades after World War II—and in keeping with the larger changes in the labor market just charted. Traditionally, unemployment was "cyclical": workers lost their jobs when production contracted and were then re-employed in lines of work similar to their previous ones when production re-expanded. Today, however, unemployment is increasingly likely to be "structural"—persistent, perhaps even permanent, and ending only when workers accept a new job that often implies major cuts in pay, hours, or both.

The popular term for this shift is "downsizing," and it captures an essential element of the change—the idea that layoffs are not the result of (hopefully temporary) drops in the demand for a firm's products but instead of the decision of employers to shed certain workers permanently to raise share prices, deal with competitive pressures, or reorganize production processes. The change can be seen most clearly in the company policies of those employers that once promised extensive job security. A 1997 poll of large employers found that 69 percent had abandoned policies of job security, such as no-layoff rules, while only 3 percent said they still had such policies. An American Management Association survey of its one thousand member companies found high and rising numbers reporting at least one downsizing wave during the 1990s even as the economy was improving. The reason given for these layoffs also changed, from overall economic conditions to a desire to restructure. Indeed, by the mid-1990s, most of the companies cutting back jobs were reporting profits even while eliminating positions—a strong indication that job cuts were structural rather than cyclical.[10]

The key difference between structural and cyclical unemployment concerns the nature of the risks faced by workers. While cyclical unemployment invariably causes temporary interruptions of earnings—which, historically, public programs like unemployment insurance have aimed to address—structural unemployment leads to permanent reductions in income and may require retraining that is both economically costly and psychologically taxing. These distinctive features of structural unemployment, in turn, have important effects on workers' up-front investment in skills and commitment to their firms.

To see the extent of structural employment, we need to look beyond the unemployment rate to studies of job loss—involuntary separation from employment due to layoffs or downsizing, rather than voluntary quits or firing "for cause." The level of involuntary job loss in the American economy is higher than most might expect. Even during the boom of the late 1990s, roughly a tenth of workers lost their jobs for reasons unrelated to their particular performance (a traditional "firing") in a three-year period. Through the early 1990s, the rate of job loss closely tracked the overall unemployment rate. Since then, however, the two have diverged sharply. Indeed, while the recent recession led to only a tiny bump in the unemployment rate, the proportion of workers losing jobs expanded substantially and did not decline even after the recession ended.

Figure 3.1 traces out the surprising trend. The light line is the official unemployment rate, which falls steadily from a peak in 1981–83, amid the worst recession since the Great Depression. The

Figure 3.1: Job Loss vs. Unemployment

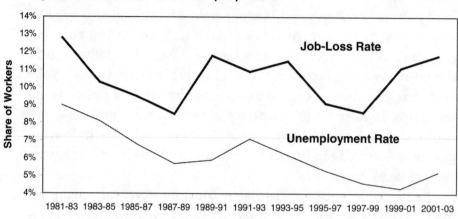

Source: Henry Farber, "What Do We Know About Job Loss in the United States?" January 2005.

line moves up a bit during the recession that began in 1991. It rises even more modestly during the downturn of 2001. Who could complain? Now look at the dark line, which is the share of workers involuntarily losing a job during the same three-year increments, according to analyses by Princeton economist Henry Farber of the Displaced Worker Survey, which began collecting data in the early 1980s. The difference is striking. Even though official unemployment has remained low through the most recent downturn, job-loss rates are now essentially as high as they were during the most severe recession the nation has seen since the 1930s.

More striking still, the costs of job losses skyrocketed during this period, reaching the highest level ever recorded since job-loss statistics started being collected on the eve of the devastating recession of the early 1980s. In the three-year period beginning in 2001—a period of economic recovery—more than a third of workers who lost jobs failed to find employment and 13 percent ended up in part-time jobs. Yet even full-time workers who found new full-time jobs—the best-case scenario, if you will—ended up earning around 17 percent less than they would have had they not lost their jobs.[11]

Statistics on the long-term unemployed tell an equally worri-some story.[12] Despite the sunny job statistics that most of us are familiar with, the share of the labor force experiencing unemployment for a half year or more—the standard definition of long-term unemployment—has in fact grown dramatically over the last generation. Indeed, compared with the late 1960s, the share of workers who experience long-term unemployment during the peak of the business cycle has more than tripled.[13] Mark McClellan's story of losing his job without a new one in sight sounds more familiar today because it is—even when the economy is roaring, there are three times as many people in the same boat.

The picture is even worse during recessions. Historically, the number of workers unemployed for more than six months—after which unemployment benefits run out in most states—peaks about six to eight months after the end of the recession. This seems unsurprising: A six-to-eight-month lag is what you would expect for a measure that requires that workers be unemployed for at least six months. Yet the last two recessions—1991 and the 2001 downturn—have seen a far different pattern. In 1991, long-term unemployment peaked nineteen months into the recovery, and in the most recent recession, it peaked *twenty-nine months* in.[14] More than two years after the 2001 recession had "ended," the number of Jeff Martinellis and Teresa Geerlings losing their jobs—and unlike Jeff and Teresa, unable to find other work—was still rising even as the official unemployment rate declined (the first time this has happened since statistics have been collected). And contrary to common perception, the long-term unemployed are older, better educated, and more likely to be professionals than the unemployed as a whole.[15]

This last point may come as a shock. After all, the general view—backed up by plenty of evidence—is that it is younger workers who've borne the brunt of the destabilizing changes in the labor market of the past two decades, especially younger workers without a college degree.[16] Compared with previous generations, today's young Americans are more likely to fall into poverty, are more indebted (in part because of the rising costs of education), and are experiencing much more variable and negative economic outcomes.

Yet the evidence is strong that established, educated workers have seen the most dramatic *increase* in the negative consequences of losing their jobs. A decade ago, during the mid-1990s expansion, workers with a college degree or higher suffered an earnings loss of less than 5 percent when they found another full-time job after being displaced from full-time employment. During the 2001–03 period, the earnings loss was an astounding 20 percent—almost twice the loss experienced by workers with *less than a high-school education*.[17] The share of the long-term unemployed who are well educated—men and women with degrees that they thought would secure their incomes forever—has risen dramatically, as has the share in white-collar jobs.[18] Increasingly, workers who had it all are finding they have nothing when their jobs disappear.

That was certainly the experience of Jimmy Richter, a thirty-year-old making nearly $100,000 at Nortel Networks when his job was cut in 2002.[19] Richter thought bouncing back would be easy, but he was wrong. No one was hiring in his field, and no one was going to pay him what he once earned, even with his college degree. On paper, the job market was tight, but every good job seemed to have hundreds of highly qualified applicants, all of them at least as skilled—and as desperate—as he. In the end, Richter swallowed his pride and took a supervisory job at a cable company for a 50 percent pay cut, putting him "back to pre-college financially," with huge debts (and, due in part to the strains of the job loss, a broken marriage). Richter was more philosophical than angry: "I used to identify myself pretty heavily through work. Now I'm just Jimmy. I have a job, and I'm glad, and I'll do the best I can at it, but that's what it is: a job."

The only truly unusual aspect of Richter's experience is how common it is at a time when the unemployment rate is so low. Why aren't employers scrambling for workers, and workers bidding up wages, when only one in twenty workers is out of a job? The answer is that many who find themselves, like Jimmy Richter, without a good job eventually give up looking for one. These are the shadow unemployed—people who want to work, who would work, but who aren't counted as unemployed because, in the parlance of unemployment statistics, they're not "actively seeking work" when they're surveyed. And however you count them, the shadow unemployed have grown.

Despite low and falling unemployment rates, the labor force participation rate of men aged twenty-five to sixty-four has actually declined in the last generation. Meanwhile, after rising sharply in the 1970s and 1980s, the labor force participation of women has leveled off and recently fallen—to an aggregate level substantially below that of men. The overall drop in male and female labor force participation doesn't reflect early retirement (in fact, workers older than fifty-five are the *only* age group that is more likely to work now than a decade ago), nor is it confined to the least-educated workers. Indeed, the largest decline in labor force participation has occurred among workers with a college degree or higher.[20]

The decline in labor force participation has greatly masked both the severity of the recent 2001 recession and the anemic "jobless" nature of the recovery that followed. This is because most of those who have left the labor force, or opted not to enter it in the first place, are not "actively seeking work" and hence are not counted among the formally unemployed. There is good evidence, however, that many of these potential workers would be in the labor force were the opportunities for them better. In 2005, according to an analysis by Katharine Bradbury of the Federal Reserve Bank of Boston, the total labor force "shortfall"—compared with similar points in the business cycle in the past—was as high as 5.1 million men and women.[21] This amount would raise the official unemployment rate to 8.7 percent, a level not seen since the steep recession of the early 1980s. Much of the disconnect between Americans' pessimism about job security and America's rosy employment figures may reflect the simple reality that many potential workers have exited the labor force out of discouragement, not because they don't want to work.

Just a Matter of Degrees?

If you find these statistics surprising, you're not alone. Much of the writing on the American labor market suggests not only that the job market is a cloudless sky of bountiful opportunities, but also that the only place where workplace hardship and insecurity still reign is among those who have failed to invest in the education and skills needed to succeed in a knowledge-based, postindustrial economy. This is certainly part of the story—the gap between workers with and without a college degree is large and growing. Yet it misses an essential fact: High levels of education may be a prerequisite for success in today's economy, but they are by no means a guarantor of middle-class security.

Just a glance at the statistics makes this obvious. Over the last generation, average education levels have risen substantially, but middle-class incomes have not. Families in the middle of the economic ladder are headed by workers much better educated than their counterparts of thirty years ago, yet these families' incomes are not similarly higher. This surprising reality is most easily seen if we concentrate on workers just starting out in the labor market— today and in the past. Between 1975 and 2002, the earnings of young male workers with just a high school diploma declined by 15 percent, while the earnings of those who had gone to college but not received a degree declined by about 10 percent. (The earnings of young women at all education levels has risen but mostly because of increased work hours.) Male college-educated workers' earnings have risen over the same twenty-seven-year period, but by a modest 10 percent—a third of a percent a year. Only young male workers with graduate training have seen a big increase in their earnings (40 percent).[22] Back in the days of my youth, a high school degree all but guaranteed a worker a stable, middle-class standard of living, but these days even a college degree is no guarantee.

To be sure, these are just the averages. Some better-educated workers do splendidly, while others barely scrape by.[23] But that's the whole point—education isn't a risk-free investment. Indeed, perhaps more than half of the rise in economic inequality in the United States involves the growing divergence of workers *with the same level of education*.[24] In other words, people with the same number of years of schooling have much more disparate economic experiences than they used to—and that means investing in education, wise as it may be, is also increasingly risky.

Risky in part because the cost of such investments has skyrocketed. A generation ago, college meant modest loans and part-time work.[25] Now it means big-time debt: Between 1977 and 2003, as the number of students enrolled in college rose by 44 percent, the cash value of student loans rose by *833* percent. In the ten years between 1993 and 2003, the percentage of students graduating from four-year public colleges with student loan debt increased from 25 percent to 58 percent. For those graduating from four-year private colleges, the proportion with debt rose from 40 percent to 70 percent. College students now graduate with roughly $20,000 in debt on average, graduate students with more than twice that, and professional students with roughly five times that. Partly because college is so expensive, moreover, a large proportion of young adults who enter its gates don't exit them with a degree in hand, even though all the research suggests that a degree is necessary for the big economic premiums (what economists call "sheepskin effects"). Not surprisingly, students who drop out are more likely to come from less privileged families and more likely to have taken on student loan burdens.[26] These students are caught in a classic double bind—after taking out loans for thousands of dollars without crossing the finish line they have no chance to reap the substantial economic benefits the actual degree might confer.

What this suggests is that many of the skills needed to excel in the new world of work are risky investments—valuable (and costly) but frequently tied to jobs and lines of employment that can seemingly disappear in an instant. Vital to success in the new world of work, and difficult and expensive to gain, advanced skills nonetheless provide no sure guarantee of economic stability. For example, knowledge industries, such as telecommunications and electronics, pay handsomely. But they are also more volatile than traditional industries, expanding more quickly during expansions yet contracting more quickly during downturns.[27] And when the loss of skilled jobs is permanent—when layoffs are not responses to cyclical market demand but the consequence of permanent restructuring—workers who've invested in the skills needed to succeed find themselves without easy avenues for deploying those skills in alternative, high-paying ventures or maintaining their former benefits. The educated rise farther, but increasingly they fall farther, too.

Ask Craig Heier, a forty-three-year-old engineer, married with three children. In early 2001, he was laid off from an e-commerce startup. Though quickly able to find another job, he was laid off for a second time a few months later. Again, he was able to find another job relatively quickly, but with a 40 percent cut in salary. Then, three months later, he was laid off again, and despite his strong engineering credentials, found no takers for his skills. Since then, Craig has been job hunting and trying to build a consulting business from his home in Oak Hill, Virginia. He has suffered from insomnia and depression, and his marriage has also felt the strain. As Karen, his wife, says, "It's been a big change from just two years ago, when we felt the sky was the limit. We thought we'd be set for years." So far Craig is hopeful about his business, and hopeful that they will be able to hold onto their house. But unexpected costs hit them hard. Under the bargain-basement health plan he bought after losing his job, a relatively minor injury ended up costing him more than $2,000. He laughs about his dream of retiring early: "My only dream right now is to get a job." Reflecting on the huge investment of time and money it took to get him where he is, he is rueful and resigned. "I'm back to where I was in 1990," he says, "trying to figure it all out, looking to start, essentially, a new career."

Who Moved My Cheese?

Should all this worry us? Richard Cox and Michael Alm, in *Myths of Rich and Poor*, think not. Yes, they concede, new economic realities have brought "sweeping changes in the way we live and work. At the same time, there's an unsettling shift from a national economy to an international one. Skills, technologies, and product lines can fall by the wayside in just a few years."[28] Yet, channeling the legions of self-help business books that tell anxious workers that change is their friend, from *Who Moved My Cheese?* to *We Got Fired! And It's the Best Thing That Ever Happened to Us!*, Cox and Alm offer this consoling advice: "*Be willing to retrain*. The average hourly wage for a computer programmer is $23.01. A typical textile worker makes only $8.25. What's more, the number of computer jobs is rising, while the opportunities in textiles are diminishing. Jobs come and go as the economy evolves, often benefiting those workers who learn new skills and keep up with economic changes."[29]

It seemed like such good advice in 1999, when Cox and Alm's book was published. Unfortunately, it looks much less sage today. Between 2000 and 2004, the computer-programming profession lost more than 180,000 jobs, about a quarter of its total employment. The outlook for the future is bleak, even though more sophisticated computer jobs requiring more advanced skills are expanding. In early 2004, unemployment among computer programmers was almost touching 10 percent, compared with around half that for the economy as a whole.

The basic story isn't so different from what has happened in manufacturing. Automation and technological innovation have made it possible for fewer workers to do more. According to the Bureau of Labor Statistics' *Occupational Outlook Handbook*, "Sophisticated computer software now has the capability to write basic code, eliminating the need for many programmers to do this routine work." Outsourcing—the movement of jobs once performed within U.S. companies to overseas subsidiaries and contractors—is another issue: As the *Handbook* notes, "Computer programmers can perform their job function from anywhere in the world and can digitally transmit their programs to any location via e-mail."[30]

To add insult to injury, many programmers who receive pink slips are asked to train their replacements in return for more generous severance pay. "It was very callous," complained Stephen Gentry, a fifty-one-year-old father of three who was still unemployed when he spoke with *USA Today* in 2004, a year after his firing. "They asked us to make them feel at home while we trained them to take our jobs." Another former programmer, Myra Bronstein, described meeting workers from India flown in for an orientation before they took her job for one-sixteenth her salary. "I was staring hard at my shoes and trying not to cry," said Bronstein. "It was hideously awkward. I felt forced. It was very deflating and dehumanizing to train your replacement. I felt sucker-punched. It was as if they handed us a shovel and said, 'Here, dig your own grave.'" She, too, was still unemployed a year after being laid off.[31]

Complaints about outsourcing have long been dismissed as much ado about very little, and indeed the scale of the practice still remains quite small.[32] Most jobs still require geographic proximity; more complex jobs are difficult to parse up, parcel out, and ship overseas. But the economists Stephen Cohen and Brad DeLong argue this may not remain the case for long: "When the offshoring of services truly hits (and it will stretch out over several decades), it is likely to deliver a much greater shock to the U.S. economy than the offshoring of manufacturing did. . . . Every job that is (or could be) defined largely by the use of computers and telephones will be vulnerable."[33]

And remember: Computer programmers are not poorly trained workers. More than 91 percent have gone to college and more than 67 percent have a degree (associate, bachelor's, or graduate). Back in the late 1990s, employers threw lavish offers and starting bonuses at young programmers just out of college: stock options, six-figure-salaries, even new cars. Today, as one disenchanted "tech" worker assessed the dismal scene, programmers are falling back to their modest status of the 1970s and 1980s, when they were "the basement cubicle geeks and they weren't very well off. They were making an honest living but weren't anything more than middle-class people just getting by."[34] Of course, those who are "just getting by" are the lucky ones—spared from the ax of automation and outsourcing, at least for now.

In the personal responsibility mantra, we are incessantly told that skills—education, on-the-job-training, commitment to a job— are the cornerstone of economic success. They certainly are. Yet skills are not costless to obtain, nor do they come without risk. Skills are an investment, and often what economists call a "specific investment"—an investment that is tied to a particular line of work, industry, or technology. And the more specific the investment, the greater the cost and dislocation if that investment is left "stranded" by economic change.

Specific investments are the backbone of strong economies: They account for innovation; they bolster worker productivity; they allow countries to specialize in the highest-value work. But specific investments also create risk for workers, because they are investments whose return depends closely on the performance not just of the economy as the whole but of specific firms, industries, and occupations. When those firms, industries, or occupations go belly-up, workers cannot easily exploit the skills they have gained and they face inevitable costs—the costs of retraining, the costs of taking a job that does not require their skills, or, worst of all, the costs of leaving the workforce altogether.

I interviewed the wife of a laid-off textile worker for this book, so I was able to ask her about Cox and Alm's suggestion to retrain. Her name is Sandy Erksa, and she works as a physical therapist and is now the family's primary breadwinner. Her husband, Dennis, was fifty-six when the textile factory he worked for finally went under after a series of increasingly desperate shuffles from one parent company to another. A chemistry major in college, he now works at a Photoworks facility as a graphics finisher, earning $10 an hour without benefits—a third of what he used to make. Sandy laughed at the thought of him going back to school at nearly sixty, but she admitted he was not doing well where he was. "It's hard for a man," she says, "He was used to having a job with a certain amount of prestige. He was good at it, a perfectionist. He got along with everybody. For him, it's been hardest when he looks at the paycheck." Then, Sandy Erksa states the obvious: "This is not what we wanted. This is not what we planned."

Service-Sector Nation

Dennis Erksa lost a high paying job at Liberty Fabrics (which, as it was slowly divested of its American workers, changed names seemingly daily—from "Liberty Fabrics" to "Sara Lee" to "Hafner" to nothing). He ended up with a $10-an-hour job in which his college chemistry degree is about as useful as his detailed understanding of how lace is made. Dennis Erksa's descent was, of course, steeper than that of many job losers, and yet it captures one of the most profound risks that workers today face: the risk of moving across sectors of the economy. Today, as the service sector continues its steady expansion and manufacturing its ongoing decline, millions of Americans have recently experienced or are about to experience this unsettling transit.

The change might be called the "postindustrial revolution," in honor of Daniel Bell's famous 1973 prediction of a postindustrial society of knowledge and service industries that don't produce physical goods.[35] Yet, unlike the industrial revolution of more than a century ago, when the movement of Americans from rural farms to urban factories changed the face of our nation entirely, the postindustrial revolution is often hidden from view. Amid all the breathless talk about rising trade and financial integration, we too often forget that the most profound transformation is taking place within our own borders, driven by forces that have affected all rich societies, regardless of their openness to foreign trade and investment. This transformation is the rise of the service sector.

The shift is etched on our economic landscape: In the late 1960s, the nation's largest employer was General Motors, which paid its workers solidly middle-class incomes ($29,000 on average, in current dollars) and provided generous benefits. Today, the largest employer is Wal-Mart, which pays roughly $17,000 on average, offers no guaranteed pension, and covers less than half its workers through its health plan.[36]

Wal-Mart and GM, of course, represent extremes. But they give a sense of the scale and scope of the change. For decades U.S. manufacturing has been in steep decline, as an increasing share of employment has moved into the service sector—industries like medical care and teaching that do not turn out physical products. In 1960 almost 40 percent of nonagricultural employment was in manufacturing. By 2002 only 14 percent was, and more than 80 percent of nonfarm work was in services. Manufacturing has not just fallen in relative terms but in absolute terms, too, with 5.2 million manufacturing jobs lost between 1979 and early 2004—over half that total since 2000 alone.[37]

One of the main reasons the rise of the service sector is such a profound change is that the skills developed in manufacturing do not transfer easily to the frequently low-productivity world of service work, endangering the economic security of those who must make the perilous leap.[38] The shift of the economy toward services thus doesn't just affect those who work in the service sector. It also threatens the jobs of millions of workers in more traditional lines of employment, whose marketable skills and workplace benefits aren't likely to move with them if they are displaced. Like Jeff Martinelli, workers who had never envisioned doing anything other than factory jobs for their entire lives face the grim prospect of moving into service jobs, from retail trade to pest control, that not only don't pay as well as their old positions but also lack the benefits they had counted on to secure their families and finance their retirements.

That's what Scott Clark faced when, after working a quarter century in a circuit-board factory, he was laid off and, after a period of retraining, found himself working fifteen-hour days as a courier for four companies—none of which provides health or pension benefits, or even a simple vacation. Asked if he could bounce back, Clark was philosophical: "I really don't know. It's just too uncertain. It really is. There's nothing there. There's nothing you can just count on. I wish there was."[39]

Uncertainty is often the name of the game in the service sector. Although service jobs are enormously diverse, ranging from mopping floors to managing investment plans, major segments of the service sector—retail trade, care-giving, customer relations—feature relatively low pay and limited benefits, with restricted opportunities for advancement. Many of these segments of the economy are also marked by seasonal employment and relatively high reliance on part-time and contingent workers and on employees who work unconventional shifts—many of whom are women.

Which brings us to another major transformation that the postindustrial revolution has wrought—the rise of a reserve army of part-time and temporary workers. In the 1950s, only about a tenth of workers were employed on a part-time basis, and formally temporary workers were virtually unheard of. By the 1990s nearly 19 percent of workers were employed part-time, and as many as 4.9 percent were employed on a temporary basis.[40] Most part-time workers are female, so it might be thought that the rise is mostly due to the increasing workforce participation of women, who are often balancing child care and work. This pattern did indeed hold in the 1960s and 1970s, but since then the rise of part-time work does not seem to have been driven primarily by growing female employment. In fact, women in their main child-rearing years grew slightly *less* likely to work part time between the late 1960s and late 1980s.[41]

Instead, the shift toward part-time and temporary work mostly reflects two other changes: the movement from manufacturing to services, where nearly all part-time and temporary jobs are found; and a marked increase in the reliance of key industries, such as retail shops, food establishments, and insurance and banking companies, on part-time work. Part-time and temporary work saves employers money for a variety of reasons, not least because these jobs generally feature low pay and low benefits (although for temporary workers, these gains may be eaten up by fees to temporary-help agencies, suggesting that here *flexibility* is the more important goal). A study comparing full-time and part-time workers *in the same industries doing exactly the same job* finds that "an individual can expect a lower wage rate if he or she decides to work part-time rather than full-time, and much lower benefits per hour."[42] As one expert on part-time employment trends observes, "The shift to part-time employment is neither a response to a technical imperative nor an outright antilabor measure. Rather, companies have shifted because they have decided cutting labor costs and enhancing staffing flexibility are more important—at least in some areas of work—than maintaining a stable workforce."[43]

There is nothing wrong, of course, with the fundamental idea that workers should be able to work part time or on a temporary basis if they want to. Indeed, opportunities for such work for those who most value it—workers in school, parents of young children, older Americans who want to continue working after sixty-five—should surely be more extensive than they are. The problem is that in today's workplace, part-time and temporary work is set up for the convenience of employers, not workers. Companies get to pay less and provide fewer benefits to workers who then often end up at the mercy of employers' staffing needs. The contingent workforce represents the apotheosis of the new employment contract—the culmination of the notion that workers are on their own, bearing all the risks and making all the investments necessary for economic success.

The Loser-Take-None Economy

Work has always been at the core of the American Dream. When the great German sociologist Max Weber wrote *The Protestant Ethic and the Spirit of Capitalism*, it was the quintessential American, Benjamin Franklin, whom he took as representative of the Protestant ethic of work and thrift.[44] More than a century after Weber's landmark work, the ethic is alive and well—at least with regard to work. We work harder than citizens of other nations, and we value work more. We are also working more hours than ever before. Indeed, our increased work hours (particularly the increased work hours of women) are the main reason most Americans' incomes have continued to rise during a thirty-year period in which workers' wages have been relatively flat.[45]

And yet, over the same generation in which we've come to work more and more, the nature of work in the United States has changed in ways that have challenged our vision of work as a guarantee of security and opportunity. The tightrope of work is higher, the winds of change that buffet us on it are stronger, but the safety net below us is tattered and incomplete.

America's program of unemployment protection has never been well equipped to deal with the risks that characterize the new world of work, and it has only grown less capable. In the original conception of the program, unemployment benefits were designed to ease workers in their transition between two jobs that paid relatively equally. Unemployment checks were meant to cope with temporary income loss, not to compensate workers for long-term earnings reductions, much less the loss of valued benefits.

The long-term unemployed weren't the central focus either. They would be enrolled in federal jobs programs or, as a last resort, given ongoing relief. In fact, under the terms of federal law, unemployment benefits have to be formally extended by Congress and the president to last longer than six months. And even though the long-term unemployed are far and away the group most disadvantaged by downturns and least capable of staying afloat, such extensions have become increasingly controversial.

In 2003, for example, Republican leaders refused to extend unemployment benefits despite the evidence of abnormally high long-term unemployment. (Workers whose benefits run out cannot reapply for benefits even if they are subsequently extended, and in 2003 more than 43 percent of people on Unemployment Insurance saw their benefits cut off before they found work—the highest rate since 1941.)[46] The conservative argument against an extension was taken straight out of the personal responsibility playbook. "A temporary change in benefits creates perverse incentives," inveighed the Heritage Foundation, "that are potentially destructive to the long-term incomes of the poorest Americans."[47]

The critics had a point: Simply providing unemployment benefits for longer periods, while necessary during downturns, is not an effective or attractive way of dealing with the main economic risk that structural unemployment represents—long-term downward mobility. There is no unemployment insurance that can help Teresa Geerling save her house or Jeff Martinelli get his well-paying job back or Craig Heier put his engineering degree to good use. There is no unemployment insurance that can deal with the permanent disappearance or erosion of benefits that can accompany job losses in America's employment-based framework of social protection. There is no unemployment insurance that can retrain workers for new jobs, much less help them cope with crushed expectations. Unemployment Insurance is vital. It is in dire need of upgrading. But it is clearly not enough to deal with the new workplace insecurity.

Tragically, our current system of unemployment insurance misses millions of the temporarily unemployed as well. Even as job insecurity has grown in recent decades, the unemployment insurance programs run by the states have contracted in reach and generosity. Between 1947 and 1995, the share of workers in covered employment who actually received benefits fell from 80 percent to less than 40 percent.[48] Low-wage workers are particularly unlikely to receive unemployment benefits. In 1995, only about 18 percent of unemployed low-wage workers were collecting anything from Unemployment Insurance. Most worked in nonunionized service jobs where employees are least likely to receive unemployment benefits. Some didn't earn enough to qualify for benefits. Others wanted only part-time jobs so they could care for kids, another disqualifying factor. Others were fired or "quit" for reasons that rule out unemployment benefits—for example, because they had to leave work because child care was temporarily unavailable.[49]

All of these growing gaps hint at a deeper issue: Even as the old model of employment has come undone, our government has not stepped into the breach. Even as corporations have abandoned the old contract, they have not forged a new contract that deals with the reality that workers constantly need to gain and upgrade skills, or the fact that women with children are now more likely to work than not. Companies are shedding or restructuring traditional workplace benefits at a dramatic rate, but few are helping American families cope with the new risks they face—the second part of our story of growing insecurity, and our next topic.

4

Risky Families

JULIE AND JERRY PICKETT represent the very definition of the two-earner, middle-class family. They live in a suburban home with three young kids, and each has long believed that both parents should be in the workforce. Julie, unlike many women of her parents' generation, always expected to contribute to her family's security through employment. For a time (ironically, it would soon turn out), she worked as a debt collector. Then, she was the owner of a small retail business. Jerry Pickett works, too—as the owner of a modest plumbing and heating company. Given her debt-collection work, Julie never let the family run more than a small balance on their credit cards.

When the Picketts had twins, however, Julie stopped working, in part because good child care was hard to find in their community. Then, Jerry's business, always seasonal, slowed down. Suddenly, the family was in debt and had to enroll in Medicaid, the health program for the poor. Even though Julie went back to work as soon as the kids entered school, the debt remained. Now, the phone never stops ringing with calls from collectors—people in Julie's old line of work. "At this point, I don't know what to do," says Julie. "I'm still paying for groceries I bought for my family eight years ago."[1]

George and Vicki Yandle's financial woes were precipitated by a tragic event: the discovery that their daughter, Dixie, had an aggressive cancer that would soon take her leg and eventually her life. The toll on her parents was enormous. Vicki, who had juggled child care and work in order to help support the family, lost her job at a local furniture store after she took time off to care for her daughter. Meanwhile, George lost his $80,000 a year job after his boss accused him of driving up the company's health premiums and of being disloyal to the firm because of his frequent trips to the hospital. After eighteen months without work, George found a new job. Yet the Yandles were still living on one-third of their previous income, caring for a dying child whose medical bills over the next six years would top $2 million. To avoid having their home foreclosed, George and Vicki even asked their grown kids to move back in and pay rent.[2]

Stories like these—and there are millions more—have become so familiar that we almost forget how distinctive they are to our times. A generation ago, families' dependence on financial contributions from women like Julie and Vicki was relatively rare. Most married women with kids stayed at home while their husbands worked for pay. Today, almost all husbands still work, but married women—even married women with very young children—are much more likely to work than not. Roughly six in ten married mothers of infant children work. In 1975, only three in ten did.[3] At the same time, the contribution of women's earnings to household income has grown dramatically. In 1970, less than a third of married couples worked roughly equal numbers of hours a week, and in about half of families, men earned essentially all of the family's income. By 2000 more than 60 percent of married couples worked approximately equal hours, and only about a fifth of families featured the *Leave It to Beaver* male-breadwinner model.[4] In the course of a single generation, the norm for married women with children has shifted from staying home to care for children to working (often full time) in the paid labor force to bolster family finances.

And bolster family finances women have. Although the median family income has grown only modestly in the last generation after adjusting for inflation, married-couple families have seen stron-

ger growth, with their median income rising around one-third between 1973 and 2003.[5] As this comparison suggests, much of the
rise in what American families take home is due not to higher wages
or salaries, but to the fact that women are working many more hours
outside the home than they once did. Indeed, without the increased
work hours of women, the rise of real middle-class incomes between
1979 and 2000 would have *been less than a fourth as large as it was*,
while low-income families would actually have experienced a substantial real income drop.[6] In short, middle-class families have gotten richer mainly because women have started working for pay or
stepped up their work hours—and this is one reason why these families' standard of living is now at greater risk.

As women with children have moved en masse from home into
the workplace, average American families are working many more
hours in paid labor, while still spending at least as much time with
their children as they did in the past. But families are managing
this difficult balancing act without some of the common supports
that working families enjoy abroad—such as paid leave to have a
child, or time off to care for sick children or elderly parents. To be
sure, there have been some attempts to improve the situation. Two
months before her daughter Dixie died in 1993, Vicki Yandle was
invited to speak at the signing of the Family and Medical Leave
Act—legislation that had been championed by feminist leaders for
years as a way of helping working parents take time off from work
after the birth or adoption of children (as well as to care for themselves or a family member in the case of serious illness). At the
ceremony, Vicki spoke of the hardship that she and her husband
had faced trying to care for their daughter and still work at their
jobs. When Dixie died just weeks later, Vicki Yandle posted a short
memorial online: "To my darling daughter Dixie, you touched the
hearts . . . of friends and relatives [and] all who crossed your path
while on this earth. I know that now you are flying free."[7]

Yet although the Family and Medical Leave Act makes unpaid
family leave mandatory for larger employers, smaller employers
aren't required to offer unpaid leave and *paid* family leave is all
but nonexistent, even among large employers.[8] Indeed, the fierce

struggle over the Family and Medical Leave Act suggests that— for all the emphasis on family values in contemporary political debate, and for all the worry about declining birth rates and an aging population—U.S. public policy treats families almost entirely as a personal responsibility, rather than a social priority. Among fourteen rich Western democracies, the United States ranks dead last in supporting mothers with children younger than six.[9] More than 160 nations in the world offer paid family leave. The United States does not, making it the only rich nation besides Australia (which guarantees all women a *year* of unpaid leave) without such a policy.[10]

Much attention has been paid to the "time bind" that both men and women feel as they try to balance the heightened responsibilities of parenting and their increased work hours.[11] Much less attention, however, has been paid to what might be called the "risk bind," the ways in which the movement of women into the workforce during a period of relatively flat earnings and rising family expenses has increased the risks to families' expected standard of living, pushing families deeper and deeper into debt—and sometimes into financial ruin. These rising risks have fallen disproportionately on women; but they are felt by nearly all Americans who've devoted themselves to marriage or taken on the responsibilities of parenthood—men as well as women, the solidly middle class as well as the working poor.

The risk bind is the major reason why American families are taking on more debt than ever before—debt that itself is becoming increasingly risky. And it is the major reason why, in a generation in which millions of Americans have gained the ultimate in private risk-sharing—two incomes under one roof—the security of middle-class families has steadily declined. The safety-net family has become the risky family.

Trouble in Two-Earner Paradise

The risky family is at odds with everything we've been told about the new world of work and family. Families are supposed to be islands of stability amid a sea of societal uncertainty. In fact, the conventional assumption about the new American family is that it serves as a form of private *risk-sharing*, allowing families to deal with shocks to income that affect one spouse by increasing the work effort of the other.[12] The analogy here might be a stock portfolio. Rather than holding a single stock (the husband's earnings), the modern family holds two stocks (the husband's and wife's earnings)—and holding two stocks is never more risky than holding one. To paraphrase the old adage of investment, two-earner couples don't put all their eggs in one basket.

The evidence on family income instability bears this point out—to a point. Singles living alone and lone parents have always had more unstable incomes than married couples with children.[13] Yet married couples with children have nonetheless seen a dramatic increase in the instability of their incomes over the last two decades—an increase that's actually larger than the rise for single parents. Indeed, what's most striking when one delves beneath the surface of the statistics is how little the increased risk-sharing inherent in the two-income family seems to have cushioned families, either against rising income volatility or other types of financial strain.

Consider personal bankruptcy. In 2001 people who were married and had kids were fully *twice* as likely to file for bankruptcy as single adults or childless couples. Even people who were married and *didn't* have kids were slightly more likely to file for bankruptcy than unmarried single adults.[14] Nor do the signs of strain end there: Families with children are more likely to lose their homes than families without children or than single adults. They're also much more likely to report being behind on their credit-card bills.[15] And they are drowning in debt, with staggering levels of indebtedness not seen among any other household type.

Clearly, something is financially amiss with the once rock-solid American family. But what? Why hasn't the rising number of two-earner families protected more Americans from the risks of financial disaster? Why are so many families going bankrupt, running up huge debts, losing their homes, or just barely making ends meet?

The answer lies ultimately in a simple fact. To most families, a second income is not a *luxury* but a *necessity* in a context in which wages are relatively flat and the cost of raising a family is high and rising. The world has not stood still, after all, as women have entered the workforce: Wages have basically flat-lined; the job market has become more uncertain; the difficulty of balancing work and family has increased; and the costs of housing, education, health care, and child care have exploded. It is families that have borne the brunt of these larger changes, and it is families that falter when, as is too often the case, the strain proves too much. The family used to be a refuge from risk. Today, it is the epicenter of risk. And increasingly, families are a source of risk all their own.

Families—or more precisely what goes on within a family, from childbirth to divorce, from sickness to disability—are a source of risk precisely because the extra work hours and income that families have gained are a necessity, not a luxury. Precisely because it takes more work and more income to maintain a middle-class standard of living, the questions that face families when financially threatening events occur are suddenly more stark. What happens when women leave the workforce to have children, as Julie Pickett did? What happens when a child, like Dixie Yandle, is chronically ill? What happens when one spouse loses his job? What happens when families themselves fall apart? And what happens to the minority of parents who don't even enjoy the private risk-sharing of marriage—who are trying to keep up with the married Joneses on a single income? How can they expect to weather the growing shocks that families face?

What's more, although having two workers in a family reduces the chance that family income will fall to zero, it increases the chance that one family worker will experience drops in or interruptions of earnings. Think about it: If every worker has an equal chance of experiencing a drop in their income, a family with two workers has a substantially greater chance of experiencing an income shock. You may never lose all the eggs when they are in more than one basket, but the likelihood of losing at least some of them is greater.

That was the story for the Grace family—an educated professional couple living in Somerville, Massachusetts. The family certainly benefited from having two earners. Peter Grace was a systems analyst; his wife, Joyce, a computer programmer working full time. But because they were both in the workforce, their expenses were high. Their youngest child was in day care, their oldest in a YMCA after-school program. Peter and Joyce had also stretched themselves thin to buy a 1,400-square foot fixer-upper in one of the hottest real estate markets in the nation—which they now wondered if they could keep.

It's not as if they were living in the lap of luxury. They had two cars, yes, but the second—a 1972 Dodge Dart—had broken down and so they were canceling the insurance on it. When they moved into their turn-of-the-century home, they had to bathe the kids in a boat cooler because the plumbing was in such disrepair. The cost of fixing the leaky roof on the place, which still lacked a kitchen sink, had required that Peter liquidate part of his 401(k). Besides the house and the now-depleted 401(k)s, the family had no savings—a legacy of long years in college, with big bills and loans to pay off.

Then, in 2002, Peter was let go by Fidelity Investments—a victim of major layoffs within the financial sector. Even with Joyce's full-time work, his unemployment check barely kept them afloat. (After months of frantic and fruitless searching, Peter was on the verge of taking a night shift at Home Depot or another low-wage service job.) And, frighteningly, Joyce's computer job was not secure either. "We don't talk about [me losing my job]," she explained, shooing her son away so he couldn't hear the conversation. "Even if they cut my hours, like they did for other people where I work, I don't know [if] I could take the eight-hour hit."[16]

The Graces are caught in the risk bind. Like millions of Americans—men and women with jobs and kids who are working hard and doing right by their families—they make up our nation's new class of highly leveraged investors. Yet what they are leveraging their futures for isn't anything grand or unusual. It is simply the dream of a good, middle-class life. Today's two-earner family tries to spread risk by drawing on two incomes rather than one. Yet, extended on credit and vulnerable to the increasingly uncertain job market, families find themselves constantly on the financial edge.

If just one family member slips, the whole financial edifice of middle-class life can come crumbling in on itself, taking the simple American dream of economic advancement along with it.

The Indebted Family

Though bankruptcy and foreclosure are the most dramatic ruptures in the thinly stretched fabric of American family finances, the day-to-day strain is best captured by a simpler fact: *American families are drowning in debt.* Since the early 1970s, the personal savings rate has plummeted from around a tenth of disposable income to essentially zero. In 2005 the personal savings rate was −0.5 percent, the first time since 1933, in the midst of the Great Depression, that the savings rate has been negative for an entire year.[17] Meanwhile, the total debt held by Americans has ballooned as a share of income, especially for families with children. As a share of income in 2004, total debt—including mortgages, credit-card debt, car loans, and other liabilities—was more than 125 percent of income for the median married couple with children, or more than three times the level of debt held by married families without children, and more than nine times the level of debt held by childless adults.[18]

Gary and Silvia Brown are a case in point. Married for thirty years, the parents of three adult children—two still in college—they seemed to have it made. By the late 1990s, they had paid off their mortgage, and both had good incomes: he was a unionized trucker, she owned a restaurant. Given all this, they didn't worry much about taking out a large second mortgage on their home to pay for their children's college tuition, which, by the time their youngest entered college, exceeded $30,000 a year.

What they didn't count on is that Gary would get injured at work and have to take early retirement, and Silvia's restaurant would fold. As a union member, Gary was much better off than most—he received $2,300 a month in pension and Social Security benefits—but his health benefits did not extend to Silvia and their two daughters. After refinancing the home again, they owed

$150,000, essentially its entire value. But they still ran up $25,000 in credit-card debt. How could they not, when 65 percent of their monthly income goes to loan payments, while 28 percent goes to health insurance costs for Silvia and the kids? Silvia eventually got a new job—which pays $2,000 a month but doesn't provide health insurance. But with Gary unable to work and Silvia already fifty, with no home equity and $175,000 in debt, the future looks bleak. "It's what life dealt us," Silvia says stoically, "and we're doing the best we can to make it work."[19]

When it comes to economic security, this may be the most troubling aspect of the debt story: Millions upon millions of families have virtually no accumulated wealth to tide them over when things go bad. The growing precariousness of family incomes would be one thing if families were building up large nest eggs to sustain them when their incomes went south.[20] Unfortunately, this isn't happening. According to the Panel Study of Income Dynamics, more than 25 percent of families in 1999 couldn't maintain even a poverty-level standard of living for three months if they were forced to spend down their wealth.

But even these estimates are optimistic, because they include housing, which is a difficult asset to turn into cash, at least if a family wants to have a place to live. If the focus is just "liquid" assets—stocks, checking and savings accounts, money market funds, and IRAs (which can be accessed for a penalty)—the picture is grim and getting worse. In 1983 just over 40 percent of families with children at home had less than $5,000 in liquid assets (adjusted for inflation); by 1998, amid the hottest stock market in American history and the fastest income growth of a generation, nearly 46 percent of families with children had not managed to save more than that minimal amount.[21] Despite much talk about the democratization of the stock market, most families do not hold stocks outside of retirement accounts—which can only be accessed for a penalty, and by risking one's retirement income. In 2004, only around 21 percent of families held stocks directly; only around 15 percent held nonretirement mutual funds.[22]

The common response to this litany of statistics is to wonder exactly why Americans are so incapable of managing their finances.

To most in the personal responsibility camp, the answer is simple: Middle-class families have abandoned the old-fashioned virtue of thrift and embarked on a reckless spending spree, confident they will be bailed out by government when the day of reckoning arrives. As *Newsweek* columnist Robert Samuelson inveighed in 2004, Americans "like to spend what they earn—and they also compete compulsively to show how well they've done. As a result, anxiety and angst become a permanent way of life, even when the economy is doing fairly well. Enough is never enough."[23] During the debate over the 2005 bankruptcy bill, which greatly tightened the nation's laws for declaring bankruptcy, conservative advocates of the legislation painted a vivid picture of feckless families running up huge credit-card debts, then asking for others to bail them out. Senator Orrin Hatch, Republican from Utah, explained that millions of Americans are bankrupt or near-bankrupt because "they run up huge bills and then expect society to pay for them." Federal Judge Edith Jones, a potential GOP Supreme Court appointee, contended that "[b]ankruptcy is increasingly seen as a big 'game,' with the losers being those who live within their means, while the bankrupts pursue more interesting and carefree lives."[24]

Yet Harvard Law Professor Elizabeth Warren and her daughter, Amelia Warren Tyagi, have thrown cold water on this condescending chorus. As they show in their 2003 book, *The Two-Income Trap*, for many middle-class families the income gains of the past few decades have been eaten up by the rising cost of basic household expenses—such as housing, health care, transportation, taxes, education, and child care.[25] Families haven't been working more hours to get ahead, in Warren and Tyagi's telling. *They've been working more hours just to break even.*

This problem is often called the "middle-class squeeze" (a term Warren coined), and it's certainly real. According to a recent analysis of consumer spending and family income, a typical two-earner family in which both partners work full time had to work 28.7 weeks in 1979 to pay for housing, medical care, college tuition, transportation, and taxes. By 2005 a typical two-earner family had to work 32 weeks just to pay these basic expenses (despite the fact that they were working about 2 weeks fewer a year to pay their taxes). After paying for these big-ticket expenses in 1980, the typical two-earner family had more than $21,000 in discretionary income left over. By 2005, discretionary income had shrunk to just over $19,000.[26]

But the squeeze by itself doesn't explain why families are at greater financial risk. Indeed, to the extent that the image of a squeeze suggests that families are caught in a static bind between costs and income, it directs our attention *away* from the mounting risks that families are facing. That's in part, ironically, because Warren and Tyagi treat family expenses in much the same way that critics of the middle class do—as "consumption" that gives no future reward.[27] This might make sense if middle-class families were spending most of their money on DVDs and designer shoes. Yet many of the big-ticket items that have come to represent more and more of family spending are best thought of not as consumption but as *investments*. They are not one-shot purchases but nest eggs that may give a big return down the line. That return, however, is risky, and precisely because families are so leveraged— both financially and in terms of work hours—they are bearing this risk with less financial flexibility than in the past.

Consider housing: Buying a good house in a good neighborhood with good schools is a wise investment in the future for most families. The children will benefit from a better education. Assuming property values stay high, families can sell their houses for more, or take advantage of the growing assortment of financial vehicles that allow homeowners to tap into rising home equity. As long as the market stays hot, families who go into debt to buy a home merely face a cash-flow problem—and one, moreover, that creditors have been creatively working to lessen through second mortgages and the like.

The problem is that there is no guarantee that the housing market will remain hot. (The sharp upward trend of the real-estate market in the past fifteen years is, in fact, even more historically anomalous than the run-up of stock prices in the 1990s.)[28] And if the air goes out of the housing bubble, families will be in serious financial trouble. What's at issue for families, in other words, isn't

just the size of the monthly mortgage check; it's the increased economic risk they are assuming as housing comes to represent more
and more of the typical family budget.

Or consider education, another classic investment in the future.
Education is a lot more important than it used to be—and a lot
more costly. Many of these higher costs have been covered by borrowing, by students as well as their families.[29] But not only is education a big investment, it is also a surprisingly risky investment.
Returns to skills have gone up, but so too has the variability of
those returns. All of which suggests that the investments that families are making in education are increasingly risky gambles.

Most of the increase in typical household wealth, moreover, has
occurred among the aging baby-boom generation, not among
younger families. Indeed, the pattern of wealth accumulation has
changed in the last generation in ways that strongly reinforce the
story of increasing financial risk for families. The economic life
cycle that most of us think of as typical ensured economic security
and upward mobility: Workers emerged from the educational system with little debt, went modestly into hock to buy a home, but by
middle-age were largely debt-free, allowing them to look forward
to retirement without undue anxiety.

Today's middle-income families, however, follow a darker path:
Deeply in debt out of college, they pay a much larger share of income to finance a home, even though they're buying homes at later
ages than in the past. Without savings, they often rely on high-
interest credit cards—America's "plastic safety net"—to weather
tough patches, or they tap into their home equity. (Between 1989
and 2001, average credit-card debt per family rose by more than
50 percent after controlling for inflation. Between 1973 and 2004,
homeowners' equity fell from 68.3 percent to 55 percent, meaning
Americans own less of their homes today than a generation ago.)[30]
And by middle-age, today's families are at the peak of their indebtedness, rather than moving into the clear.

We can see this in the Panel Study of Income Dynamics, which
has asked questions about wealth on a regular basis since 1984.
Young families whose heads grew up in the 1940s and early 1950s
entered middle-age (age thirty-five to forty-four) in 1984 with a

median household wealth of $56,271. For young families whose heads grew up in the 1960s and early 1970s, by contrast, the middle-aged situation reached in 2003 was not nearly as bright: The median family held only $31,800, or $24,471 less (all these numbers are in 2003 dollars).[31] At the same time, according to a recent study by the think tank Demos, the youngest of adult Americans are piling up vastly more debt than their parents did at the same stage of life, particularly credit-card debt. In 1992, 7.9 percent of young adults (aged twenty-five to thirty-four) faced "debt hardship"—spending more than 40 percent of their income on debt payments, including mortgages, student loans, and minimum credit-card payments. By 2001 the percentage facing debt hardship was 13.3 percent.[32]

Not surprisingly, the gap in wealth between young and old families has grown: In 1984, median household wealth of older families (whose heads were age fifty-five to sixty-four) was four and a half times the median for young families (age twenty-five to thirty-four). By 2003 it was nearly *thirteen and a half times* as great.[33] And rising debt and falling wealth for younger Americans haven't been accompanied by higher consumer spending. To the contrary, young Americans in the 1990s (so-called Generation X) spent less than their baby-boomer parents did in the 1970s. "With the possible exception of having a larger array of entertainment and other goods to purchase," write two economists, "members of Generation X appear to be worse off by every measure."[34]

The message, in short, is that middle-class families are not merely more in debt than they used to be, their debt is increasingly tied up in risky investments in education and housing. Families are facing much greater insecurity not just because they have inflexible budgets but also because the things they are spending their budgets on entail much more significant risk.

All this would be one thing if the only risks families faced came from the investments they made. But, of course, families also face risks to their earnings just like everyone else. Job loss does not distinguish between those who have children and those who do not. Skills are no less fragile just because you have decided to join in holy matrimony or take the plunge into parenthood. But there is a risk for which the distinction does matter—and this risk is a threat to families' increasingly rickety finances that few rarely think of in connection with economic insecurity: the birth of a child.

Baby Blues

After Peter Grace lost his job at Fidelity and the family was struggling just to get by, Joyce Grace didn't want her son to hear about money troubles. But when it comes to two-earner families, money troubles and kids often go hand in hand. Two-earner moms and dads are not simply workers, after all. They are also parents. And because they are, the trade-offs posed by the new world of work and family become all the more stark. If both parents work, who stays home when a kid gets sick? If both parents work, what happens to family finances when one leaves the workforce to raise a new baby or care for young children or elderly parents? These are questions whose answers often mean the difference between staying afloat or sinking for today's middle-class families.

The assumption of the economics literature is that all of the services that stay-at-home moms used to provide can be purchased privately—that a sick kid can be cared for by a babysitter, an elderly parent by a nursing home. But the love of a parent or child is not something that can be bought in the marketplace, and in many cases it is nearly impossible to arrange affordable and adequate substitutes for family care. When both parents work, events within the family that require the love and care of a parent produce special demands and strains that traditional one-earner families did not face.

At the root of the dilemma is the simple reality that raising children is long, hard (and, yes, terrifically rewarding) work—costly in terms of both time and money. Over the last generation, the expectations on parents have grown dramatically, even as the costs of parenthood have risen and the tangible rewards have evaporated.[35] Parents are expected to devote eighteen years of their lives and tens of thousands of dollars to provide continuous guidance, love, education, and care to each of their offspring. Indeed, our society depends on these massive investments to flourish and grow. But most of the costs of raising children are not borne by the societies that reap the benefit; they are borne by parents. The result is a wholesale transformation of the economic effects of kids. In the not-so-distant past, children were an insurance policy for parents— an additional worker on the farm, a helping hand when parents grew older. Today, for all the joy and love children bring into a family, they are, in simple economic terms, a risk—and a risk that parents bear almost wholly on their own.

We are not used to thinking of children in this way (and thankfully so, or few of us would probably take the plunge into parenthood). The facts, however, are clear. According to the 2005 calculations of the U.S. Department of Agriculture, raising a single child to age eighteen will cost almost $237,000 for a middle-income family. For two children, this works out to an average of 37 percent of family income per year for eighteen years. Children can be a blow to family *incomes* as well. Although many women continue to work through pregnancy, some cannot. And most mothers and fathers want to spend at least limited time away from work with their new children after birth—time that is almost always unpaid, when it is provided at all. Little surprise, then, that fully a quarter of "poverty spells" in the United States—periods in which family income drops below the federal poverty line—begin with the birth of a child, or that the presence of children in the household is the single best predictor that a woman will end up filing for bankruptcy.[36]

The strains are felt even by families that manage to stay afloat financially. Whatever the measure, families with kids are consistently closest to financial meltdown. Consider a deceptively simple question: "If you were to lose your job, how long could you go without a job before experiencing significant financial hardship?" In April 2003 the Gallup Poll asked a random national sample of employed Americans exactly this. The results were shocking: 70 percent of Americans said they could last no more than *four months* with serious financial hardship. But here is an equally shocking finding, based on a statistical analysis of the survey responses: Those who had children were about 50 percent more likely than those who didn't to say they would experience financial hardship after only a *week*. Indeed, as figure 4.1 shows, once basic demographic characteristics, like age and education, are taken into account, people with kids are both significantly more likely to say they can make it no more than a month without their job and significantly *less* likely to say they can make it for a year or more. Financially speaking, parenting is no picnic.

And, ultimately, parents *have* to do much of the vital task of raising kids on their own. Simply put, child-rearing is not easy to outsource. The core issue here is not the quality of day care—the best quality day care is very good, if often prohibitively expensive; and what research has been done does not suggest that formal child care is itself harmful (bad child care is another matter, but formal caregivers do not have a monopoly on that). The core issue is that raising kids requires serious parental investment even when high-quality child care is available, and high-quality child care is often financially out of reach for even middle-class families.

Parents recognize the value of this parental investment, and they act on this recognition. A striking finding of time-use research

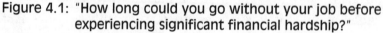

Figure 4.1: "How long could you go without your job before experiencing significant financial hardship?"

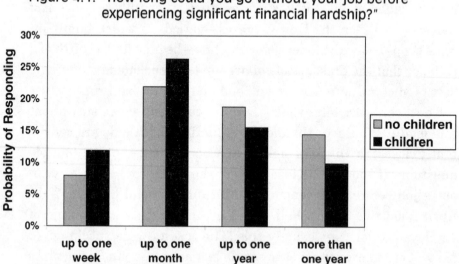

Source: Gallup Poll Social Series, April 2003, 1,000 adults. Analyzed with ordered probit model, controlling for age, education, race, income, marital status, and gender (all respondents were employed).

is that parents today spend at least as much time with their children as they did in the mid-1960s, when most families featured the stay-at-home-mom model. True, women are spending much less time on housework, but their overall time with their children has remained remarkably stable and may actually have risen slightly. Men, by contrast, are clearly spending *more* time with their children than they used to—more than a third more, in fact, than in the mid-1960s—though still substantially less than women. In balancing work and family, in sum, parents have largely preserved the precious time with their children that is so crucial. What they have sacrificed is time with each other and their communities, time spent doing other household chores, time for themselves, and time sleeping.[37]

Though children are always a serious commitment, they are an especially serious commitment when they are ill or disabled. Estimates range widely, but as many as 18 percent of American children are thought to have a chronic physical, behavioral, or developmental condition that requires special care and services.[38] The toll of caring for these children is great, as the Yandles will testify. Parents of such children are much more likely to earn incomes that leave them in poverty than are parents with healthy children, even when other factors that might affect household income are taken into account. But families with ill or disabled children are doubly disadvantaged because they must spend more on health and social services for their children on their smaller incomes. "Families with exceptional children," one recent study concludes, "are at exceptional risk of economic hardship."[39]

Parents, of course, also have parents of their own, and they are getting older and more in need of care, too. Of the 22 million Americans who are caring for elderly parents, 40 percent are parents themselves.[40] These are members of the so-called Sandwich Generation, caught between their duties as parents and their duties *to their* parents. In 2002 nearly 9 million elderly Americans reported at least one disability that limited their ability to perform basic activities or live independently. Most of the care these older Americans receive comes from family members, and the family members who are most likely to assume this care-giving role—more likely even than spouses—are daughters and daughters-in-law. Daughters who are caring for their frail parents spend nearly 100 hours per month providing assistance on average (215 hours if they are the primary caregivers). And, again, these numbers represent just the time commitment. Frail older Americans typically have relatively limited wealth and extremely low incomes, and Medicare and private health insurance do not cover most long-term health services. (Medicaid for the poor does cover some services, but only a very small share of frail older Americans who are not institutionalized are covered by it.) The financial and time costs of caring for older parents can thus be substantial, and they are costs that are rapidly rising for working families as the population ages.[41]

Linda Sylvester is a case in point. At the age of forty, she found herself caring for three elderly parents (her parents and her mother-in-law) and three teenage sons. Her mother, who is blind, lives in the Sylvesters' home. Her father, who has Alzheimer's disease, lives in a nursing home. Her mother-in-law, who still lives nominally on her own, is frequently bedridden with arthritis. When the stress and headaches began to be overwhelming, Linda quit her job as a dental hygienist, relying on her husband, Chuck, to earn the family's living. "I always feel guilty that I don't do enough," Linda says. "I don't go to the nursing home enough. I don't help my mother-in-law enough. But then I have my own kids, and I want to make sure I spend time with them."[42]

As Linda's story suggests, the unavoidable investment of time that raising children or caring for older parents entails does not come from both spouses equally. Although men are more involved in caregiving and housework than they once were, women still do the lion's share of both—and bear the greatest cost. For all their huge gains in status, education, and earnings, women today still remain much more financially at risk than men. The gap in earnings between working women who have kids and those who do not—what economists call the "wage penalty for motherhood"—remains surprisingly and stubbornly large.[43] Women are the ones most likely to have their incomes and careers disrupted, the ones most likely to work in jobs with low pay and few benefits, and the ones most likely to work part time or on a temporary basis. Not surprisingly, they are also the ones most disadvantaged when families themselves fall apart.

When Families Fail

Divorce is rarely discussed in connection with the shift of women from home to work—perhaps out of resistance to the suggestion that family breakup might be driven by simple economic calculations. Yet there is little doubt that the greater ability of women to support themselves and children outside of marriage (despite the endurance of a substantial gender gap in earnings) is an important factor in the post-1960s increase in divorce rates. Across the Western world, divorce has become more common precisely when and where women's participation in the labor force has expanded.[44] This is not to suggest that law and culture (much less love) are immaterial, only that the increased instability of American families over the last thirty years has an important connection to the expansion of female economic autonomy.

The probability of a first marriage ending in divorce or separation within ten years rose from about 14 percent in the early 1950s to more than 30 percent by the late 1980s, where it's largely stayed since.[45] This is not just an American problem—divorce rates have risen in all nations in which women have gained economic opportunities. Compared with a generation ago, the ability of women to sustain themselves economically outside of marriage has certainly increased; yet the financial effects of divorce on families, and especially women, are frequently devastating. In a world in which two earners are needed to live a middle-class life, parents working and raising kids mostly or entirely on their own face truly dire circumstances.

Those parents, of course, are overwhelmingly women, which is one reason why women experience much more severe economic drops after divorce than do men. A wealth of studies has documented that women see a drop of between 30 and 55 percent in family income when they divorce, with the biggest drops occurring in high-income families and among women who had been married for many years before divorce.[46] This is not because women's earnings fall after divorce—women generally work longer and make more. Rather, it is for two obvious reasons: Men usually contribute more to family incomes, which means divorce hurts women more than men, and women usually end up assuming the lion's share of child-rearing, which means they must bear these costs largely on their own. As a result, a startling 25 percent of young women (age twenty-six to thirty-five) who divorce experience catastrophic income losses that reduce their income to 150 percent of the poverty line or less. The corresponding figure for men is roughly 4 percent.[47]

Ann Brash was the child of a divorce, but her own life had been relatively free of hardship—until, that is, she and her husband divorced, leaving her to take care of her two kids on her own. Ann had gone to college but, like two-fifths or so of college attendees, never received her degree (she eventually did by passing an exam to obtain extra credits). Ann scraped by, homeless for a time, working as an editor for a small-time publisher, yet always insistent that she would spend time with her children, who eventually got into prestigious colleges.

Yet things went from bad to worse. Her car broke down, and she bought a new one to get to work. The deal had seemed good, but it left her with unmanageable car payments. Ann quickly fell into debt, relying on credit cards to keep going. As her credit worsened, the interest rates offered became higher. Ann finally decided to declare bankruptcy, but found that she could not even afford the almost $1,000 worth of fees that she had to pay to get the process started. The financial counselor she went to told her she had no choice—she had to stop paying her credit-card bills altogether. After seven months, she had saved up enough money, and filed for bankruptcy. But even without her debts, she is barely scraping by. "One half of the biweekly check goes to rent," she explains. "The other half to the car. Then there are the utilities and transportation costs to get back and forth to work. We're not having Christmas this year, though we will try to have a meal. I'm sorry, I don't mean to complain."[48]

Men may not experience the large drops in income that women do when they divorce, but the costs of divorce for them are rising. The familiar assertion that men always do better after a divorce is simply false—true only among the dwindling minority of families in which men earned almost all the family's money before the marriage ended. When earnings within marriage are more even (as they are for an increasing share of families), and especially when fathers have at least partial custody of children, men also suffer economically from divorce, and these losses appear to be long-lived, rather than temporary.[49] One important reason for these losses is that mandatory child-support payments have become more common, meaning that divorced men cannot easily shirk their responsibilities for their children, as they once frequently did.

Still, despite all these changes, divorce still remains much more threatening financially for women than for men.[50] Moreover, women who work longer hours are actually more likely to divorce than women who work shorter hours or do not work at all.[51] This is a new—and striking—development: In the 1960s and 1970s, two-earner couples and one-earner couples were about equally likely to break up. By the 1990s, however, two-earner couples were about 40 percent more likely to break up than one-earner couples.[52] Once again, when it comes to divorce, the increased economic opportunities of women have been something of a double-edged sword.

The Right Choices Are Risky

Strong families are the backbone of strong societies. And yet, strong families do not magically emerge. They take hard work and commitment, and they require investments—of love, of course, but also of time and money. These investments are ingrained in our nature, but they are also ingrained in custom and common sense. We are told that we should raise children in strong and stable families, that we should commit to long and healthy marriages, that we should invest in good schools for our kids and good homes for our families.

These investments are crucial and increasingly costly. Yet they have also become more uncertain, and families have been left to cope with the risk on their own. The response has been the greatest run-up of private debt in American history, as families have leveraged themselves ever more aggressively to maintain a middle-class standard of living, while working more hours than ever before.

This might seem like a simple story of bad choices, a morality tale about how we've placed work and material goods above family (or in rarer cases, the other way around). Yet at root it is an economic story. Children today are an economic risk rather than a reward, and the severity of that risk has increased. Two-earner families mark a great cultural shift, to be sure. But it is a shift that has been reinforced by an economic reality: the need for two incomes to live a middle-class life. For two-earner parents forced to pay more for basic household expenses while shelling out hard-earned income for services that stay-at-home moms once provided, the idea that choices are all that matters rings hollow.

To the Personal Responsibility Crusade, strong families are built on good personal decisions. If a family can't afford to have kids, it shouldn't. If it gets into hot water, it must be its own fault. But the stories and statistics we've explored show just how unrealistic this view is. People sometimes do make bad choices, but how can that explain the millions of middle-class families straining to make ends meet? How can it explain the dilemmas and hardship faced by the Picketts or the Graces or Ann Brash or Linda Sylvester or the Browns? And what answers does it offer to those strained families when the bottom suddenly falls out?

Forming a family and having kids is indeed the most personal of decisions. Yet when Americans build strong families, it has profound benefits for society as a whole: stronger neighborhoods, more productive workers, new generations of leaders and scientists, explorers and artists. These benefits, however, do not come without cost. They are paid for through the sacrifices that families must make, the risks that families must bear, usually without much compensation or assistance. As these risks and sacrifices increase, Americans increasingly find themselves forced to choose between economic security and having a family and children. This is a choice that truly deserves to be called "bad."

5

Risky Retirement

THE IMAGES STILL HAUNT US: Families holding folded flags, crying before open graves, processing the nightmare in the weeks after the tragic events of September 11, 2001. Ellen Saracini was among the mourners. Her husband, fifty-one-year-old Victor J. Saracini, was the captain of United Airlines Flight 175, the second plane that crashed into the World Trade Center. Victor was a former navy pilot and, according to one neighbor, "a great guy, a man's man," a fierce protector of his wife and two teenage daughters who surely "fought to the end."[1] Victor had protected his family even in their time of loss—through his life insurance and the generous widow's pension that Ellen received from United Airlines. For Ellen and the girls, the money was welcome. It would pay for college and support Ellen's parents, who lived in an assisted living facility.

Four years later, however, the value of the pension on which the Saracinis were now reliant was cut by more than half. After two years in bankruptcy, United announced that it had reached a deal with the courts and the Pension Benefit Guaranty Corporation (the federally authorized agency that insures traditional pensions) to default on all its pension plans—a retreat from $9.8 billion in commitments. United's was the largest pension failure in American history. Ellen—and her family—would see the majority of her widow's pension disappear. Like most pilots (but unlike most workers whose pensions are insured by the Pension Benefit Guaranty Corporation), Victor had earned a pension larger than the amount fully insured by the agency. There was also the fact that his employment had been "terminated" at fifty-one—well before the agency's threshold of sixty-five for full benefits. Today, Ellen Saracini describes her situation as "double jeopardy." Yet she talks mostly about the problems of other United workers. "My own situation is not a crisis," she says. "But a lot of other people have real hardship— medical costs they won't be able to afford, houses they won't be able to keep. . . . Everyone was affected by September 11, just to different degrees, and now everyone is affected by this decision . . . just to different degrees. Each one is drastic in the eyes of the person it touches."[2]

The collapse of United's pensions may have been drastic, but it was not without precedent. Just a few years earlier, Bethlehem Steel had also dumped its cash-strapped plans on the Pension Benefit Guaranty Corporation (other recent defaults include US Airways, Polaroid, and Kemper Insurance). Yet the thought on almost everyone's mind was the collapse in 2001 of Enron—a high-flying energy conglomerate that, before its fall, was America's seventh largest corporation.[3] By the time of United's collapse, the word "Enron" had become shorthand for the risks faced by workers holding a retirement account when a company goes under.

The basic problem at Enron was simple: More than 60 percent of Enron's pension assets were in the company's soaring stock, and when Enron went under, so too did workers' pensions. With Enron's share price plummeting seemingly overnight from $90 to just 26¢, thousands of workers not only lost their jobs but most of their retirement savings as well.[4] One of these workers was Charles Weiss, a well-paid technical manager who saw almost all of the $300,000 in retirement savings he had built up vanish in an instant. "They ruined us," Weiss laments. "What Enron did was perpetrate financial terrorism on the employees and shareholders of the company." Another former employee, Tom Padgett—who, at age fifty-nine in 2001, was ten years Weiss's senior—lost even more. In late December 2000, his pension assets were more than $600,000. A year later, they were

$11,000. "Betrayal is a good word for what Enron did to me," Padgett says. "There are other words, but you couldn't print them."[5]

The irony is thick: United and Enron—the old-economy transporter and the new-economy trader—have merged together in popular perception as symbols of the increasingly precarious state of American retirement security. But the obvious analogies can mislead. Each company was mismanaged; each fell into bankruptcy; each saw its pension collapse. And yet the reasons for the collapse and the story of what happened next are starkly and revealingly different.

Despite the scale of United's default, most of the airline's employees will eventually receive all of the benefits they were promised at the time of the plan's disbandment. Highly paid workers and those who do not reach the age of sixty-five before benefits are paid—a group that, tragically, includes Victor Saracini—will receive less. Even so, historically, nine out of ten workers get full benefits when their plans are taken over by the Pension Benefit Guaranty Corporation.[6] Those pensions, moreover, are based on strict formulas that protect workers even if the stock market drops or they live longer than expected in retirement. And although United won the right to default on its plan, it only did so after a legal fight in which both sides—the corporation and its workers— were allowed to make their case.

Now look at the Enron debacle. Most workers caught in the company's implosion lost much more than even the most unfavorably treated United employee. It's easy to criticize employers for overinvesting in company stock—until one realizes that overinvesting in company stock is one of the most common errors that pension holders make, that Enron employers actually invested less in their own company stock than many workers do today, that Enron matched employee contributions to the plan with company stock (and required that such matches be held till age fifty), and that, when the end was near, it actually "locked down" its plan, preventing workers from reshuffling their holdings—just one example of the plan's mismanagement that would come to light.[7]

The most important difference, however, is the simplest: Enron's retirement plan was not a traditional defined-benefit pension of the sort that United offered. It was a 401(k), and 401(k)s, like other defined-contribution plans, are completely uninsured—for the simple reason that they don't offer any promises to insure. A 401(k) pension plan is akin to a private savings account. If it grows, all the money is yours. But if it dwindles, all the losses are yours, too. There is no agency looking out for you. Nor is there any guarantee that you will get an adequate benefit for your entire retired life. For all the pain and dashed expectations experienced by United's employees, their plans were protected by a government-backed agency, and the terms of their plans were defined in precise language with legal force. The most highly paid of United's workers lost a great deal, to be sure; many others had to cope with the reality that they would no longer be able to accrue the large pensions they had come to expect. But Enron's unfortunate employees got *nothing*—no insurance, no guarantees, no compensation. *They were on their own.*

This contrast is fundamental, because American retirement security is looking more and more like Enron. As recently as twenty-five years ago, more than 80 percent of large and medium-sized firms offered a defined-benefit plan; today, less than a third do, and the share continues to fall.[8] Companies are rapidly "freezing" their defined-benefit plans (that is, preventing new workers from joining the plan), and shifting them over to alternative forms (such as the so-called cash-balance plan) that are more like 401(k)s. Meanwhile, 401(k) plans have gone from nothing to a national obsession, their total assets rising from zero to roughly a fifth of our nation's economy. If workers get a pension today, they get a 401(k). Three digits and a letter spell the future of American retirement security.

And that is what is so worrisome. Traditional pension plans are hardly risk free. Yet they have three essential elements that make them especially vital for retirement planning for ordinary workers: they are mandatory for covered employees, making them a form of forced savings; they are professionally managed under rules that prevent common errors like overinvesting in company stock; and they pool the key risks to retirement income and shift them onto employers. Much ink has been spilled comparing the returns of 401(k)s and old-style pensions. (According to a study of returns between 1985 and 2001, the dinosaurs have actually won, earnings returns that exceed those of their upstart competitors by about 1 percent a year.)[9] But the central issue for retirement security isn't the return, but the risk. Some people do well with 401(k)s; others—like Charles Weiss, who saw most of his $300,000 in assets vanish, and Tom Padgett, who lost almost twice that—do poorly. The difference, in a word, is risk.

The difference is also who is bearing the risk—thousands, even millions of Americans jointly or each account-holder individually. The Personal Responsibility Crusade has had perhaps its greatest success in the area of retirement security, where responsibility for almost all the management and risk of private retirement planning has shifted onto workers and their families. Though added almost haphazardly in the late 1970s, little Section 401(k) of the tax code—and its siblings, from Individual Retirement Accounts to tax-free education savings plans to Health Savings Accounts—have become the guiding template for conservatives' grand plan for an "Ownership Society."[10] The last guaranteed pillar, Social Security, is the next battlefront in the campaign to shift from guaranteed benefits to individual accounts.[11]

The debate is momentous, and it is about more than when people should retire, or how they should invest, or even whether Social Security should be reformed. It is about risk. To understand the real debate, we need to understand why guaranteed private pensions and Social Security were created in the first place. Then we need to understand why—in an age of growing economic insecurity—such guarantees remain more vital than ever, and ever more at risk.

The Problem of Expectations

To grasp why pensions exist—and why 401(k)s work so poorly as guarantees of retirement security—it helps to talk with Susan Lemoine. In many ways, she seems an unlikely person to worry about retirement. Her husband, John Lemoine, used to work at AT&T making more than $70,000 a year. The Lemoines have four kids, now all teenagers. She is only forty-one—more than a decade younger than John—and she works as a paralegal. But Susan Lemoine says, "I will work until the day I die."[12]

Susan is not alone in her pessimistic thinking. After consistently falling for decades, the participation of older Americans in the workforce is rising, and many older Americans who are still working say they cannot afford not to. Between 50 and 60 percent of adults, according to recent Gallup Polls, fear that they aren't prepared for retirement—the highest level of concern about any financial topic.[13] And like Susan, more and more think that they will have to postpone their retirement or, more rarely, forgo it altogether.

How can this be? Retiring without adequate income would seem the easiest risk of all to avoid. Virtually everyone but Supreme Court justices expects to retire at some point. Retirement does not, one would think, drop into people's lives unannounced. It creeps up slowly, usually with plenty of advance warning. And it is an event so common that the AARP has 35 million members.[14] So why are so many Americans unprepared and fearful?

The answer is *expectations*. As routine as retirement is, it actually involves a relatively complex set of calculations—ones that, unfortunately, intersect with serious biases in the way people think about risks and the future. Consider the variables that a relatively young worker has to consider: How much will I make in the coming years? How much of my pre-retirement income do I need to live in retirement? When will I retire, and how long will I live after I retire? Will I marry, will I have children, and how much will that affect my savings? What are the likely long-term trajectories of the stock and bond markets and the cost of living? Will I change or lose jobs? Will my health remain good? Will my employers offer me a pension and of what sort? And what's going to happen to Social Security?

Importantly, most of these questions involve the long term—at times, the very long term. What's more, many of the variables we have to consider—like future longevity and stock-market returns, much less the fate of Social Security—are inherently uncertain. Few workers in 1950 would have predicted that fifty years later people would routinely live into their eighties. Workers who cashed in stocks in August 1987 would not have known that those who did so four months later would be receiving back more than a quarter less, on average, than those who had cashed in earlier.[15] Four in ten retired workers today report that they left their jobs earlier than planned because of layoffs, health problems, or sick family members.[16] These are precisely the sorts of considerations that, as behavioral economists have found, people both routinely and systematically misperceive and regularly fail to incorporate into their planning. Traditional pensions address this problem by shifting many of these uncertain risks onto employers, who promise a guaranteed pension in retirement based on years of work, pay, family size, and the like.

Traditional pensions also deal with another problem that behavioral economists have recently highlighted: *procrastination*. When sacrifices must be made in the present to ensure well-being in the relatively distant future, many people tend to be myopic—they act in ways that they end up regretting in the future. Myopia of this sort seems to be wired deeply into the human psyche, but it is an even greater problem when current resources are scarce. With today's families often cash strapped, it is understandable why short-term sacrifices are so hard to make, even if they have large long-term gains. This is one reason why people so often "tie themselves to the mast"—as Ulysses did to resist the sirens in *The Odyssey*—constraining their short-term choices in order to do the right thing for the future.[17] Traditional pension plans do this: Because the employer contributes on workers' behalf (in effect, paying workers in the form of future, rather than current, income), they essentially force workers to save.

All this is to explain why Susan Lemoine's story isn't as unusual as it might seem. Her plight reflects the problem of expectations—or rather, dashed expectations. Her husband, John, was forced to take early retirement at AT&T, and although in the years afterward he worked more than one job to supplement his pension (as a maintenance worker at Sam's Club, then a part-time X-ray technician and full-time security guard), he eventually had to stop working because of an auto accident. If Susan had known John would lose his well-paid job at AT&T, she might have acted differently. Maybe she would have gone back to school or spent less time with the kids. And John might have saved more if he had understood that he was going to have to leave the workforce prematurely, or that AT&T, along with other large companies, was going to cut back on retiree health coverage, or if he had anticipated just how costly health care was going to be when he hit his fifties. They might even have had fewer kids.

The fact that people with good incomes and good jobs face trouble planning privately for retirement suggests how serious the problem of expectations is. Traditional pension plans and Social Security developed as a means of dealing with the problem of expectations for middle-class and working-class Americans, who had always faced the greatest risk in planning for retirement. Now, with traditional plans nearly extinct and Social Security under siege, this uniquely American solution is in doubt. And the model that has rapidly replaced it—tax-free accounts that are not only heavily tilted toward the affluent but also transparently incapable of solving the problem of expectations—is putting more and more Americans at risk.

Securing Retirement

In 1875 a railroad freight-forwarder named American Express adopted a radical innovation in workplace benefits: the formal pension plan.[18] Before American Express's move, retirees did sometimes receive help in old age, but workers had no right to benefits, which were given (or withheld) solely at the discretion of the company. This was pretty much how it stood even after 1875. Although formal plans grew in number in the early twentieth century, most salaried and wage workers were still on their own when it came to retirement.

In the popular story of what happened next, these early pension plans were devastated by the Great Depression, making clear the need for a federal Social Security program. The truth is more complex—and crucial to grasp if we are to understand what is being lost today. Formal private plans actually weathered the Depression surprisingly well. Indeed, soon after Social Security was passed, most companies that operated private plans began to build their plans on top of Social Security, a practice known as "integration." In effect, integration meant that workers received pensions from their employers that took into account Social Security payments. If their Social Security benefits were higher, their private benefits were lower. If their Social Security benefits went up, their private benefits went down.

Over the following decades, Social Security expanded dramatically to become the primary source of retirement income for most workers. But for the better paid and the unionized, private pensions were a big supplement, boosting retirement income for these workers to European levels or higher. In return for working for a firm for a certain number of years, companies promised workers that they would add whatever was needed on top of Social Security to provide a generous guaranteed income for workers and their families throughout their retired lives.

The highpoint of this distinctly American system was 1974, the year that the Employee Retirement Income Security Act, or ERISA, was passed. ERISA was designed to make private pension plans a secure counterpart to Social Security, in part by creating the Pension Benefit Guaranty Corporation, the insurance program for private plans that bailed out United's pensions. The act put in place strict rules to ensure that workers would be guaranteed their full benefits, just as they were with Social Security. The law was, in the words of Jacob Javits—the Republican senator from New York who was the legislation's tireless champion—"the greatest development in the life of the American worker since Social Security." Under the law, Javits grandly predicted, "private plans will develop more rapidly than in the past because the Congress will have assured that pension promises are kept and reasonable expectations built on these promises are not disappointed."[19]

Soon after ERISA passed, however, it became clear that Javits's sunny proclamation had not foreseen a momentous shift in the world of private pensions—the unexpected emergence and explosion of the 401(k). The result was a transformation as profound as the one that Javits had confidently foreseen, yet ultimately far less happy for the cause of American retirement security.

Ted Benna's Revolution

Ted Benna is not an unassuming man. He is quick to tell reporters of his pivotal role in the development of the 401(k). He clearly relishes his familiar moniker, "father of the 401(k)." He is tireless in his defense of his cherished offspring, insisting that few 401(k) plans have any difficulties to speak of. Yet even Ted Benna admits that he had no idea he would spawn a revolution when in 1981—thanks to his friendship with a Reagan-administration cabinet secretary—he was able to petition the Reagan administration to rule on the legality of what we now know as the 401(k) plan.

Nor, it seems, did anyone else see the revolution coming. When Congress added Section 401(k) to the tax code in 1978 to resolve some long-standing disputes over profit-sharing plans offered by employers, no mention was made of the new tax provision, except a brief note in the congressional report on the 1978 legislation indicating that the effects of section 401(k) would be "negligible."[20] It is no understatement to suggest that this may have been the least prescient prediction in the history of the American Congress.

The essence of the 401(k) is often thought to be investment in stock-market mutual funds, and indeed 401(k)s created the modern mutual-fund movement. But the hallmark of 401(k)s—the point on which Benna pressed for clarification in 1981—is that they let workers set aside *their own* earnings for retirement. 401(k)s are thus a world apart from traditional defined-benefit pension plans. The account is in an *employee's* name and under an *employee's* control. The *employee*, not the company, decides whether and how much to contribute, at least up to federal limits. Workers who leave a company take their accounts with them, either in the form of a single payment or by "rolling over" their holdings into an IRA or another 401(k). The money, with some important restrictions, is theirs, and it's still tax-free.

To American corporations—and American conservatives—the appeal of the unexpected new possibilities of Section 401(k) was immediate and powerful. Traditional defined-benefit plans were instigated by employers for two main reasons. First, by guaranteeing long-service workers that they would receive a generous pension, defined-benefit plans helped employers foster and retain loyal and skilled lifetime employees.[21] With the demise of the old employment contract, this rationale no longer carried the weight it once did. The second reason for traditional defined-benefit pensions was even less relevant as the 1980s rolled on—unions. Organized labor had always been a crucial force pressing for defined-benefit pensions. But as unions grew less common, employers had less reason to care what they thought. Thus went another motive for traditional pension plans.

If the old virtues of defined-benefit plans seemed less compelling to employers, the one singular virtue of 401(k) plans became all the more irresistible: 401(k)s are dirt cheap. In the late 1970s, employers devoted nearly 3.5 percent of workers' payrolls to pensions. By the late 1980s, they were contributing around 1.5 percent.[22] Most 401(k) contributions, after all, are made by workers, not employers. And many workers offered 401(k) plans—roughly a third—contribute nothing to them, meaning that even those employers that match employee contributions are completely off the hook.[23] It is no secret, either, which workers are most likely to contribute: those with the highest earnings. But in contrast to traditional plans, employers don't have to worry much about how skewed their 401(k)s are toward the best-paid workers, because any skew is merely the result of workers' choices.

If employers were the biggest beneficiaries of Section 401(k), they were hardly the only ones. Mutual funds and investment banks embraced 401(k)s as the Second Coming. One financial planning publication seemed unable to find sufficient praise: "A cultural icon, a measure of our financial well-being, and a symbol of democratic power—individuals of all walks of life own Corporate America through their 40l(k)s."[24] In 1999 *Money* magazine offered up a

breathless history of mutual funds and the 401(k). "Over the full
sweep of time, mutual funds have shown that they are probably the
greatest contribution to financial democracy ever devised," the review began. Then—in a sign of just how little understood the origins of 401(k)s are even among enthusiasts—*Money* placed the
creation of 401(k)s in 1975 (they were created in 1978), said they
were part of ERISA (they were not, and ERISA was passed in 1974),
and stated that ERISA "passed after years of advocacy by Ted
Benna" (poor Jacob Javits; he never stood a chance).[25]

Although the initial creation of 401(k)s in 1978 seems to have
been mostly inadvertent, it did not take long for conservatives to
wake up to their potential as a way of cutting taxes and privatizing spending. Conservatives had initially placed their faith in Individual Retirement Accounts, which dramatically expanded as part
of Reagan's tax cuts in 1981—the same year that the Reagan IRS
granted Ted Benna's petition to create the first 401(k). With Democrats in control of the House of Representatives, conservatives had
limited success expanding tax breaks for IRAs and 401(k)s in the
1980s. But after Republicans took both houses of Congress in 1994,
IRAs were expanded, and the uses to which they could be put were
loosened, making IRAs closer to all-purpose, tax-free savings accounts that could be tapped for favored big-ticket expenses, like
college or the purchase of a home. After George W. Bush captured
the White House in 2000, Republicans also successfully pushed
for a major expansion of 401(k)s, increasing how much could be
put in the accounts and making sure that this amount would automatically rise in the future.

To be sure, not all advocates of 401(k)s and IRAs had grand policy
visions in mind. Tax-free accounts, after all, represented a big tax
break especially valuable to the well off—and, hence, especially
attractive to antitax conservatives, whatever the long-term effects.
Yet the potential political benefits of the 401(k) and IRA revolution were never far from the minds of leading advocates. As early
as 1983, Stuart Butler—the Waldo of the conservative policy movement we met earlier—had co-authored a strategy memo in which
he called for expanding tax-free private accounts into "a small-

scale private Social Security system," while mobilizing "banks, insurance companies, and other institutions that will gain from providing such plans to the public."[26] In the first Bush administration, officials described the expansion of 401(k)s as a strategy of "empowerment" that "would create a framework within which individuals are free to do the best they can do for themselves."[27] By the time the second President Bush was campaigning for Social Security privatization in 2005, he was speaking of a "401(k) culture"— a culture that, not coincidentally, was wholly in keeping with his vision of a conservative ownership society.[28] Asked why conservatives should support 401(k)s, a Heritage Foundation economist said simply, "When citizens have a vested interest in the economy and own more property (or investment assets), the more . . . politically conservative your society will be."[29]

In the eyes of Wall Street and Washington, section 401(k) was the harbinger of a joyous new era. Unfortunately, it would be the first era since Social Security's creation when, instead of expanding, retirement security began to slip away.

The 401(k) Bait and Switch

At the end of the 1990s, Americans could legitimately have many doubts about their retirement security. But one thing that nobody with a defined-contribution pension plan to his or her name could doubt was that the stock market had been beneficent.

Between 1994 and 1999, the Dow Jones Industrial Average increased from 3,600 to more than 11,000. Like the fortunate child born into wealth, the 401(k) was fathered at the beginning of an almost twenty-year period of unusually consistent and rapid stock-market growth—an anomaly that is unlikely to be repeated anytime soon. Surely there could not have been a more auspicious environment for Ted Benna's brainchild to take root and grow.

All the more remarkable, then, that as 401(k)s grew like Topsy and the Dow soared, the retirement wealth of most Americans hardly rose at all. In fact, the median American family headed by someone aged forty-seven to sixty-four saw its retirement wealth fall significantly during this period. So at odds with received wisdom is this statement that it must be repeated: *Over the fifteen years between 1983 and 1998, the typical family approaching retirement saw the wealth earmarked for its retirement decline, not rise.* The stock market skyrocketed, 401(k)s exploded, but the typical family saw its retirement wealth drop.

To be sure, defined-contribution accounts grew handsomely during this period, especially in the 1990s. Yet, at the same time, median defined-benefit holdings declined as employers stopped offering defined-benefit plans. So too did expected Social Security benefits, thanks to the cutbacks in Social Security passed in 1983. When all the gains and losses are added up, the median family approaching retirement—that is, the family exactly in the middle of the retirement wealth distribution—ended the 1990s with 11 percent *less* in retirement wealth than the median family had in 1983. And the story gets worse. The proportion of near-retirement families that are likely to live on less than *half* of their prior income in retirement increased substantially between 1989 and 1998—from less than 30 percent to more than 40 percent. In other words, more than two out of five families nearing retirement are likely to be living on less than half of what they are living on now—a sharp increase in less than a decade.[30]

If these results prompt incredulity, rest assured: this is a natural response. Throughout the bull market of the 1990s, commentators crowed that contemporary 401(k)-empowered Americans were the first to truly share in the fruits of the stock market's bounty. In one sense, the claims were true: More Americans than ever invested in the stock market through their retirement accounts, but what was often left out is how unequal the scale of these investments was.

We are told that the "average" American has tens of thousands of dollars socked away in a 401(k), but in fact roughly three-quarters of account holders have less than the widely cited average of $47,000. The median among account-holders—which is a better measure of what's typical—have around $13,000.[31] And all these figures include only those who *have* 401(k)s, when only half of workers have access to a defined-contribution pension plan, and only around 40 percent contribute to one. Overall, around 70 percent of defined-contribution pension and IRA assets are held by the richest fifth of Americans.[32] And even those who do contribute adequately tend to make common investing errors, like putting their money in low-yield bonds, neglecting to rebalance their accounts periodically, and overinvesting in their own company's stock.

In the personal responsibility mantra, all these are failures of individual choice: failure to find an employer who offers a plan, failure to contribute, failure to contribute adequately, failure to manage accounts well. "It's kind of a severe doctrine," said one Treasury Department official during the first Bush administration when asked about the potential risks posed by 401(k)s. "It's rough, because you're not protecting people against themselves. They have the responsibility."[33]

But who ends up having the "responsibility" for bad outcomes under 401(k)s is not random: It is in fact lower-income workers who are least likely to receive a plan or contribute to it—in part because of the distorted way in which 401(k)s are subsidized. The tax breaks for 401(k)s are worth the most to high-income people. Unlike traditional pensions, moreover, 401(k)s can be used to save money for one's heirs. High-income workers also don't have much need for a guaranteed income in retirement, precisely the feature of old-style plans that most workers valued above all.

The all-too-common failure of workers to contribute to or properly manage 401(k)s also reflects well-understood biases in retirement planning that, we've seen, are deeply ingrained in the human psyche. Studies suggest, for instance, that simply automatically enrolling workers in 401(k)s, rather than requiring that they opt in, doubles initial enrollment in 401(k) plans, increasing it to nearly 90 percent.[34]

Yet most crucial of all, all these choices are simply not an issue with traditional defined-benefit pensions, which have essentially 100 percent participation rates for covered workers. Workers forced to save, save. Workers not forced to save, don't, or don't save enough. Yes, failure to save for retirement is a personal choice, at least for workers with access to 401(k) plans. But the structure of 401(k)s

explains much of the choice: 401(k)s are almost tailor-made to produce insufficient retirement savings for ordinary workers—and,
indeed, this is one reason they're so cheap for employers to run.

One lawyer active in pension litigation—a burgeoning field as
more and more workers at companies like Enron, WorldCom, and
Global Crossing suddenly lose their pensions—told me about a trade
association meeting at which 401(k) providers were, in his words,
"enthusiastically peddling their wares." A panel at the conference
focused on strategies to motivate workers to participate. After the
standard hortatory presentations, a human resources manager
stood up and asked a blunt question:

> Am I missing something? How am I supposed to get my workers to
> contribute more? A typical participant at my company is forty-five, has
> two kids, makes $60,000, has no defined-benefit pension, and has maybe
> $50,000 in his 401(k), tops. When I show him the fancy projections
> you're telling me about, suggesting he needs a million dollars to have
> anything like the life he's living now, he just says, "Forget it. What's
> the point?" So how am I supposed to get him to contribute more?

There was a long silence. Then, one panelist was brave enough to
jump in. If the typical worker only had $50,000 at age forty-five,
the panelist responded, that's his own fault—he can't retire. But,
of course, $50,000 is more than most account holders have in their
401(k)s. If this worker—who has a 401(k) and who's put away a
substantial sum—can't retire on his 401(k), few workers can. The
lawyer who told me the story described the conference as akin to
"an auto show at which half the cars don't have engines."

The risks posed by 401(k)s go beyond the participation problem
to encompass nearly all of the managerial and savings responsibilities imposed on workers. Consider one of the most distinctive
features of defined-contribution plans: the ability of workers to
take their pension as a "lump sum," that is, in the form of cash,
when they leave an employer. As a means of protecting retirement
wealth, this is of considerable benefit to workers who change jobs
frequently—but only if they save the money. Unfortunately, "most
people who receive [lump sum distributions] do not roll over the
funds into qualified accounts," such as IRAs and other 401(k)s.[35]
They do not roll over the funds despite the fact that they must pay

income taxes on all their benefits, as well as a penalty of 10 percent if they are younger than fifty-five.

How could people be so foolish? A clue is provided by research on what affects workers' use of lump sum distributions. Workers who are laid off are 47 percent less likely to roll over their pension distributions. Workers who relocate to obtain a new job are 50 percent less likely. And workers who leave work to care for a family member are 77 *percent* less likely. "Overall," as one economist concludes, "the evidence suggests that pension assets have been used to buffer economic shocks to the household."[36] Here, then, is another private response to economic insecurity—but one that leaves families more vulnerable to one of the greatest risks of all: retiring without adequate income.

Which brings us back to the crucial issue—risk. All of these faults of 401(k)s would be one thing if defined-contribution plans provided secure income guarantees in retirement. Yet entirely the opposite is the case: 401(k)s put all the major risks and responsibilities—market risk, outliving one's savings, deciding how much to contribute and how to invest those contributions—onto workers themselves. As 401(k)s have expanded and traditional defined-benefit plans have eroded, the nation has in effect engaged in a vast experiment to see how Americans fare in a world in which retirement planning is an individual responsibility and in which families bear the resulting risks on their own. It is now clear that this experiment has had dire side effects.

After all, defined-contribution pensions did not simply add to the menu of options that workers already had. Some fortunate workers receive both defined-contribution and defined-benefit plans, but most workers—especially younger workers—have only one choice if they're lucky: a 401(k). In 1983 only about 6.6 percent of families' private pension wealth, on average, was in defined-contribution plans, like 401(k)s; by 1998 more than half was. For households headed by workers younger than forty-seven, the shift was even more stark, from around 10 percent of pension wealth in the defined-contribution system to 62.5 percent.[37] This means, in effect, that the private retirement fortunes of all but today's oldest workers are dependent on the fate of 401(k)s. And this means, in turn, that these private retirement fortunes are dependent on the future of financial markets.

To be sure, there is nothing that requires that 401(k)s be invested in stocks. Workers are free to buy bonds or a conservative mix of stocks and bonds, and indeed a significant share of workers invest their 401(k)s too conservatively for their age, placing their money in no-stock portfolios.[38] Still, the investment gurus are right that stocks deliver a higher overall return. The problem is that this return comes with higher risk, and 401(k)s place all of this higher risk on workers, offering little of the investment guidance and none of the protections against economic loss that are inherent in defined-benefit pensions.

Sometimes, the losses can be staggering, as one unlucky employee of MCI discovered. Laid off after WorldCom acquired MCI in 2001, Jim Horner (not his real name) had worked for MCI for more than twenty years as a skilled technician, during which time he had built up $900,000 in his 401(k) retirement account. In his fifties, without a college degree, and with his skills no longer valued, he had had a rough time finding a new job and was now working behind the counter at a relative's ice-cream parlor. In 2003, a check for around $800 arrived from the now-bankrupt WorldCom. Jim feared the company was trying to buy him off, although he'd never thought of joining in the legal actions against the telecommunications giant whose "creative accounting" had destroyed the company's stock and thousands of jobs. But the check was something less sinister, and more tragic. It was his 401(k). The plan's policy was to send a lump-sum payment to all former workers when their plan balance fell below a minimal level. Jim's near-million-dollar pension—which, like the 401(k)s of many others in the company, was invested in company stock—was now his, all $767.14 of it. Although I can't use his real name, I have seen a copy of his 401(k) payout stub, and it is chilling:

Birth Date:	xx/xx/48
Employment Date:	xx/xx/79
Plan Entry Date:	xx/xx/80
Reason:	Termination xx/xx/01

Effective Date:	xx/xx/03
Options:	Lump Sum Payment
Total Shares/Units:	11,937.4735
Total Payment Amount:	$950.93
Federal Income Tax Withheld:	$191.79
Net Distribution Amount:	$767.14

Jim's situation is, of course, extreme. But the risks posed by the stock market are much bigger than most 401(k) enthusiasts recognize. Even under highly favorable assumptions, workers who invest their private accounts in the stock market during their working lives will receive wildly divergent pensions, depending on whether they retire when the market is up or down. According to one analysis that stacks the deck in favor of private accounts (assuming, for example, that they have no administrative costs, that everyone who uses them invests in a broad stock-market index fund, and that it's possible to purchase a fairly priced "annuity" paying a lifetime income at retirement), the biggest pension received by a worker is *five* times as large as the smallest, with the rate of return varying from as low as 2 percent to as high as 10 percent—a highly risky basis for retirement planning.[39]

But, of course, in the real world, it is not so easy to turn a retirement account into a lifetime guaranteed income of the sort that Social Security and defined-benefit pensions provide—which brings us to the second big risk of defined-contribution plans: outliving one's assets. To protect against this risk requires purchasing an annuity, yet annuity markets are notoriously prone to failure. The main reason they're prone to failure is that the people most likely to live a long time after retirement are the people most likely to purchase annuities, so insurers generally charge very high rates for a guaranteed income (as much as 10 percent higher than what an "actuarially fair" cost would be).[40] Hard as it may be to believe, a 401(k) account with a balance of $65,000 will purchase an annual guaranteed benefit of only around $5,000 at age sixty-five.[41] Little surprise, then, that most people don't use their 401(k) accounts to buy an annuity—an understandable decision that nonetheless places them at serious risk of outliving their assets.

Again, the true effects of the 401(k) revolution have yet to be seen. We will know them with certainty only when today's younger workers start retiring. But the signs are already troubling. Among Americans aged sixty-four to seventy-four in 2005 (that is, those born between 1931 and 1941), nearly a third lost 50 percent or more of their financial wealth between 1992 and 2002—a rate of wealth depletion that will soon leave them confronting a complete exhaustion of their assets, a much-reduced standard of living, or both. The rate of wealth depletion was even higher among those who reported they were in poor health.[42] These results suggest that while much attention has been paid to the accumulation of assets *for* retirement, far less has been devoted to the issue of how Americans managed their assets *in* retirement. Defined-benefit plans and Social Security ensure that workers receive a relatively stable income as long as they live. There are no such guarantees when it comes to IRAs and 401(k) plans, and every reason to think that many retirees will exhaust their accounts well before they die.[43]

That has been Elinor Sheridan's experience. She retired in 1998, when the stock market was booming. But because she started working after raising her children and then suffered through a divorce, her private defined-contribution account was small—around $60,000. Over a quarter of that total disappeared overnight when the stock market dropped in 2000; Elinor exhausted the rest by the time she was in her seventies. Now, she lives on Social Security and the tiny defined-benefit pension that she earned working for seventeen years for a hospital—which together provide less than $20,000 a year. Despite being in her seventies, she is trying to get back into the workforce. Ironically, her job title when she was at the hospital was "risk manager."[44] When it comes to retirement, all of us are risk managers today.

Social Insecurity

The transformation of private retirement pensions from relatively secure income guarantees into individualized private accounts makes a guaranteed foundation of retirement savings all the more important. And as defined-benefit pensions vanish, Social Security is, for the vast majority of Americans, the only guaranteed pension left. Yet the role of Social Security has actually declined in the last twenty years. The wealth represented by expected Social Security benefits fell in the 1980s and 1990s.[45] Looking forward, Social Security is expected to replace a smaller share of pre-retirement income than it did in the past.[46] And, of course, all these estimates assume that Social Security will pay promised benefits—an assumption that is safer than Social Security's doomsayers believe, but which still hinges on favorable economic and demographic trends and some adjustments in the program.

You would think that the greater risk of private retirement pensions would cause political leaders to embrace Social Security even more warmly. Of course, if you thought that, you would be dead wrong. At the same time that private pensions have grown more risky and uncertain due to the decline of defined-benefit pensions and the expansion of defined-contribution plans, critics of Social Security have argued that the program should be reformed to look more like, well, defined-contribution plans.

This is the essence of current proposals for "privatizing" Social Security, which have moved from the radical fringe of American debate to its very center. Back in the early 1980s, when Ronald Reagan was swept into power on a wave of dissatisfaction with the economy and its governance, the idea of privatizing Social Security was briefly raised but quickly beaten back. After the rebuff, Stuart Butler declared ruefully to an audience of would-be privatizers, "if we are to achieve basic changes in the system, we must first prepare the political ground so that the fiasco of the last eighteen months is not repeated."[47] Preparing the ground, it turned out, meant not only expanding private retirement and savings accounts, but also mounting a major public campaign to decrease trust in the traditional Social Security program—by engaging in what Butler called "guerilla warfare against both the current Social Security system and the coalition that supports it."[48]

Guerilla warfare was a team sport. In what would become a standard cycle, trumped-up complaints against Social Security moved from conservative intellectual circles to policy experts in antigovernment think tanks into the mouths of Republican politicians—becoming, as in a childhood game of "telephone," more grandiose and inaccurate at each step of the journey. Thus the respected Harvard economist Martin Feldstein wrote a series of highly influential—and, it soon became clear, highly flawed—analyses arguing that Social Security was not only inherently unsound but a massive drag on the economy.[49] His complaints were picked up by anti-Social Security policy experts who dumbed them down for a broader audience and trumped them up for the press-release world of Washington. Within a matter of years, these talking points became the standard mantra of Republican leaders: Social Security was going broke; it was drastically reducing national savings; it was bad for widows and blacks; it was a form of fiscal child abuse that allowed greedy seniors to rob from the younger generation.[50]

The claims were often as preposterous as they were powerful. (How, for example, could Social Security so grievously disadvantage women when they received so much more back from the program relative to what they had paid in than did men? How could the program be running on empty when Republicans were calling for using the surplus in the program's trust fund to pay for new tax cuts?) But the plausibility of the Chicken Little chorus was less important than its overall impact. What Social Security had going for it, besides the fact that people liked its basic goal, was that millions of Americans had paid into it and expected to get back what they had been promised when they retired. Convincing Americans that the chance of getting full Social Security benefits was lower than the chance of aliens landing on Earth—as one humorous but completely bungled anti–Social Security survey suggested most younger workers felt—made the task of blowing up the present system that much easier.[51]

Still, the reality that workers expected to get back what they had paid in was the softest of soft underbellies of all plans for privatizing Social Security. The problem is this: Since the late 1930s, Social Security has paid benefits with the revenue raised by current workers' contributions. Money from one generation of workers finances the retirement of their parents and grandparents. If, however, Social Security is to become a system of private IRA-style accounts, into which current workers put some or all of the money that they would have paid in taxes, the trillions needed to pay promised benefits have to come from somewhere else—or, more precisely, from new taxes, new benefits cuts, new borrowing, or some mix of the three. This fundamental dilemma is all the more acute because advocates of privatization know that the one thing they cannot do is threaten the benefits of the presently retired and those nearing retirement. Without a commitment to honor past contributions into the traditional system, Butler warned in 1983, "we can never overcome the political opposition to reform." Yet this commitment, he quickly added, "necessarily place[s] constraints on the mechanisms that can be used to move the country towards a private system."[52]

What was completely swept under the rug in the campaign to sell the public and politically skittish leaders on privatization was how serious those "constraints" were. The costs of switching over to a private system came to be known as "transition costs," as if these were small and temporary hurdles to a win-win outcome. Yet these "transition costs" could run into the trillions and stretch out for decades into the future.[53]

And they were indeed real costs. Advocates of privatization could have simply said that benefits for retirees were too high and had to be cut, with the savings going into private accounts. But they knew all along that this was a losing strategy. Instead, they said private accounts would simply give all Americans the choice of obtaining higher returns in the stock market, without imposing serious burdens on anyone—a claim that was doubly false. The truth was that once the euphemistically labeled transition costs were taken into account and reasonable adjustments were made for the administrative costs of millions of new investment plans, Social Security provided a competitive rate of return. More important, the only way to pay the "transition costs" was to take something away from someone—either retirees in the form of lower benefits, all Americans in the form of higher taxes or reduced spending on other valued ends, or future generations in the form of new gov-ernment debt. The free-lunch mantra simply denied basic rules of accounting.

More crucial still, the entire case for privatization bypassed the most fundamental issue of all: economic risk. Social Security, after all, is an insurance program, not a private investment account. It offers a guaranteed benefit in retirement that is more generous to families with low lifetime incomes, whose heads are disabled or pass away, and who have the good fortune to live a long time after retirement (elderly widows are the chief example). The program protects families not just against these risks but also against the risk of large drops in their assets due to stock-market or housing-price instability as well as the risk of unexpected inflation, which can devastate families on fixed incomes.

Virtually all of these protections would be undercut or elimi-nated by privatization. Workers would see their guaranteed bene-fits largely replaced by the returns on their accounts, which could vary greatly from person to person. Those disabled before retire-ment, those who end up living a long time after retirement, those with low incomes, those who retire when the stock market drops—all might end up with less than they would have enjoyed had they received the guaranteed benefit. In short, a social insurance pro-gram would be replaced by a system that shifted much more risk onto the shoulders of individual workers and their families.

Critics of Social Security sometimes scoff at this observation, noting that Social Security, too, is risky because it will need addi-tional funds to pay promised benefits and because politicians can change the program at any time. The first point—about the program's potential funding problems—is valid but misguided as a basis for privatizing Social Security, because privatization will do nothing to help the program pay full benefits, and indeed will make it harder for it to do so.

The second point—about the risk of political intervention—is almost certainly wrong, as well as more than a little disingenuous. Social Security could be changed at any moment, but the popular view of the program as the "third rail" of American politics suggests that politicians don't wake up every morning eager to change it. Indeed, the only politicians trying to upend the program today are precisely the ones invoking the specter of politicians trying to upend the program. (It is like a mugger telling you to give up your wallet because someone might take it.) In any case, a system of private accounts would be open to similar sorts of political chicanery, because, as already noted, these accounts would be created by, funded by, and regulated by the federal government.

Social Security—because it pools risk across millions of citizens and uses the power of government to guarantee against the major threats to family income during (and, in some cases, before) retirement—simply does not have the kind of inherent uncertainty built into it that private accounts would. According to one reputable calculation, based on historical and global stock returns, half of Americans who set up private accounts would fail to do better than they would under Social Security even if they used the conservative investment strategy (50 percent bonds/50 percent stocks) suggested by the President's Commission to Strengthen Social Security. Meanwhile, the least fortunate 10 percent of accountholders would each lose at least $49,980 in net retirement wealth. Losses like this are simply inconceivable under the present system.[54]

Given all this, it is remarkable how successful the Personal Responsibility Crusade has been in taking on the most popular and triumphant of America's bulwarks against insecurity. The reason for this success is clearly not the inherent appeal or plausibility of the case. Even after two decades of softening up the public, critics of Social Security seem to have fallen flat in their most concerted attempt yet to convince Americans that the program should be partially privatized. Intellectually, the case for reform is riddled with errors and non sequiturs that are so obvious and embarrassing that few nonbelievers would take the case seriously if it were not so influential among current political leaders. To be sure, Social Security has been weakened by its long-term funding gap, but, as we've seen, this would only be worsened by privatization plans.

The success of the Personal Responsibility Crusade in assaulting Social Security must instead be chalked up to the savvy, coordinated strategy of the crusaders themselves, who have boxed in the program by building up an alternative intellectual movement and programmatic infrastructure that covertly strikes at the heart of Social Security's insurance functions. In 1980 conservative policy advocate Peter Ferrara forthrightly said, in an anti–Social Security manifesto funded by the Cato Institute, that Social Security's insurance function should be handed over to the private sector and the rest of the program shunted off to the welfare system.[55] By 2005 when George W. Bush became the first president to take on Social Security, a frontal attack on America's most popular social program had come to be portrayed as the system's logical and costless continuation.

Reclaiming Retirement Security

The argument of advocates of privatization is exactly the opposite of the notion that Social Security needs to remain a vital foundation of retirement security. It is that Social Security should jump on the 401(k) bandwagon and expose workers to even more of the risk that Social Security was originally designed to protect them from.

The plight of ordinary Americans like Charles Weiss, Tom Padgett, Susan Lemoine, Jim Horner, and Elinor Sheridan reminds us just how foolish such a move would be. Over the last twenty years, the nation has shifted more and more of the risk and responsibility for retirement planning from employers and government onto workers and their families. Some Americans have done extremely well under this uncertain new system. Many others, however, have barely budged upward, and the majority have basically stood still or fallen. All of us, however, are facing far greater risk in planning for our postwork years.

The promise of private pensions at their heyday was a secure retirement income that, when coupled with Social Security, would allow older Americans to spend their retired years in relative comfort. That promise, it is clear, will no longer be kept. But reforms to our private pension system could make private retirement accounts work far better as a source of secure retirement income. And the promise of Social Security *can* be kept—if we recognize and safeguard its vital role in providing economic security for American families.

6

Risky Health Care

ARNOLD DORSETT was an American success story. An air conditioner repairman, he earned more than his father ever did—almost $70,000 a year, thanks to a relentless schedule of eighty- to ninety-hour workweeks. He owned a good home in the suburbs. His young wife, Sharon—training to be a nurse when they met, and hoping to return to school soon—stayed home to care for their three kids. Arnold was driven, a striver. He was also, it turned out, the father of a young boy who was sick and getting sicker.

Zachary had not been healthy since his birth—one reason why Sharon had never gotten that nursing degree and Arnold was working so hard to pay the bills. But it was not until Zachary was eight that he was diagnosed with an immune system disorder that promised even bigger medical costs down the road. By then, the bills had already crushed the family's finances. Despite having health insurance and refinancing their home, the Dorsetts had run up nearly $30,000 in outstanding credit-card balances and could no longer make their car or mortgage payments. In March 2005 they succumbed to the inevitable and filed for bankruptcy, becoming one of the 425,000 to 700,000 Americans a year whose bankruptcies are medically related.[1] It was not an easy choice. Losing their house they could accept. Losing their pride was a different matter.

"I make good money, and I work hard for it," Arnold Dorsett told the *New York Times*. "When I filed for bankruptcy, I felt I failed."[2]

Crises like Arnold Dorsett's rarely make the headlines as they did in this case. The health woes of everyday families have simply become too numbingly familiar. Every thirty seconds, someone files a bankruptcy claim that's due in part to medical costs and crises.[3] Most who file have insurance, almost all are working. But insurance and employment aren't always enough.

Consider the grim statistics. Among *insured* Americans, 51 million spend more than 10 percent of their income on medical care.[4] One out of six working-age adults are carrying medical debt, and 70 percent had insurance when they incurred it. Of those with private insurance and medical debt, fully half have incomes greater than $40,000, and of this group a third are college graduates or have had postgraduate education.[5] Meanwhile, millions upon millions of otherwise fortunate Americans find themselves uninsured at some point, and often at several points, during their lives. Everyone has heard the numbers: 46 million Americans without health insurance, the vast majority of them in working families.[6] But the uninsured are a constantly shifting group that includes many more people than that. In the two years beginning in 2003, a stunning 82 million people—one out of three nonelderly Americans—went without health insurance at some point. Most were uninsured for at least half a year; more than half were uninsured for at least nine months.[7] And yet these ordinary Americans at extraordinary risk have for years remained largely unnoticed, an inconvenient blot on the heralded success story of the American economy.

In the last few years, however, the financial maelstrom that engulfed the Dorsetts has started to move from the back pages to the front pages. Anxious conversations in corporate boardrooms and around kitchen tables have gradually grown into a national debate about America's crumbling infrastructure of health financing. The players in the discussion range from the giant old-economy manufacturer GM, which estimates it spends around $1,400 per finished vehicle on health costs, to the sprawling new-economy behemoth Wal-Mart, which has come under increasing fire for its stingy health benefits even as its medical costs grow.[8] The players include state governments alarmed about the rising cost of the Medicaid program for the poor, and national officials sharply at odds about the future of Medicare for the aged. And they include families like the Dorsetts, who never thought they'd be in the dark shadows of America's shiny high-tech system. "My friends don't understand it," Sharon admits, describing her bankruptcy. "They think, How could it get so bad so quick? Unless you have a sick kid, you don't know what it's like."[9]

Sadly, more and more Americans know what it's like—from the parents of sick children to elderly Americans trying to afford prescription drugs to workers struggling to pay their health premiums (or finding their employers don't offer health benefits at all). In the last half decade, the unraveling of American health insurance has accelerated at a frightening pace. Since 2000 the proportion of employers offering health coverage to their workers has fallen by nearly ten percentage points, and the proportion of employers that finance the full cost of coverage—once the norm—has plummeted, from 29 percent to 17 percent for individual health insurance and from 11 percent to 6 percent for family health premiums.[10] Meanwhile, premiums have shot up—increasing at *five* times the rate of inflation since 2000, while most workers' wages have barely increased at all. In just the last four years, the share of moderate-income Americans who lack health coverage has risen from just over one quarter to more than 40 percent.[11] A system that was barely treading water is now sinking fast.

This is not the first time American political leaders have debated the future of the United States' distinctive system of health care financing. Again and again in the twentieth century—most recently in the 1990s—efforts to make health insurance an integral piece of the American social fabric were stymied. But today, medical costs and insurance are at the heart of insecurity in the United States, and a growing number of corporate and political leaders, and everyday Americans, know something must be done. Unfortunately, a new barrier now stands in the way of broad risk protection in American health care—the Personal Responsibility

Crusade and its chilling call for individualized Health Savings Accounts that could topple the already-fragile structure of American health insurance.

Sick Markets

Health care in the United States is better than ever. Astounding advances in research and clinical practice have meant that diseases that once killed or hobbled almost everyone they struck can now be effectively treated and sometimes cured. Basic medical care is more refined and capable, if not always more available. Americans live longer than they used to; they are less likely to spend their later years with debilitating conditions; and they have a much larger range of treatment options, at least when they have the money to pay for them. Americans are hardly alone: The differences across rich countries in the quality of medical care today pale in comparison to the differences between present medical technology and the options of a generation ago.

The problem is, health care is also more expensive than ever, and this rising cost is creating pervasive insecurity in the United States. The dirty little secret about America's $2-trillion-a-year medical complex is that it is enormously wasteful, ill-targeted, and inefficient. The best American medical care is very good, but the insurance framework through which that care is financed is very bad—and exorbitantly expensive. The United States spends more as a share of its economy on health care than any other nation. Indeed, its public programs, which cover less than half the population, cost more per American than citizens in other rich nations pay per person for their *universal* programs.[12] On top of this staggering direct cost, nearly $190 billion a year is spent indirectly in the form of federal tax breaks for employer-provided health benefits.[13] And yet all this spending has not bought Americans the one thing that health insurance is supposed to provide: security.

Health insecurity is not confined to one part of the population. It is experienced by all Americans: those who are insured as well as those without coverage, those near the top of the economic ladder as well as those near the bottom, those who are healthy as well as those who are sick. What creates insecurity is the *possibility* of large economic shocks not covered by insurance—a possibility that has been rapidly mounting. Those who lack insurance face insecurity, but so too do those who risk losing coverage when they change or lose jobs. Those who are impoverished face insecurity, but so too do those with higher incomes who experience catastrophic costs. Those who are sick face insecurity, but so too do healthy families who are just one sickness or injury away from financial calamity. As health costs have skyrocketed and the share of Americans with stable health benefits has eroded, health insecurity has become a problem faced by all Americans—fortunate and unfortunate alike.

At the root of the problem is the peculiar, and peculiarly flawed, character of health insurance markets. In many areas of economic life, we expect the free play of the competitive market to allocate resources in more or less efficient and productive ways—at least given basic limits and protections. Markets don't necessarily give us the outcomes that we consider just or fair. But when they function well, they give us efficient outcomes, making sure that those with the desire and the means to purchase something get the best product at the lowest possible cost. Or so the argument goes when it comes to healthy markets, but the market for health insurance is anything but.

To start with the most fundamental issue, health care is not like other goods. Most of us think it's fine that some people can't buy fancy clothing or fast cars, or have to eat at home instead of going out to splendid restaurants. But most of us draw the line at basic health care. Someone who is gravely ill or injured needs treatment— period. This "rule of rescue" builds on a broader conviction: that everyone in an affluent society needs to have at least some protection against conditions and events that cripple their ability to participate as citizens and workers.[14]

And since health care isn't an optional luxury, it's also an expense that almost everyone wants to have insurance against. Health insurance was once called "sickness insurance"—for a simple reason: the main cost of health care used to be the time spent out of the workforce due to sickness. Today, however, the costs of medical treatment vastly dwarf the forgone earnings due to sickness, mostly because medicine can do so much more than it once did. In 2003, according to my own analysis of data from the Medical Expenditure Panel Survey, nearly 40 percent of Americans had medical expenses (covered by insurance or not) that exceeded 10 percent of family income, a third had expenses that were larger than 20 percent, and more than a tenth had expenses that exceeded their *entire income*. There is simply no way that families can finance expenses like this on their own. Insurance, like basic health care, is not optional.

Yet, precisely because insurance is necessary and widespread, patients are not sensitive to the costs of health care in the way that they are to the costs of other goods. Economists love the facetious example of restaurant insurance. If the cost of eating out was paid for by insurance, they note, we'd eat out a lot more often, pack a lot more in, and order the most expensive items on the menu. The analogy is far from perfect, but the point is valid: Health insurance greatly reduces the incentive to economize; it is *supposed* to. And this, in turn, drives up costs, making insurance all the more vital. When insurance is widespread, we can't expect the price of services to be the main constraint on spending. Cost control requires restraint through other means, whether private insurance review, professional self-policing, or public spending constraints.

All this would be less of a problem if the insurance market in health care worked smoothly, but it does not. When insurance is for discrete, discernable risks that are easily assessed and not easily faked, private insurance markets perform splendidly. Unfortunately, the health insurance market isn't at all like this. Perhaps the biggest difference is that the likelihood of needing insurance and the magnitude of future health costs are very difficult for insurers to estimate. As a result, insurers frequently know less— much less—about applicants' need for insurance than applicants themselves, and this gives rise to the great bugbear of private insurance markets: "adverse selection."[15]

Adverse selection is a fancy phrase for a simple fact—people who most need insurance are most likely to buy it. The problems begin when insurers try to protect themselves against adverse selection. One obvious response is to try to weed out or charge exorbitant rates to the highest-risk groups. Yet the ability of insurers to do this is limited by knowledge, by technology, and sometimes by law. And, of course, these practices undercut the ability of those who truly need insurance to obtain it. The other response is to raise premiums, but this simply reduces the number of people who have coverage. It cannot eliminate adverse selection, because at any premium, those most likely to need coverage are most likely to see it as in their interest to pay the premium.

The upshot is that insurance markets plagued by adverse selection tend to become highly fragmented and incomplete, or fail to function at all. Many people who want and need insurance can't buy it at a premium they're willing to pay, and exclusions and gaps in coverage are endemic. In the worst-case scenario, known to insurance aficionados as a "death spiral," insurers continually jack up rates to deal with adverse selection, driving healthier subscribers from the plan, which in turn sets off another round of rate hikes and another exodus of lower-risk patients, eventually sealing the insurance plan's doom.

Thankfully, American health insurance isn't in a death spiral of this sort. But it is experiencing a steady erosion—a death march—as Americans find it increasingly difficult to afford the ever-rising tab for health insurance and medical services. The epicenter of this transformation is the crumbling of America's employment-based system of health financing, which arose in the mid-twentieth century as a distinctive response to the challenge of health insecurity in the United States. As health care costs have exploded in an increasingly competitive business environment, this old, odd bargain has come undone—and the Great Risk Shift has relentlessly played out.

The Not-So-Accidental System

Americans don't think twice about the fact that, unless they're economically disadvantaged or older than sixty-five, they have to obtain health insurance through their employers. And yet, America's employment-based system was scarcely a natural market development. More important, this system is far from the norm. Indeed, the United States is the *only* rich capitalist nation that relies on employers to voluntarily provide health insurance to working-age citizens and their children.

The modern roots of America's distinctive system go back to the New Deal. Health insurance had been a political issue at the state level before the 1930s, but efforts to create insurance programs on a state-by-state basis had all foundered. The Great Depression, however, brought the issue to the national level, and in a new form. For the first time, the cost of medical care, not lost wages, was the concern, and President Roosevelt's top advisers believed strongly that some kind of government-backed insurance system was needed. As the Social Security Act was being finalized, one internal report to Roosevelt declared, "[T]he problem of medical care should not be regarded as being a third or fourth item in a general program for economic security. . . . [T]his part of the program is equally important . . . and equally feasible."[16]

It may have been equally important, but it was not equally feasible. Doctors, insurers, and employers all were hostile to the idea, while organized labor expressed only tepid support. Many around Roosevelt believed the rest of the Social Security Act could be taken down by the fight and convinced him to put off pressing for action. Within a few years, however, Roosevelt was bogged down in Congress and leading a nation that was heading into the most fearsome war the world had ever seen. Government health insurance, as one account put it, was an "orphan" of the New Deal.[17]

But the orphan had siblings—in the private sector. Pressed to come up with an alternative to a public program, the American Medical Association softened its once-virulent opposition to voluntary insurance plans that would pay for doctor's care. Meanwhile, Baylor University Hospital in Texas became the big bang of modern health insurance when it pioneered the first Blue Cross plan for hospital care. Blue Cross was not really a normal commercial plan. It was instead a powerful example of private social activism, driven by true concern over the ability of workers of modest means to afford increasingly costly hospital care. For decades, in fact, Blue Cross plans did not even charge different rates to subscribers based on their likely medical costs. It pooled all risks on equal terms, just as Social Security did.

Employers were the crucial brokers in this emerging private system, for it was employers that soon became the virtually exclusive means by which workers obtained health benefits. The reasons for this were many. Employers provided a stable base for marketing and administering plans, and most firms had both healthy and unhealthy workers, allowing risks to be pooled within the workplace. By the 1950s, moreover, champions of the private sector in government had managed to ensure that health benefits received the same sort of favorable tax treatment that retirement pensions did. For employers, then, health insurance was an increasingly good deal: It bought them loyalty, healthier workers, and federal tax breaks.

It also bought them an insurance policy of their own—against national health insurance, which foundered in the fierce political debates of the 1940s in large part because private workplace insurance was so rapidly expanding. Between 1940 and 1950, enrollment in private health insurance rose from 12 million to 76.6 million, reaching for the first time a majority of Americans. To this day, we live with the legacy—a system in which most working Americans receive coverage from their employer, or not at all.

Yet we also live with another legacy: Medicare and Medicaid, which cover the three groups least capable of obtaining insurance in the private market: the aged, the disabled, and the poor. No other country in the world began its government insurance program with such vulnerable groups. The norm was to cover manual workers first, then move up the income ladder to reach all or most citizens. But focusing on the aged proved to be just the trick for frustrated American health reformers, allowing them to present their goals not as a radical break with the past but as a simple continuation of the expansion of private insurance.[18] In 1965, at the height of Lyndon Johnson's Great Society, the strategy paid off with the passage of Medicare and Medicaid. It was the first and last great expansion of public health insurance in American history.

Insurance-Sclerosis

The years just after Medicare and Medicaid passed were the high-water mark of American health coverage. Already, however, signs of strain were showing, and the cracks only grew in the years to come.

There was, first, the abandonment of broad risk-pooling by private health plans. Charging similar rates to all subscribers had been a hallmark of the founding philosophy of Blue Cross. It was also a central reason why most states gave Blue Cross plans special exemptions from normal insurance rules. Yet after World War II, commercial insurers moved into the workplace market to poach Blue Cross customers, offering lower-risk groups reduced premiums. Under fierce competitive pressure, the Blue Cross plans started doing the same—varying premiums based on the expected cost of enrollees, and thus ceasing to spread risk as broadly as they once had across the population.[19]

Another change was equally harmful to broad risk-pooling. When Congress passed the Employee Retirement Income Security Act in 1974—the bill reshaping American pensions—it included a small provision that turned out to be a huge loophole. The provision essentially said that companies that paid for their workers' health costs directly (a practice known as "self insurance"), rather than contracted with insurers to foot the bill, could escape all state regulation of health insurance. What made the provision a loophole is that, unlike in pensions, ERISA didn't impose any new requirements on the health plans it freed from state control. Not surprisingly, larger corporations rushed to fill this regulatory vacuum by setting up their own self-insured health plans, and by the early 1990s more than two-thirds of American companies—and essentially all the largest—self-insured.[20]

Smaller companies were less fortunate. For them, self insurance posed big risks. Because they had so few workers, they couldn't spread risk easily within the firm, and they weren't as capable of managing the administration of self-insured plans. Moreover, when big firms self-insured, many of the most stable, lowest-risk working groups exited the insurance system, raising premiums for those firms too small or too cautious to self-insure—and helping to drive up the number of uninsured, which hit 38 million in 1992.[21]

The situation of Kerry Kennedy, the owner of a small furniture store in Titusville, Florida, showcases the growing dilemmas. Titusville, best known for the Space Center, is a historically conservative city, founded by a Confederate general. Yet Kennedy was supportive of ambitious government action to help the uninsured, and he was committed to providing insurance to his workers. In 1992, however, Kennedy was informed by his insurer that his premiums would ratchet up to a level he couldn't afford, because two of his workers were "high risk" because of their advanced age. Those two workers were his mother and father, who founded the store and still worked in it.

If the story sounds familiar, it should. President Bill Clinton told it in a speech to a joint session of Congress in September 1993, on the eve of the introduction of his ill-fated Health Security Act. Many lessons have been taken away from the spectacular defeat of President Clinton's plan: Americans hate government; national health insurance cannot survive on American soil; corporate America will never support any government action to rein in health costs or boost the number of insured. The Health Security Act—1,342 pages long and based on an intricately complicated theory known as "managed competition"—was certainly dead on arrival. But it succumbed not to some inexorable law of politics that makes any government action to deal with the problems in American health insurance an impossible sell. Instead, it was an already-crippled creature dropped into the den of wolves that America's ultra-expensive medical complex had spawned.

First were the self-inflicted wounds. Rather than press for something relatively modest as a down payment on larger changes, Clinton's health policy wonks constructed a grandiose process for developing an ideal plan that could bridge all the major ideological and political divides. Rather than build on existing programs, insiders in the process denigrated them as flawed and insufficient. One memo on Medicare by a top architect of the Clinton plan declared that "Medicare's entire history should be a lesson on how not to structure a national health program," ignoring that Medicare was the *only* national program the United States had and one that was overwhelmingly popular.

Instead of a simple and popular Medicare-like system with free choice of doctors, the idea of managed competition relied on the massive expansion of tightly managed health plans like HMOs, about which Americans expressed little enthusiasm. The resulting grand scheme was so complicated, so intricate, so unwieldy it could be portrayed as anything opponents wanted, and fearsome caricatures of liberty-robbing, big-government monstrosities were soon unleashed—to little clear retort. Not surprisingly, public support for the plan plummeted after Clinton's stirring speech.

Hobbled, the plan was then crushed under the weight of interest-group and conservative resistance. It had tried to appease all the major groups—insurers, large employers, doctors, hospitals. (One unintentionally hilarious White House memo fretted early on that the plan could "get so many people on board that our boat may sink from its own weight"—which at least got the outcome right.)[22] The problem was that all these groups still had plenty of incentive to fight, and plenty of money and other resources to wage that fight. No other nation has tried to transform a medical-industrial complex as large or as costly as the American system, or to do so as thoroughly. Once the battle heated up, even ordinary Americans sympathetic to the cause grew wary, fearful they would lose their own benefits without something better in return.

In the end, the Clinton plan's failure flowed from hubris, and the hubris flowed from a bowdlerized Marxist notion of internal contradictions. Advocates of the Clinton plan argued, rightly, that the American system of health insurance was at war with itself. Lack of broad coverage drove up costs, which reduced coverage, which in turn accelerated costs even more. But where the theory went terribly wrong was in assuming that the only outcome of this internal war was a victory for more extensive risk-pooling. What the Health Security warriors missed, what would soon rise from the ashes of their defeat, was an alternative vision pointing to a very different endgame: the Personal Responsibility Crusade and its call for a system of individualized health insurance free of the entanglements of either government health programs or workplace benefits.

HRC vs. PRC

The battle over the Clinton health plan marked the end of an era. It was not, of course, the end of the era of rising costs or declining coverage, as those who proclaimed that the system was healing itself so loudly insisted. It was the end of the era of conservative me-too-ism on health care.

In the 1970s, conservatives shifted from arguing against any government action in health care to claiming that it should be designed to support and bolster broad-reaching private insurance.[23] At the decade's opening, President Nixon called for mandating that all employers provide health benefits. By its closing, Stanford economist Alain Enthoven—a free-marketeer who advocated universal insurance—had come up with the notion of managed competition that eventually became the basis for Clinton's proposal. Even in the early 1990s, roughly half of Senate Republicans called for using tax breaks and regulations to extend existing private insurance to nearly all Americans.

What linked these proposals was a belief that broad risk-pooling in health insurance was essential but needed to be achieved through private means. In essence, these proposals called for extending and improving America's existing system of private risk-pooling, without too much government interference or intervention.

When President Clinton put Hillary Rodham Clinton in charge of formulating his reform plan, it therefore wasn't completely far-fetched to expect that his effort would eventually attract moderate conservative allies. But what he hadn't counted on was the Personal Responsibility Crusade, emboldened by the opportunity to stake out a starkly different vision of the future of American health insurance. A debate that began as a dispute among differing proposals for expanded risk-pooling thus quickly became an ideological battle over the idea of risk-pooling itself. Round 1 of the battle—HRC vs. PRC, if you will—saw the Personal Responsibility Crusade emerge not just victorious but with a powerful new alternative to private risk-pooling: Medical Savings Accounts.

At the center of the battle was a once-obscure congressman named Newt Gingrich. Entering the health care fight, Gingrich had only recently taken over the position of minority leader in the House. Yet, already, he was the undisputed leader of the increasingly powerful, vocal, and recalcitrant conservative wing of the GOP. But Gingrich didn't simply want Republicans in Congress to say no to the Clinton plan. As it became clear that the plan could be taken down—perhaps with the Democratic Party in tow— Gingrich began to outline an ambitious, antigovernment agenda, which moved to center stage when Republicans unexpectedly captured both houses of Congress in 1994.[24] And on this agenda was a bold new initiative that Gingrich was calling Medical Savings Accounts.

Newt Gingrich was not the father of Medical Savings Accounts. The basic idea had been around at least since the early 1970s, when economists first began to take a long hard look at America's insurance system. Economists were not of one mind about either problems or solutions, but most agreed that the widespread presence of health insurance in the medical sector was a, if not *the*, major cause of high and rising costs.[25] Some economists took this conclusion to indicate that health insurers need to exercise more vigilant oversight of patients and medical providers. Yet an influential wing argued quite the opposite: Citing the problem of moral hazard, they argued that health insurance should be cut back to bare-bones catastrophic coverage, requiring that patients pay for care directly so as to encourage greater economy in treatment choices.

This position found its champion in the private sector in the person of J. Patrick Rooney, chairman of Golden Rule Insurance.

Rooney was a huge donor to Gingrich and his causes.[26] He was also a tireless advocate for Medical Savings Accounts and helped convince Gingrich and many conservatives in the House to press for them.[27] Meanwhile, conservative think tanks spewed out supportive ideas, ranging from souped-up accounts that would cover a whole range of consumer expenses to integrated plans for transforming American health insurance into a wholly individualized framework of tax breaks and individual accounts.[28] The ideas included a proposal eerily similar to plans for Social Security privatization, allowing workers to decide whether they wanted to contribute their payroll taxes to Medicare or put them in a medical IRA for their retirement (and, of course, go without Medicare).

Legislation was slower to come. Republicans held hostage a plan to improve the portability of health coverage in the mid-1990s until President Clinton gave in to their demands to create limited new tax breaks for Medical Savings Accounts. In 1997 a massive overhaul of Medicare created a pilot Medical Savings Account program for the elderly—which, like the rest of the legislation, proved an abject mess. Undaunted, enthusiasts recast Medical Savings Accounts as "Health Savings Accounts," and flexed their muscles again during the debate over a prescription drug benefit for Medicare beneficiaries. Indeed, the only way in which President Bush and Republican leaders were able to get conservatives to sign on to a prescription drug bill in 2003 was by throwing billions of dollars at such accounts—billions that, of course, could not be spent on the legislation's putative goal of providing prescription drug coverage.

While Health Savings Accounts became a near-theological aspiration of the Right, most policy experts remained skeptical. They noted the obvious: Health Savings Accounts would be attractive mainly to healthy and well-off Americans who didn't fear exposing themselves to the risk of uncompensated costs. If adopted broadly, such accounts would undermine risk-pooling in the private sector, because they would allow these workers to escape from group health plans, leaving their costlier colleagues behind. The exodus, if unchecked, could leave old-style group plans beset by a death spiral of adverse selection—as wave after wave of people jumped ship: first the healthiest, then the healthiest of those left behind, and so on. [29] Ultimately, Health Savings Accounts could tear apart the already tattered fabric of risk-pooling in the private sector.

There was another big problem with Health Savings Accounts: Nobody except their promoters really liked them. Even when they were authorized, employers rarely offered them, and workers who signed up for them hated them. The 1996 demonstration project had authorized 750,000 Medical Savings Accounts—a cap that conservatives had complained would kill the goose that lay the golden egg of health insurance freedom. By 2004, however, fewer than a tenth that number of accounts had been established.[30]

The distinct lack of public enthusiasm for Health Savings Accounts was driven home to me when I interviewed a young woman who actually markets HSAs for a large insurance company—let's call her Jane Doe. Jane admitted to me that while she loved the company for which she worked, she now led something of a double life. Her company had automatically enrolled all its workers in an HSA, and Jane—despite being young, healthy, and savvy—found the plan frustrating and inadequate. In other words, Jane spent her days selling a product to employers and individuals that she found awful and was convinced would hurt the traditional insurance that her company used to focus on.

Jane's story isn't all that unusual: A survey done in 2005 found that just 42 percent of enrollees in account-type plans were "very" or "extremely" satisfied, compared with 63 percent of workers in traditional coverage.[31] Nonetheless, the number of HSA enrollees is rising. By November 2005 roughly 2.4 million people were enrolled in HSAs, and estimates in early 2006 showed the number up to 3 million.[32] Perhaps more important, employers seem to be warming to HSAs. A quarter of large employers say they will offer such plans in 2006, and almost half are considering them for the future.[33] Meanwhile, 300 financial service companies have already started to provide HSA accounts and 150 more plan to offer them soon.[34] Said one health economist in 2004, "Wall Street is licking its chops at managing the money."[35]

Also licking its chops around the same time, it turned out, was the 800-pound gorilla in the American labor market, Wal-Mart. In October 2005 an internal Wal-Mart memo leaked to the press showed the company wanted to restructure its health benefits—long under fire, because they covered so few so incompletely—to reduce the costs and risks faced by the company.[36] The memo, written by Wal-Mart's executive vice president for benefits, called for "limited risk initiatives" and moves to reduce "cross-subsidization" within the health plan offered to Wal-Mart's wage workers (called "Associates"). To weed out less healthy Associates, the memo said, workers had to be made to do physical tasks even if they weren't usually part of their job. The retirement and life insurance plans, already meager, had to be cut. And, above all, Wal-Mart needed to "move all Associates to . . . consumer-driven health plans to help control cost trends, while allowing Associates to build up Health Savings Accounts."[37]

The move toward HSAs by the nation's largest employer would mean a major change in America's insurance system. It would also signal the culmination of a major shift in the strategies and arguments of conservatives. The Right once embraced private insurance precisely because it pooled risk without government intrusion; but as private insurance has grown less capable of pooling risk across America's working population—both because of the sharp decline in its reach and because of the dramatic change in employer and insurance practices—conservatives have not tried to save what they once championed. Instead, they have called for government intrusion to further fragment private risk-pooling and undermine old-style workplace insurance. Just as private accounts in Social Security threaten to exacerbate the increasingly uncertain world of pensions, Health Savings Accounts are poised to make the increasingly risky world of private health insurance even more fragmented and frightening.

Medi-Scare

The annals of American medical history are full of ironies, but few are as rich as the fact that HSAs have been pursued by their advocates mostly through Medicare reform. Medicare, after all, is the nation's one great source of health security—the only health plan that pools risk nationally not on the basis of work status or military service but essentially on the basis of citizenship. When it was created in 1965, in fact, advocates of Medicare believed it would be the stepping-stone to universal coverage.[38] Medicare did expand to the disabled and people requiring dialysis, but it has otherwise been caught in a holding pattern—increasingly criticized as costly and outmoded, and increasingly insufficient as a source of health security for older Americans.

Which brings us to another dirty little secret of American medical care: Despite Medicare, the aged are still at grave risk because of rising health costs. Built on the model of Blue Cross in the 1960s, Medicare has gradually fallen behind the private sector in the breadth and generosity of its coverage. No health plan designed today would fail to put limits on out-of-pocket costs paid by patients. Yet Medicare still does not include such limits. No health plan designed today would exclude routine coverage for prescription drugs. Yet until recently Medicare did. And, as will be discussed, its faulty drug-coverage plan—enacted in 2003 and implemented disastrously in 2006—still leaves gaping holes.

While Medicare coverage has remained largely unchanged, the cost of care for the elderly has exploded. Meanwhile, employers have increasingly sought to cut back their own provision of health insurance in retirement. (Between 1988 and 2004, the share of employers with 200 or more workers offering retiree health coverage fell from two-thirds to just over one-third.)[39] And the private market for insurance to supplement Medicare—so-called Medigap insurance—has eroded as insurers find it harder and harder to maintain private risk-pooling in the supplemental market. Today, seniors are actually paying a larger share of their income on medical care than they did at the time of Medicare's passage.[40] In 2000 they spent an average of $3,526 out-of-pocket on medical costs—or 22 percent of their incomes—with low-income seniors spending nearly a third of their incomes. Mortgage and credit-card debt has risen dramatically among Americans older than sixty-five, and between 1992 and 2001 seniors represented the fastest-growing group of bankruptcy filers, with their filing rate tripling over the period.[41]

Kathleen Frazier knows all about the medical problems facing older adults. She's only fifty-eight, but she qualifies for Medicare because she is disabled. So does her husband, a former IBM worker, who is seventy. Unfortunately, the couple realized a few years back that they could no longer afford the ever-more-expensive retiree health plan her husband had been guaranteed in return for agreeing to retire early in 1987, during one of IBM's many restructuring efforts. Instead, they signed up for a new drug plan through a Medicare HMO (at a cost of $270 a month, rather than Medicare's usual premium of around $50). But Kathleen's costs quickly exceeded the spending limit in the plan, and the couple now has to pay for Kathleen's medication out of pocket. "We pay the rent because my seventy-year-old husband is working full time at $9 an hour," Kathleen says.

Although Medicare's ability to fulfill its promise is ever more in doubt, efforts to upgrade Medicare have mostly failed. Instead, the program has been pilloried as an out-of-control entitlement that needs to be reformed top-to-bottom so that senior citizens have greater incentives to choose care wisely—which means, it turns out, further undoing the broad risk-pool that has been the program's greatest source of success.

After all, controlling Medicare spending can only be done in one of two ways. The first way is controlling how much Medicare pays for services—which Medicare has actually done slightly better than the private sector since the early 1980s.[42] The second is by shifting more of the costs and risks of care onto Medicare beneficiaries. Given that Medicare coverage is substantially less generous than the norm in the private sector and that most elderly and disabled Americans have modest incomes—median income of the aged is around $19,000—shifting costs and risks would seem the very last option to embrace.[43] And yet, this is precisely what many critics of Medicare now call for, under the guise of an innocuous-sounding idea known as "premium support."

Ironically, premium support—now a darling of the Right—is similar to the managed competition plan President Clinton embraced in 1993 to conservative denunciation. In essence, people who are enrolled in Medicare would be given a fixed amount to either buy into traditional Medicare coverage or purchase a private alternative. Much as in a defined-contribution pension plan, Medicare would cease to guarantee a specific benefit at a particular price but rather offer a guaranteed level of support ("premium support") for the purchase of private options or traditional Medicare coverage.[44] If a particular plan costs more than the premium-support amount, the remainder would be the responsibility of Medicare beneficiaries—even if those beneficiaries remained in the traditional Medicare program.

Like the Clinton health plan, the premium-support relies on a great number of heroic assumptions and delicate institutional choices, none of which is likely to come together very well in practice. This is not just speculation: In 1997 a balanced budget deal between Clinton and congressional Republicans moved toward the premium-support idea by expanding the range of private health plans offered by Medicare and the incentives for seniors to enroll in them. The reforms were an unqualified bust. Overwhelmed by the confusing array of options in some regions, without any alternative options in others, seniors largely steered clear of the new plans. Meanwhile, despite attempts to sweeten the pot for private plans, many insurers pulled out of the program, leaving those seniors who had enrolled in private plans to obtain drug coverage stranded.

The most spectacular failure of faith-based reliance on the private sector was the new Medicare drug benefit, passed in 2003. The plan was full of contradictions from the outset. Its GOP advocates insisted that they could obtain drug coverage cheaply by relying on the private sector. But the costs of the program mushroomed as it made its way through the legislative process, even as the scope of the coverage came to look more and more limited. In the end, the bill had to be slammed through Congress in the dead of night, after holding the House vote open for an unprecedented three hours (most votes last only 15 minutes) so that

Republican leaders could threaten and cajole. The chaos was rep-
licated upon implementation. Confused by the array of options and
dismayed by the drug coverage's limits, many seniors did not or
could not sign up. Four months into the new program, as the dead-
line for enrolling without a penalty loomed, only 8.6 million more
seniors had drug coverage than had had it before the new legislation's passage in 2003.[45]

The main reason for the divorce between the high costs of the
new insurance and its meager benefits is simple: Republicans insisted that Medicare stay out of the business of directly providing
drug coverage. Independent analyses based on the experience of
other programs suggested that Medicare would likely obtain steep
discounts on drugs if it purchased them directly. But the pharma-
ceutical industry went all out to head off the threat—even poach-
ing the Republican who wrote the legislation in the House as its
new lobbying chief upon his retirement (negotiations began while
the bill was being written). The end result was a program that
spent billions but did little to relieve the growing risk on seniors'
shoulders.[46]

The premium-support approach, however, promises to shift more
risk onto senior's shoulders—which is why it is such a central challenge to the basic social insurance philosophy of Medicare. To understand this, it helps to remember that the costs of health care
are extremely concentrated on the small portion of Americans who
incur major health expenses in any given year.[47] As it is currently
constructed, Medicare essentially pays for the high costs of these
unfortunate Medicare beneficiaries by spreading the costs across
all Medicare beneficiaries—and through taxes, across all Americans. Yet if Medicare were a system of multiple private plans competing with the traditional Medicare option, then it would be much
harder to spread costs in this way. Some plans would get a healthy
group of patients. Others, almost certainly including traditional
Medicare, would not. Even with adjustments to account for this
fact, the premium-support approach would still create a substantial amount of sorting of patients that would undermine the ability of traditional Medicare to pool risks and perhaps even to survive.

Again, these are not idle speculations. The entire history of private health insurance in the United States—from the abandonment of broad pooling by Blue Cross to the hypersegmentation of the market in the 1980s and 1990s because of the exodus of large employers from the private risk pool—illustrates the dangers. Advocates of premium support often point to the Federal Employees Health Benefit Program. But analyses suggest that there are huge discrepancies in the premiums of plans within the federal employee's program due simply to the health of the patients they enroll.[48] Such discrepancies would be much greater, and much more worrisome, in the context of Medicare, especially if they meant that senior citizens who wanted to have a free choice of doctor and a simple insurance plan—both hallmarks of Medicare—were not able to enroll in the program they once benefited from because of its higher cost.

At heart, then, proposals to "modernize" Medicare by introducing premium support are really about shifting the risk of rising health costs from the government onto senior citizens. And this shift will not be a one-time occurrence. If Medicare moves from a guaranteed package of benefits to a system that merely provides a fixed amount of support, then it will be much easier down the road to control Medicare costs by simply trimming the level of the fixed contribution. This is all the more true because Medicare beneficiaries would suddenly face very different premiums and enjoy very different benefit packages, undermining the unified constituency of beneficiaries that has made direct cuts in Medicare so difficult in the past. If these changes came to pass, traditional Medicare—the program in which most senior citizens are now enrolled and with which most are overwhelmingly satisfied—could well "wither on the vine," as Newt Gingrich famously predicted during the budget battles of the mid-1990s.[49]

The Medicaid Band-Aid

While Medicare has been caught in a holding pattern, America's other major health program, Medicaid, has significantly expanded over the past two decades. Today, Medicaid covers a fifth of America's kids and pays for 40 percent of childbirths. It pays for two-thirds of elderly residents of nursing homes and, before the Medicare drug legislation, for the prescription costs of 6 million indigent seniors.[50] Along with the Earned Income Tax Credit for the working poor, Medicaid is now the leading example of a program that helps lower-income workers and their families struggling to get ahead.

Shannon and Derek Combs are just such workers, and their family has benefited greatly from California's health programs for lower-income residents. Their daughter, Kelsey, is covered by the Healthy Families Program, and Shannon herself has Medi-Cal coverage, because she's pregnant with the couple's second child. In a floral print dress, her blond hair hanging in ringlets around her shoulders, Shannon does not look like most Americans' stereotype of public-assistance recipients. And in a sense she isn't—because her assistance will last only as long as she's pregnant. She and Derek, resident managers of a storage-unit facility, have both been uninsured for as long as they can remember. Derek, thirty-one, has been healthy enough to pay for all his care out of pocket. But Shannon recently suffered from bleeding ulcers. Even though she was throwing up blood, she resisted regular checkups. Eventually she had to have emergency-room surgery, which left her with $9,000 in unpaid bills. Now, Derek is facing his own quandary. His teeth are decaying but he can't afford fillings, root canals, and crowns, so he will probably just have them pulled at $25 each.[51]

For all of Medicaid's value to struggling families like the Combs's, Medicaid is still a Band-Aid on the festering wound of health security, hamstrung by its structure from doing more and vulnerable to demands that it should do less. In the first place, most of Medicaid's spending does not do what most people think it does—provide basic health security to families like Shannon and Derek's. Instead, it funds care for the elderly poor in nursing homes, the blind, and the disabled. These three populations account for the lion's share of Medicaid spending. This spending is of course valuable, but it means that most of the debate about Medicaid misses the point. Cast as a dilemma concerning generosity toward the able-bodied poor, Medicaid's dilemma is more accurately a problem of letting every unmet health need fall on a single, cash-strapped program, straining its ability to provide basic health security to its original target population.[52]

Worse, Medicaid is limited in its ability to provide basic health security by its very structure. As a gap-filling program designed to reach populations without access to workplace health insurance, Medicaid faces two serious contradictions once it begins to reach beyond the truly impoverished. The first is known in health-policy circles as "crowd out"—the reality that covering low-income workers through Medicaid will mean that some workers who would have gotten private health insurance receive public coverage instead. There is nothing wrong with crowd out in principle. Low-income workers often don't have access to workplace policies, and the coverage they have is often inadequate, costly, and insecure. Yet crowd out nonetheless creates a basic conflict between expanding public coverage and maintaining existing private protections—a conflict that becomes more acute the more people the government tries to cover. In effect, crowd out sends a clear message: Cover *only* the poor. Trying to reach most Americans means heading down a slippery slope marked by rapidly diminishing returns.

The second contradiction is that, despite Medicaid's expansion over the last two decades, it is still viewed as a program for the indigent by many Americans. And understandably so: Medicaid pays medical providers low rates, so many shun Medicaid patients altogether. A great deal of Medicaid spending is funneled into crumbling community medical institutions. Applying for Medicaid is often hopelessly complex. Partly as a result of this complexity, millions of Americans eligible for Medicaid do not enroll in the program. But even when enrolled in Medicaid, families often find themselves without coverage soon after they enroll, because they briefly lose official eligibility or more often, they fail to follow cumbersome and frequent reapplication processes.

Shannon Combs had not known, for example, that Medicaid covers low-income pregnant women. She learned it only when she visited a doctor at the beginning of her pregnancy—not from the doctor, who had told her she would have to pay him $3,200 for a

normal delivery (half of it up front), but from a pregnant receptionist who happened to be on the program. When she went to sign
up, she was shuffled from office to office—first a program for the
medically indigent that turned her down, then four visits to the
Medi-Cal office because, she says, "they kept asking me to bring
new papers with me." "It seemed," Shannon recalled, "like obstacles
were being put in front of me left and right."

The statistics are dismal. Medicaid is now officially available to
every child in poverty in America; yet the share of children who
are uninsured has remained remarkably constant in the face of
the expansions.[53] One reason why Medicaid has faltered is that it
is financed in substantial part at the state level. Unlike the federal government, a state generally cannot spend more during downturns to deal with the increased needs that accompany recessions.
States therefore tend to cut back programs for the less advantaged
precisely when the number and plight of the less advantaged are
greatest. This further compromises health security during periods
of economic hardship.

All this is more worrisome because the expansion of Medicaid
seems to have run its course. Criticism of Medicaid was often
muted in the past. In recent years, however, state governors and
Republicans in Washington have spearheaded efforts to scale back
Medicaid. In Texas, about a third of children eligible for the state
children's health program were cut off in a single year. In Missouri,
state leaders have sought to end Medicaid altogether, eliminating
health insurance for as many as 100,000 people. But rather than
fill the growing breach, the federal government is pulling back. In
each of his last six budgets, President Bush has sought to cut Medicaid spending substantially and shift responsibility to the states
so they can hike co-payments and make the tough choices about
who gets care and who doesn't. In 2005, Republicans in Congress
responded by cutting Medicaid spending.[54]

A Simple Plan

American political leaders are convinced that any proposal for
universal health insurance would be DOA. Yet Americans are more

receptive to the idea than ever, and there just might be the will today to bring back what we have lost—broad risk-pooling in American health insurance.

The solution is right under our noses: Medicare. As we've seen, Medicare *does* need upgrading; Medicare *does* do too little to help the nonelderly. But the answer isn't to tear down Medicare; it's to build up the program to make it a stable foundation for providing health care for all Americans without access to good coverage. Making Medicare available to all Americans without workplace insurance would, in a single stroke, help Medicare *and* broaden health security. Though requiring new financing up front, this solution would actually lessen Medicare's long-term cost problem because it would make program spending less sensitive to the demographic distribution of the population. By increasing the share of health spending financed by Medicare, it would also give the government greater leverage to control costs.

Perhaps most crucial, expanding coverage to the uninsured through Medicare would powerfully link the health security of elderly and the young—the fate of Kathleen Frazier and the fate of Shannon Combs. No longer would young workers without insurance support elderly citizens with good coverage. And no longer would advocates of expanded insurance coverage feel that improving Medicare was at odds with their ultimate aims. Instead of simply making Medicare more like insurance for workers, *this* Medicare reform strategy would also make insurance for workers more like Medicare: secure, affordable, and simple.

But wouldn't Americans reject a huge federal program called Medicare? The idea seems convincing—until one realizes that there already is such a program, it's called Medicare, and Americans absolutely love it. Indeed, many Americans don't even think of Medicare as a government program, as is suggested by the (perhaps apocryphal) story of an elderly constituent who reportedly jumped up at a congressional town-hall meeting and declared, "Keep government out of my Medicare."

To be sure, none of this will be easy. So far has Medicare drifted from the larger goal of universal security that advocates rarely mention the two in the same sentence. But the two should be spoken of together. We can preserve and improve Medicare for future generations and finally make health insurance secure for all Americans. Or we can leave each bobbing separately in a sea of hostility to the ideal of insurance—an ideal that once fired enthusiasm for the goal of security for all Americans and could do so yet again.

Conclusion

Securing the Future

THE GREAT RISK SHIFT has played out like a slow-motion car crash projected onto thousands of screens at once. There is the twisting steel, the acrid smell, the broken bodies, the lost dreams. But the time frame is extended, the fallout scattered. David Lamberger fights to keep his home in Michigan. Elinor Sheridan looks for a job at seventy because she can't live on Social Security alone. The Combs family worries about what will happen when Medi-Cal coverage for Shannon ends. Julie and Jerry Pickett try to put out of their minds the endless phone calls from the debt collectors. The Dorsetts file their bankruptcy papers before taking Zachary to the doctor.

We can see the common thread that unites these stories only by looking at them through the lens of risk. Risk is the reason the sunny view of America's economy that is prevalent among today's popular commentators so completely misses what's going on. Yes, we are richer than we once were—though most Americans are only modestly richer. But we are also at much greater economic risk: Our incomes rise and fall more sharply. Our health care is less secure. Our pensions put more of the risk and responsibility on us. Our public programs of insurance have grown more threadbare. Our jobs and our families are more financially perilous. All of these mounting risks add up to an ever more harrowing reality: Increasingly, all of us—even those of us with good jobs and good pay, with children and spouses, with homes and college degrees—are riding the new economic roller coaster. And yet most of us seem to feel that we are riding it alone.

Rather than drawing Americans together, the Great Risk Shift has played out family by family, workplace by workplace, debate by debate. Indeed, the one identifiable political movement that has emerged out of the Great Risk Shift is dedicated *not* to reversing the slide of Americans into greater and greater insecurity but abetting that slide by shifting more risks and more responsibility onto Americans' fragile finances.

Say this for the Personal Responsibility Crusade: It has a vision and a goal. Critics of public and private programs of insurance know what they are against, and they know what they are for: greater personal responsibility and individual self-reliance, propelled by aggressive government policies that erode the bonds of shared fate and undermine the systems of social insurance that once linked Americans across lines of class and economic vulnerability.

There can be no turning back the clock on many of the changes that have swept through the American economy and American society. Employers are not going to provide the mini–welfare states of the past. Unions are not going to magically reemerge to cover a third of the workforce. The competitive strains on American employers are not going to go away. And the tide of red ink facing government will not evaporate naturally.

Nor can we transport ourselves back to a wistful image of the New Deal, when men and women committed to social insurance began constructing many of the institutions of risk-pooling that are now in tatters. But accepting these changes does not mean accepting the new economic insecurity, much less accepting the assumptions that lie behind the current assault on insurance. Personal responsibility has its place: Americans will indeed need to do much to secure themselves in the new world of work and family, but they should be able to do it in a context in which government and employers act as a help, not a hindrance. And they should be protected by an improved safety net that fills the most glaring gaps in present protections, providing all Americans with the basic financial security they need to reach for the future—as workers, as parents, and as citizens.

An "insurance and opportunity society" will not be costless, though its long-term rewards will vastly exceed its short-term costs. It will not be uncontroversial, though it rests on sensible ideas from a wide range of thinkers and leaders. And it will not be easy to achieve, though it can and must be sought. What it *will* do is restore a simple promise to the heart of the American experience: If you work hard and do right by your families, you shouldn't live in constant fear of economic loss. You shouldn't feel, as Teresa Geerling and David Lamberger and so many others do, that a single bad step means slipping from the ladder of advancement. The American Dream is about security and opportunity alike, and rebuilding it for the millions of middle-class families whose anxieties and struggles are reflected in the stories told in this book will require providing security and opportunity alike.

So get wise, get mad, and get even. First, get wise. You need to prepare yourself and your family against economic risk. After all, you will be the one buying your home, making your educational choices, forming your family, thinking about your insurance options, planning for your retirement. Now is the time to start making those choices with the new risks you face in the front of your mind.

Next, get mad. The Great Risk Shift is driven by powerful forces, but it isn't inevitable, and Americans should demand better. We don't need to accept that we have to deal with risk all by ourselves. We must speak out.

Finally, get even. We can reshape our economy and policies to achieve the ideals we believe in, rather than letting our economy and policies reshape our ideals. A basic foundation of insurance can, in fact, provide huge economic and social gains.

Get Wise

What can you do to steel yourself against the ongoing shift of risk? Taking stock of the new realities is the first step. The Great Risk Shift has seeped into so many aspects of our lives that many of us have still not recognized how much it has changed our assumptions, or at least should change them. If you're like most people, you never expected to face the risks to your income, your job, your health care, and your retirement as great as those you face today.

The extent of insecurity in the United States is routinely missed. The new insecurity doesn't look like the old insecurity—grainy Dorothea Lange photos of Depression-era men and women, their weathered faces projecting despair and helplessness. Those who experience it have homes, cars, families, degrees. They've usually tasted the fruits of success, if sometimes only fleetingly. They very rarely end up on the streets or in shelters. For most, insecurity is a private experience, hidden away behind closed doors, felt in quiet despair.

If this private experience seems wholly foreign to you, count yourself lucky. If it strikes all too close to home, know that you are not alone. And if, like most Americans, you're worried but not desperate, and want to know what you can do to protect yourself and your family, remember that recognizing risk is the first step to dealing with it—and the time to start dealing with it is now.

Seeing Risk

The silence of the insecure is not the only reason we often fail to recognize the magnitude and frequency of economic risk. Studies consistently suggest that we are good at some kinds of risk assessments and very bad at others.[1] Unfortunately, the kinds of risks that we face today—diffuse, interwoven, mounting, uncertain— are precisely those we are most likely to overlook. Economic losses for families are often like system failures in engineering—they cascade from seemingly small events into major crises. Yet few of us worry much about the small events that can set off the chain.

No doubt you are aware of some of the larger realities of risk in the United States. Yet have you sat down and thought about what you would do if you lost your job, or your child or spouse or parent became seriously ill, or you became seriously sick or disabled, or the housing market in your area headed downward? How long could you go without your present income? How well do your present insurance policies protect you? How secure are your finances against unexpected shocks?

Take a moment to take stock of your financial situation. The main focus should be the big picture: How prepared are you if your income and expenses suddenly become anything but stable? This may seem an imponderable question: How can you plan against events that are highly uncertain (and hopefully pretty unlikely)? The answer is, that is what managing risk is all about—seeing the "unforeseen," and preparing for it. Recently, for example, Southwest Airlines has shot ahead of its competitors because it locked in low fuel prices through so-called hedges, purchasing the right to buy fuel at a fixed price even if prices went up, as they have. Southwest had the cash to buy the hedges, and it recognized that the reduction in risk that hedges represent was well worth the extra spending in the short term.

Sitting down and thinking about how you would stay afloat financially if things—and perhaps many things—took a turn for the worse is a lot like the process that Southwest went through in deciding to buy fuel hedges. You need to decide what the risks you face are, then think about whether and how you can reduce them, and finally whether the cost of reducing them is worth it or within your means.

So what are the main risks you face? As this book has shown, the two great threats to your finances are drops in or interruptions of your income, and major unexpected expenses, particularly health expenses. And, ironically, these risks hit you hardest when you have extended yourself financially to achieve your dreams. Investing in your home, in your family, in your education, in specialized skills for your job—these are the choices that give you the most back, but they are also the ones that put you at the greatest risk, especially when the retirement savings you've been depending on or the pay from the job that you still held last week are gone. Does that mean you shouldn't take any of these risks? Far from it: The risk is there precisely because the rewards are so high. But you should have your eyes open, and you should be prepared for the downsides.

Saving Yourself

What can you do to prepare? The first, and most obvious, step is to save, and as we've seen in this book very few of us do much saving. One reason we save less than we should, the research suggests, is that rises in home values (and in the 1990s stock values) made us feel richer as our home prices (and retirement funds) grew.[2] But remember, these riches are uncertain. They can materialize only when you cash in your retirement fund or sell your home. There is no free lunch. If you pull equity out of your home, you are selling part of your home and probably putting yourself at greater financial risk. If you borrow against your 401(k)—or, worse, use a lump-sum payment to finance current spending—you are undercutting your retirement and probably putting yourself at greater financial risk.

So what should you do? The most important piece of advice is to heed the lesson of loss aversion—what you once thought were items you could easily do without will, with time, become items you can only painfully do without. To prepare, then, you need to turn the growing instability of family incomes to your advantage. When your income unexpectedly rises, don't treat that money as license to ratchet up your expectations. If you put these unexpected gains aside, you will be much better prepared for unexpected losses.

All this may seem perverse. Money is money, and economists have long argued that if we're rational, our spending is driven by our "permanent income"—the income level we have once the transitory up and down shocks are factored out. Don't believe it: We all spend more when we think we're richer, even if our riches our temporary, because we all use simple rules of thumb to judge our work and spending behavior.[3]

The trick is to use these common rules of thumb to your advantage. Most of us separate our income and spending into categories: essentials, luxuries, money for retirement, money for the kids' education, and so on. Behavioral economists call these "mental accounts," and while it might not make sense for *homo economicus* to treat unexpected windfalls differently from all other income, it makes perfect sense for you to wall them off from your normal income and spending.

Mental accounts are even better when they are real accounts, so create a rainy-day fund that you put money you earn and don't want to spend into *before* it ever enters your checking account or pocket. But call this account your "sunny-day" fund, because it's where you put the money you didn't expect to get: the unexpected raise, the year-end bonus, the money from relatives or friends, the money you'd set aside for a big purchase that you end up not having to make (or convince yourself you don't have to make).

It goes without saying that you should, if you can, be contributing as much as possible to tax-favored retirement accounts (and you should be putting this money in broad index funds that have low administrative costs and a mix of investments appropriate to your age and comfort with risk, and *never* in the stock of the company you work for). But the reason isn't just to prepare for retirement. Again, the research on savings behavior strongly indicates that pre-committing resources—tying yourself to the mast, as Ulysses did to resist the sirens—is crucial to saving. For all their faults, 401(k)s have one notable virtue: Once you sign up for them and designate your contribution rate, the money goes into the account before it goes into your paycheck. While this money will ideally be yours in retirement, you can, in a pinch, use 401(k)s and other retirement savings vehicles as a temporary stopgap measure before you retire—and you should if the alternative is more dire than having to live on a modest retirement income.

The other reason why pre-committing resources for retirement is valuable is because you can temporarily stop pre-committing them if you face unexpected expenses. If you are setting aside even a small share of your income for retirement, that's a safety valve you can release by postponing your contributions for a while (especially since there are now substantial tax incentives allowing workers nearing retirement to "catch up" on their retirement savings).

Precautionary savings, however, has major limits. Retirement, for example, is probably the easiest future contingency to prepare for, and the target of most of our nation's savings incentives. Yet most of us still find preparing for retirement intensely anxiety-producing and difficult. How can we expect to prepare for more immediate and unpredictable risks simply through savings? The answer is that most of us can't, and this is where borrowing and insurance come in.

Give Me Credit

Americans often see debt as a badge of shame, even as they pile it up. But borrowing is as American as apple pie, and wise borrowing makes sense. Without credit, almost no one could buy a home or finance their education or weather short-term economic shocks. Without credit, establishing a family or starting out in a new career, much less starting a new business, would be immensely more difficult, often impossible. Borrow when you must, without guilt or feelings of failure, but borrow smart.

Many Americans today are not borrowing smart. The explosion of credit cards, adjustable and no-interest-down mortgages, second loans, and subprime lending—over the same era in which the financial risks facing Americans have exploded—has created a frightening new landscape of debt in the United States. America's current extraordinary levels of debt are deeply worrisome, not only because they are tied up in ever more risky financial vehicles but also because they suggest that debt (and, increasingly, high-interest debt) is being used just to maintain a middle-class standard of living and weather the shocks that were once dealt with through public and private insurance.

Limiting debt, especially high-interest debt, is therefore essential advice—and like most essential advice, hard to follow. Instead of extending yourself to buy a fancy house that leaves you with no discretionary income after the mortgage is paid, start with a simple home and work your way up. Stick with transparent, straightforward financing arrangements whenever possible. Long-term fixed-interest loans are much easier to plan around than loans that backload the interest charges and leave your payments at the mercy of fluctuating interest rates. Simple car loans—or better yet, no car loans—are better than lease arrangements that are complex and full of unexpected charges. You already have enough risk in your life; don't pile on risk by taking on variable and high-interest credit, or signing up for deals that aren't clear, and try to avoid using debt to finance things that decline in value over time (like cars and unlike prudent investments). Remember that no financial institution lends you money out of the goodness of its heart, and just because someone is willing to lend you money doesn't mean you should take it. If the interest rate is exorbitantly high, creditors think you are either a sucker or a high-risk client. Don't be a sucker or a high-risk client.

The most serious financial error that Americans commonly make is overextending themselves to buy a house. This is understandable and sometimes unavoidable, but it is dangerous. Homes are valuable investments; they represent most of most Americans' wealth. But a mortgage is a highly unforgiving loan. And as one in sixty American households a year have learned in the last few years—households like that of David Lamberger—the consequence of falling behind on a mortgage can be severe. Although your mortgage payments will almost certainly be your largest monthly expense, they shouldn't be so large that you can't see yourself paying them if you or your spouse take a pay cut or face unforeseen expenses—because, as emphasized, these cuts and expenses happen to many more of us than we think.

Borrowing for college or other forms of education is also a good investment. But like other investments that involve risk, the choice should be made wisely. I teach at Yale, so I may run into trouble for reporting that a good state education is almost every bit as valuable as an Ivy League degree—and much less expensive.[4] The most important thing is actually getting the degree, and since financial difficulties are one of the major reasons students fail to finish college, the most important thing is finding a school you can afford.

Saving and borrowing are twin sides of the same coin—they are ways of extending the impact of financial commitments over time. But there is a third and final way to deal with risk on your own that is fundamentally different: insurance.

Insurance Assurance

If you count up the number of insurance policies you have, you may be surprised. Auto insurance, health insurance, homeowners insurance, life insurance—in ways both big and small we shield ourselves against risk by buying pieces of paper that promise to protect us when things go bad. But few of us stop to think about why these policies work—and sometimes don't work. Insurance is a deceptively simple invention that took millennia to emerge.[5]

All insurance has the same fundamental characteristics: It pools individually unpredictable but collectively predictable risks that are too large to protect against easily on one's own. This simple description also suggests when insurance is the best deal for you and your family. First, you shouldn't buy insurance if you can easily manage the costs on your own. Not only do you not really need insurance in these cases, the only people who will buy such insurance are those that are either ridiculously risk averse or know they will need protection. Second, insurance is usually a better deal when the risks it is covering are closer to individually unpredictable and collectively predictable. Term life insurance is generally quite reasonable for healthy people, and if you have children, or a spouse determined to never work, you should have it. Private disability insurance is a more difficult call, but usually a good deal for higher paid workers.

Long-term care insurance, by contrast, falls toward the other end of the spectrum and is often not a good deal, especially for younger workers. The basic problem is the uncertainty that insurers face in writing contracts that cover medical costs twenty or thirty years in the future. Underwriting future U.S. medical costs is an enormously risky commitment, and insurers have approached it with all the relish that most of us approach a root canal. Most long-term care insurance contracts are riddled with exceptions, qualifiers, and limits that make it quite likely that someone who's spent years paying for a policy is not much better off than someone who hasn't planned ahead. The market works better the closer to potentially needing long-term care you are, but then, of course, you also know a lot more about your likelihood of needing care and insurers assume that, so rates are extremely high and policies can sometimes be difficult to find. By all means, explore your insurance options, but do so fully aware of the market's shortcomings.

And make sure you do not forget your public insurance options. Far too many Americans don't take advantage of insurance programs for people like them. Medicaid isn't just for the poor, and there is no shame in using it if you qualify. If you lose your job because of foreign trade, you may be able to receive assistance that is not available to most unemployed workers. If you have a long-term medical problem that prevents you from working, you may be eligible for federal disability insurance. In nearly all cases, however, *you* need to apply. To find the fragments of the American insurance patchwork that may be able to cover you and your family, speak with others who are going through what you are. Like the receptionist who told Shannon Combs about Medicaid coverage, important information can be found in surprising places (including the website for this book, www.greatriskshift.com).

We can do much on our own, in short, to see and prepare for the new risks we face. But the limits on what we can do on our own are still huge. Compared with individuals and their families, government and employers have major inherent advantages when it comes to managing risk. We can soften the blow of the Great Risk Shift by wisely planning our finances and our future. But to halt the massive transfer of economic risk onto our shoulders requires joining together and demanding that our government, our employers, and our leaders wake up to huge and growing dislocations that their actions—and their failures to act—are causing.

Get Mad

If the first thing we need to do is to get wise, the second is to get mad—really mad. If you are like most Americans, you are dissatisfied and anxious, aware that something is rapidly changing but unsure of how to deal with the new realities. Yet the anxiety and dissatisfaction most of us feel is diffuse and undirected, and too often it pulls us away from shared conversations about the future rather than pulling us in.

Why aren't we up in arms about the Great Risk Shift? Part of the reason, as we've seen, is that the shift of risk onto our shoulders has been steady and cumulative—at least until recently. Only now are we starting to recognize the breadth and depth of the problem that we face. Moreover, economic risks are hard to perceive. They run headlong into the cognitive biases that we've developed over thousands of years to protect us against visible and immediate threats to our safety while keeping us from being overwhelmed by the buzzing, blooming confusion of our environment. And even when we perceive risks, they often come at us as shots out of nowhere. Nobody slaps a label on our uncertain economic experiences that says, "Made in Washington, DC" or "Brought to you by your local employer." And few of us would know what to do with the information on the label anyway. Seeing economic risks as dropping from the sky is partly a way of protecting ourselves from our own sense of individual powerlessness.

What's more, most of us still strongly believe in the idea of upward economic mobility, whatever the statistics tell us about the reality. Willy Loman aside, we rarely embrace the tales of loss that are as much a part of the American Dream as the ubiquitous tales of success. Consider a *New York Times* poll done in 2004, when most Americans were downright livid about the state of the economy.[6] Eighty-four percent of Americans in the poll described themselves as working, middle, or lower class. Yet an amazing 45 percent believed it was very or somewhat likely that they would become financially wealthy in the future. Even as Americans are anxious about their finances, they subscribe to what might be called the Lake Wobegon view of their economic fortunes (after humorist Garrison Keillor's fictional town in which "all of the children are above average"). When it comes to our economic future, all of us, it seems, are above average.

Our reluctance to join together and voice our concerns also reflects the very nature of the new uncertainties we face. Once, we were protected from many of the most severe economic risks of modern capitalism by the combined energies of our employers and our government. In the last generation, however, all of us have increasingly come to perceive, rightly, that "it's up to us" to succeed in a highly individualized and uncertain economy.[7] Employers have cut back on the generous benefits they once provided as a matter of course, and many government programs have grown more threadbare. The job market has grown more uncertain, particularly for more educated workers, who were previously insulated from workplace insecurity. And as women have entered the workforce in record numbers, families also feel more strained and insecure than ever as they try to balance work and family.

These trends produce real anxiety and hardship, as we've learned, but they also produce a greater sense of self-credit for economic success—and a greater sense of self-blame for economic failure. Though often criticized as an empty slogan, the "ownership society" is actually a highly coherent prescription that responds to the major changes in the economy and society that have promoted this widespread sense that we're on our own. What the ownership society represents (whether in the form of private accounts in Social Security or medical savings accounts or new tax breaks for savings and investment) is a call for individual management of economic risks. It speaks to the increasingly common view that all people have going for them in today's economy is their own efforts, choices, and sacrifices.

The Achilles' heel of the ownership society, as the dismal fate of President Bush's proposal for Social Security privatization suggests, is that it does not speak to the other side of our convictions—the widespread sense that economic risk has shifted too extensively onto the shoulders of working families, that some basic foundations of economic security need to be reestablished to deal with the risks and challenges of the twenty-first century. President Bush gambled that Americans imbued with the ethos of individualism and self-reliance would fail to recognize the risks that private Social Security accounts represented, or that they wouldn't be overly concerned about the growing economic uncertainty in other aspects of their lives. He made the wrong bet, and his misstep has created an opportunity to reverse the rapidly rising tide of economic risk.

To seize the opportunity, the ideals and institutions of economic security need to be refashioned for the twenty-first century. And this in turn requires—and this may be the biggest challenge—that Americans come to see politics and government as ultimately on their side. One reason growing economic insecurity hasn't shaken American politics as much as it might have is that we think we are on our own in the new world of work and family. And when we think we are on our own, we are much more likely to support those who tell us that fighting economic insecurity is just a matter of increasing personal responsibility and coming up with more and more tax-favored accounts that allow us to grapple with economic risks by ourselves.

The starting point for a new vision is a simple but forgotten truth: economic security is a cornerstone of economic opportunity. Like businesses, people invest in the future when they have basic protection against the greatest downside risks of their choices. The worker who fears being laid off at any moment may be more productive in the short run. But in the long run, insecure workers tend to underinvest in specialized training; they are more reluctant to change jobs; they try to minimize their sense of job commitment to protect themselves against psychological loss. Similarly, the family barely scraping by may work more hours; but in the long run insecure families are not going to be able to make the investments in education and other keys to their future that they should. And, of course, none of these costs include the huge emotional, psychological, and economic losses absorbed by workers and their families when they lose their incomes, their homes, and their dreams.[8]

Students of U.S. public opinion have long marveled at our seemingly inconsistent embrace of government programs of insurance, on the one hand, and the ethic of rugged individualism, on the other. Americans are "operational liberals" and "philosophical conservatives," the political psychologists Lloyd Free and Hadley Cantril once argued.[9] They want to have their welfare state cake and eat their free-market capitalism, too. But why not? If we are to be encouraged to invest in new skills, strong families, new jobs, and everything else that makes upward mobility possible, we need a broader umbrella of basic insurance, not a more tattered and narrow one. Back in 2003, President Bush said that it was the job of government to provide "the economic environment in which risk-takers and entrepreneurs create jobs."[10] Apparently, he thinks the only folks taking economic risks are the well off and corporations, not everyday Americans.

There is a huge void in American politics just waiting to be filled by public leaders who can speak convincingly about the need to provide economic security to expand opportunity. Pollsters regularly report ten to fifteen-point advantages for security-opportunity messages over various versions of President Bush's low-tax ownership society. Polls also suggest a consistent preference among voters for a role for government that promotes security in the context of expanded opportunity, as opposed to a government role that keeps taxes low to promote self-reliance.[11] Most Americans are more worried today about Big Insecurity than they are about Big Government.

Get Even

As we work to even out our nation's imbalanced priorities, our first priority should be Hippocrates' "Do no harm." Undoing what risk-pooling remains in the private sector without putting something better in place does harm. Allowing companies to underfund their defined-pension plans, as new pension "reforms" now on the agenda would, does harm.[12] Piling tax break upon tax break permitting wealthy and healthy Americans to opt out of our tattered institutions of social insurance does harm. And though simplifying our tax code makes eminent sense, making it markedly less progressive through a flat tax or national sales tax would do harm. A progressive income tax, after all, is effectively a form of insurance, reducing our contribution to public goods when income falls and raising it when income rises.

The acid test that major social policy reforms should have to meet is this: Do they substantially increase the risk on Americans' already burdened shoulders? If the answer is yes, then our response to these proposals should be no. Most private account proposals fail this test. By putting "more skin in the game," they also make Americans more insecure. Accounts can help Americans manage their finances. But the incentives have to be right, and the incentives embodied in the ownership society are exactly backward. Providing choice within public programs and giving people the tools they need to secure themselves are surely valuable goals. Yet these goals need to be achieved in ways that are consistent with providing basic financial security. Government can often "row, not steer"— but government should not be punching holes in families' financial lifeboats at the same time.

Nor are private insurance markets going to emerge spontaneously to deal with the most pressing risks that we face. Although markets work splendidly in most areas of commerce, insurance markets often fail precisely when we need them most. The problem of adverse selection, for example, often makes it difficult for private insurers to provide good benefits at a premium that lower-risk people are willing to pay. (Adverse selection, it will be recalled, occurs because people who most need insurance are most likely to enroll in it.) Many of the risks that we most want to protect ourselves against—unemployment during severe downturns, for instance, or unexpected inflation that erodes our retirement benefits—are hard to insure against because they are "systemic," they occur to many people at once and are thus particularly difficult for private insurers to effectively cover. And some risks, like the cost of long-term care thirty or forty years down the line, are just too, well, risky for insurers to take on. As a result, insurance for these sorts of long-term, uncertain risks is usually incomplete and inadequate. To insist that we must wait for the private sector to deal with the Great Risk Shift is to hold Americans' security hostage to an unfounded hope, not a realistic aspiration.

Smart Modernization

Yet while we should work to preserve the best elements of existing policies, we should also recognize that the nature and causes of insecurity, and beliefs about how insecurity should be addressed, have all evolved considerably. During the New Deal, economic insecurity was seen largely as a problem of drops in or interruptions of male earnings, whether due to unemployment, retirement, or other costly events. Even as working women became the norm, the special economic strains faced by two-earner families were largely neglected. So too were the distinctive unemployment patterns that became increasingly prevalent as industrial employment gave way to service work—for example, the shift of workers from one economic sector to another, which often leads to large cuts in pay and the need for specialized retraining.

Flaws in existing policies of risk protection have also become apparent. Our framework of social protection is overwhelmingly focused on the aged, even though young adults and families with children face the greatest economic strains. It emphasizes short-term exits from the workforce, even though long-term job losses and the displacement and obsolescence of skills have become more severe. It embodies, in places, the antiquated notion that family strains can be dealt with by a second earner—usually a woman—who can easily leave the workforce when there is a need for a parent at home. Above all, it is based on the idea that job-based private insurance can easily fill the gaps left by public programs—when it is ever more clear that it cannot.

This means the emphasis should be on portable insurance to help families deal with temporary interruptions to income and big blows to household wealth. It also means that these promises should be mostly separate from work for a particular employer—a commitment that moves seamlessly from job to job. If this sometimes means corporations are off the hook, so be it. Indeed, providing new sources of economic security to workers will offer the greatest help precisely to those employers that have already made the greatest commitment to their workers' security, leveling the competitive playing field and improving the financial health of many now-embattled corporations. In time, moreover, employers will pay their workers more to compensate for fewer benefits, and there are plenty of ways to encourage their contribution without having them decide who gets benefits and who does not.

By the same token, however, we should not let massive social risks be borne by institutions incapable of effectively carrying them.

Bankruptcy should not be a backdoor social insurance system; private charity care should not be our main medical safety net; credit cards should not be the main way that families get by when times are tight—and not just because these systems are prone to abuse and predation but also because they were not designed to bear the burden they now carry, much less to carry it effectively. To be sure, the principle of "do no harm" may dictate protecting even incomplete and inadequate safety nets when nothing better is possible. The ultimate goal, however, should be a new framework of social insurance that revitalizes the best elements of the present system while replacing those parts that work least effectively with stronger alternatives geared toward today's economy and society.

Dealing with Risks to Workers

Nowhere is the need for both restoration and reform more transparent than when it comes to our protections for the unemployed. Unemployment insurance has eroded dramatically in the last generation—state by state, recession by recession, worker by worker. But ideas for restoring it are not hard to find, and the cost would be comparatively modest. In fact, there is evidence that unemployment insurance more than pays for itself in terms of higher economic productivity, because it encourages workers to take the time to match themselves to jobs for which they are truly suited.[13]

Restoring strong national standards that require all states to cover workers who've worked for a minimum time would go a long way toward filling the gaps in the present program. So too would an automatic trigger that extends benefits beyond their usual six-month cutoff (on a progressively reduced basis to encourage workers to find new jobs) when long-term unemployment makes up a substantial share of total unemployment. Long-term unemployment benefits could also be provided in the form of retraining vouchers to use for the purchase of private educational services. Workers who opt for retraining vouchers would receive more support than those who simply want cash, which would encourage the long-term unemployed to invest in new skills.

Unemployment insurance, however, isn't designed to deal with the most serious risk of losing a job—not temporary interruptions in income, but long-term declines in earnings power and standard of living. There is now broad agreement among economists that some form of wage insurance is needed for workers displaced by trade or reengineering within an industry who end up not being able to find a new job with pay or benefits comparable to their old one.[14] These proposals are vastly superior to restrictions on company hiring and firing, which can lead to labor-market inflexibility. They are also vastly superior to placing heavy restraints on trade and financial flows in our dynamic, open economy—which is why even the most ardent free-marketeers often support wage insurance.

The details of wage insurance proposals differ, but they have in common that they would provide a supplement to wages to encourage workers to take new jobs even if those jobs pay less than previous ones. To discourage workers from failing to search aggressively for a higher-paying job, such assistance should only cover a portion of the wage loss that follows a job switch, and it should decline gradually over time. But such policies should not be available only for workers displaced by trade, as is true of most existing government help for displaced workers. The experience of losing a job is just as devastating if your job disappears forever as it is if your job heads off to a country where labor costs are lower, and your wages should be protected in either case.

Unemployment insurance could also be the platform for dealing with the most serious work-family conflict faced by many Americans today: the difficulty of taking time off when children enter our families. Encouraging states to provide several weeks of paid leave to care for newborns, newly adopted children, and newly placed foster children would, in a stroke, greatly reduce the strain that working Americans face when they decide to start a family. This is not a pie-in-the-sky idea: California has already made the leap, and the results are encouraging. Nor is the California experiment very costly: less than $2.25 per worker per month. Illinois is considering a paid-leave policy that would cost less than 60¢ per worker per week.[15]

The Family and Medical Leave Act was greeted with derision by personal responsibility crusaders when it was first proposed. Congressman John Boehner, now the Republican majority leader in the House of Representatives, declared, "We don't need the federal government further strangling the free enterprise system in this country."[16] But the free-enterprise system has clearly survived. In 2000, 90 percent of employers covered by the law said that it had had a positive or neutral effect on their profitability, and many said they experienced gains, mainly due to better employee retention and productivity.[17] Yet the act still does not apply to 45 percent of workers in the United States, and there is little reason that it should not be extended to the vast majority of those now outside its protections.[18]

Nor is there any strong reason that the United States should not emulate Great Britain and institute a "Right to Request" law that allows parents with young children to petition for altered work hours from their employer—to be granted at their employer's discretion. As work-family expert Karen Kornbluh reports, the British policy has been an unqualified success, with no major problems reported by employers even though roughly 800,000 parents successfully requested a change in hours (86 percent of all petitions were granted).[19]

Securing Retirement

If young workers need assurances to raise the next generation of Americans, they also need assurances to plan for their own future. The incentives for higher-income Americans to save have ballooned with the expansion of tax-favored investment vehicles (with more on the way if current proposals for new and expanded tax-free accounts are enacted). Yet most Americans receive relatively modest benefits from these costly tax breaks. In the words of one knowledgeable commentator, our incentives for savings are "upside down," delivering most of their benefits to people who have substantial income and assets (and who are therefore most likely to simply shift their savings around to avoid taxes, rather than to save more) and virtually nothing to the vast majority of Americans who most need to save.[20] Replacing the current welter of tax breaks for nonretirement savings with a single Universal Savings Account that is most generous for Americans of ordinary means would go a long way toward restoring the balance.

Yet the biggest challenge today when it comes to personal savings is preserving a system of broad, guaranteed retirement pensions, including Social Security. For workers who expect to retire in thirty or forty years, defined-benefit pensions are already a thing of the past. But defined-contribution plans, such as 401(k)s, are failing miserably to provide a secure foundation for workers' retirement. Safeguarding our one guaranteed system, Social Security, is thus all the more essential.

The future financial threats to Social Security are well known, if often exaggerated. But dealing with them does not require abandoning the core elements of the program: guaranteed benefits tied to lifetime income provided as a right when workers reach retirement for the remainder of their lives. The funding shortfall within the program can be relatively easily closed by making Social Security benefits and the payroll taxes that fund it modestly more progressive—that is, more generous for lower-income workers—while bringing in the last remaining uncovered workers and tying benefits to future longevity, so that fortunate generations that live longer than the last receive slightly less from the program than now promised. Also important, over the long term, is shifting the financing burden of Social Security away from an exclusive reliance on payroll taxes toward a dual reliance on wage-based levies and capital income. Dedicating the proceeds of a reformed estate tax to Social Security, for example, would not only improve the program's fiscal standing but also even out its sources of financial sustenance between wages and capital gains.

Even with these changes, today's workers will need other sources of income in retirement, and 401(k)s as they are presently constituted are not the solution. Too few workers are offered them, enroll in them, or put adequate sums in them—a reflection of perverse incentives built into their very structure. Instead, we should create a Universal 401(k) that is available to all workers, whether or not their employer offers a traditional retirement plan. Employers would be encouraged to match worker contributions to these plans, and indeed government could provide special tax breaks to employers that offered better matches to lower-wage workers.

Since Universal 401(k)s would be offered to all workers, there would cease to be any problem with lump-sum payments when workers lost or changed jobs. All benefits would remain in the same account throughout a worker's life. As with 401(k)s today, this money could be withdrawn before retirement only with a steep penalty. Unlike the present system, however, 401(k)s would be governed by the same rules that now protect traditional pension plans against excessive investment in company stock. What's more, the default investment option under 401(k)s would be a low-cost index fund with a mix of stocks and bonds that automatically shifted over time as workers aged to limit market risk as workers approached retirement.

After all my criticism of 401(k)s, it may come as a surprise that I think Universal 401(k)s are the best route forward. But the difference between Universal 401(k)s with strong incentives for contributions and the present system are profound. Moreover, I would make one dramatic additional change that would fundamentally improve 401(k)s, transforming them into a source of guaranteed retirement income: Under my proposal, government would automatically turn workers' 401(k) accounts into a lifetime guaranteed income at age sixty-five—unless workers specifically requested otherwise and could show they had sufficient assets to weather market risk. To help workers plan ahead, 401(k) balances would be reported to account holders not simply as a cash sum but as a monthly benefit amount that workers would receive when they retired if they had average life expectancy—just as Social Security benefits are reported.

Because these new annuities would be provided directly by the federal government to nearly all Americans at retirement, there would be little worry about the problems of adverse selection and high administrative costs that plague annuity markets today. Interestingly, this proposal is not so different from an idea that was seriously considered by the developers of the Social Security Act in 1935, who argued that the post office should sell low-cost annuities to those who needed them. In essence, Universal 401(k)s along these lines would bring back something close to a guaranteed private pension, with government, rather than employers, pooling the risk.

Medicare Plus

Health care is at the epicenter of economic insecurity in the United States today, and for two interwoven reasons: Health care costs have exploded while coverage has dwindled. The only way to address these twin problems is to address them simultaneously, broadening coverage so as to exercise effective control over costs.

To see why both costs and coverage must be tackled at once, consider the fiscal situation of Medicare, which is far more dire than that of Social Security. Medicare's costs are certainly rising rapidly. But the main reason they are has little to do with Medicare and much to do with American health care. In fact, since payment controls were first introduced into the program in the early 1980s, Medicare's costs per patient have risen slightly slower, on average, than private health insurance spending per patient—despite Medicare's older and less healthy population. In recent decades, Medicare has contracted with private health plans to provide insurance to some beneficiaries—which, if you believed the rhetoric about Medicare's inefficiency, should have cut costs. Yet every reputable study has shown that Medicare loses money when beneficiaries enroll in private plans (in large part because the beneficiaries who enroll in private health plans are healthier than those who do not).[21]

This is not to deny that Medicare faces serious strains. Because it covers only the aged, its spending will be driven up by the retirement of the baby-boom generation in the coming years. Medicare spends hugely different amounts on patients in different parts of the country, reflecting long-standing but unnecessary regional variations in medical costs and practice patterns that Medicare could do much more to reduce than it does. And Medicare has moved much too slowly to introduce measures that might make it better able to judge the efficacy of treatments and coordinate care for the chronically ill (although, revealingly, it still remains ahead of most of the private sector on both scores).

But, as we've seen, the common critique of Medicare—that it is overly generous—is completely untrue. Medicare coverage is substantially less generous than the norm in the private sector. A private plan with Medicare's current benefit package would cost about $2,300 for a single nonelderly adult, compared with a current average for private plans of about $3,600 with the sort of benefits negotiated at the typical workplace.[22] What's more, Medicare provides this relatively ungenerous coverage for less than the private sector would charge for the same benefits. If we as a nation cannot "afford" Medicare, then we as a nation cannot afford to provide basic health care to the aged.

Few Americans, I am certain, are ready to accept this dismal conclusion—not at least in the world's richest nation. And rightly so: Almost every other advanced industrial country provides insurance not just to the aged but to all citizens, while spending much less on a per-person basis than the United States' incomplete system does. Many of these nations, furthermore, have much older populations than we do, have citizenries that go to the doctor more often, and have better basic health outcomes. Yet their overall health spending remains far below ours and, in many, has also been growing more slowly.

What's more, it is crucial to recognize that today's Medicare *is* very different from the model of thirty or forty years ago. That's because Medicare now allows beneficiaries to choose among a growing variety of private managed-care and fee-for-service options— choices that meet with overwhelming popular approval so long as they do not increase the cost of staying in the conventional Medicare program.

The problem is, Medicare is available only to the aged and disabled. This means that Medicare has only a limited ability to control costs because its reach is so restricted. It also means that paying for Medicare inevitably pits the needs of younger Americans against the needs of older Americans. And it means that Medicare's cost are highly sensitive to the share of the population that is older than sixty-five. The United States is the only nation in which the day someone turns sixty-five, most of their health care costs suddenly turn up on the government's budget.

Expanding Medicare to people younger than sixty-five would, in a single stroke, solve all three problems. It would increase Medicare's ability to control costs (as well as its ability to monitor and improve the quality of care). It would even out the nation's commitments between young and old. And it would make Medicare's future costs less frightening, because they wouldn't spike as the baby-boom generation retires. Of course, Medicare would have to be upgraded to work for younger Americans, putting more emphasis on prevention and limiting out-of-pocket costs—but this would be good for older Americans, too.

How could this be done? Very simply, in fact. All employers would be given an affordable choice: They can provide insurance at least as generous as an improved Medicare program, or pay a modest amount to Medicare to help finance coverage for their workers, who would then be automatically enrolled in the program. People enrolled in Medicare would pay a small additional premium based on their income and family size, and they could choose among a range of private plans as well as traditional Medicare.

I have developed this proposal, which I call "Medicare Plus," in considerable detail, and its costs and effects have been carefully estimated by the leading private firm that does such analyses.[23] (In the July of 2006, legislation based on this proposal was introduced by Congressman Pete Stark of California.) The bottom line is straightforward and promising: roughly half of Americans would be enrolled in Medicare and half in employer-provided insurance, virtually no one would remain uninsured, and the cost would be slightly more than $114 in additional health spending per person a year—with these costs quickly erased by the savings produced by the new system. Employers that now provide insurance would experience substantial savings, since many pay much more than what the new system would charge (5 percent of wages). Yet the costs for firms that do not now provide insurance would be modest.

Expanding Medicare in this way wouldn't eliminate private employment-based insurance. It would simply give employers a new choice while requiring that they make at least a minimal commitment to financing coverage for their workers. In higher-wage firms and unionized industries, companies would still see it as in their interest to provide broad coverage—although some might decide it was better to supplement the new Medicare Plus program than to provide coverage directly. But the new framework would ensure that everyone who works has secure health insurance, that many more workers have a choice of health plan (including a plan with free choice of doctors and specialists), and that firms that now struggle to provide health benefits or can't provide them at all have an attractive, low-cost option for doing so. Because the new Medicare Plus program would cover approximately half of Americans, moreover, it would have strong leverage to bargain for low prices on behalf of covered Americans and their employers.

And over time the program could evolve in different directions, depending on how employers and Medicare Plus fared in controlling costs. If employers came under greater financial strain in their management of health costs, they would have the option of Medicare Plus. If, however, they improved their ability to control costs, they would be more inclined to provide coverage on their own. Rather than a constant tug-of-war, this system would create a constructive public-private dynamic that would result in the sector best able to control costs enrolling the largest number of patients— and without the health security of ordinary Americans held in the balance.

Universal Insurance

I have left for last the most inclusive and novel idea for dealing with the rising economic risks facing Americans—"Universal Insurance." Universal Insurance is a new insurance program that would protect workers and their families against catastrophic drops in their incomes and budget-busting expenses. The guiding principle behind Universal Insurance is that working families should have access to more than the highly segmented programs that now characterize American social protection—programs that not only leave glaring gaps but also lack the ability to respond flexibly to a rapidly changing world of risk. Instead, we should work to create a framework of insurance that covers all working Americans, that moves seamlessly from job to job and state to state, and that deals with the most severe risks to family finances, regardless of whether they fit neatly into existing program categories.

The basic structure of Universal Insurance is not complicated. (The details are another matter, and for those who are interested, this proposal is available in much more precise form, along with my own cost and coverage estimates, on this book's website: www.greatriskshift.com).[24] If you experience catastrophic expenses or a large drop in income due to a variety of common risks, Universal Insurance covers a share of the loss.[25] Universal Insurance is a stop-loss program, filling the gaps in other public insurance benefits. [26] In other words, Universal Insurance applies only if existing public policies do not adequately protect family incomes.[27] How much is covered by Universal Insurance depends on your income and the extent of the loss, with coverage more generous the farther down the income ladder you fall. Thus, higher-income Americans do receive protections but only if their incomes drop substantially. Protections for middle- and lower-income Americans kick in more quickly and are more generous.

Universal Insurance will not simply provide relief to workers and families hit by severe economic shocks, although it will surely do that. It will also provide workers and families with the basic foundation of economic security that they need to look toward the future with confidence and invest in their own economic advancement. Just as the right kinds of economic protections for investors and entrepreneurs are the key to business development, the right kinds of protections for workers and their families are the key to encouraging economic opportunity.[28]

The goal of Universal Insurance—and of the other reforms I have outlined—is simple, understandable, and direct: *economic security for all working Americans*. No complicated flowcharts. No fifty-point programs. Just one overarching vision of a new social bargain: If you work hard and do right by your families, you shouldn't be insecure. *Providing security to expand opportunity*—this is the key not only to undoing the Great Risk Shift but also to reclaiming the ideal of shared fate in the twenty-first century.

A Time for Vision

All these changes, of course, will not come without costs, and they certainly won't come without political struggle. Yet against the cost, one must balance the savings. Billions in hidden taxes are currently imposed by laws that facilitate bankruptcy, mandate emergency-room care, and bail out the politically sympathetic when things go bad. The elimination of these expenses must be accounted for when tallying up the bill, as should the huge drain that our current system imposes when people don't change jobs, don't have kids, don't invest in new skills because they fear the downside risks.

Nor should we forget the principles at stake. If we acquiesce to the "creative destruction" of American-style capitalism, then we also have to accept that many Americans, at one point or another, will be hit with disasters they cannot cope with on their own. Providing protection against these risks is a way of ensuring that the dynamism of our economy is politically sustainable and morally defensible. It is also a way of ensuring that Americans feel secure enough to take the risks necessary for them and their families to get ahead. Corporations enjoy limited liability, after all, precisely to encourage risk-taking. But while today we still have limited liability for American corporations, increasingly we have full liability for American families.

New ideas and proposals are essential, but they are not enough. More than anything else, I hope that the facts and ideas in this book will help spark a broad debate about how we as a nation should deal with the pressing economic risks of the twenty-first century. Today, Americans feel a loss of control over the circumstances that govern and shape their lives, and they are turning inward as a result, taking to heart the clear message of recent trends that they are on their own in the insecure new world of work and family. This is a threat to our nation's future, and to the vision of America that generations of Americans have held dear.

The philosophy behind the reforms that we need is one of constructive change guided by an abiding spirit, the spirit of shared fate. Today, when our fates are often joined more in fear than hope, when our society often seems riven by political and social divisions, it's hard to remember how much we all have in common when it comes to our economic hopes and values. Indeed, we are more linked than ever, because the Great Risk Shift has increasingly reached into the lives of all Americans—from those in the upper middle class like Andrea Case to those among the working poor like David Lamberger. What the ever-present risk of falling from grace reminds us of is that, in a very real sense, all of us are in this together. The Great Risk Shift is not "their" problem; it is our problem, and it is ours to fix.

Acknowledgments

IN WRITING A BOOK ABOUT RISK, the greatest risk is getting lost. Risk appears in an enormous range of places, from the minutia of pension funding to some of the biggest trends in our society. It cuts not just across topic areas but also across conventional disciplinary boundaries, touching on political science, sociology, economics, law, psychology, history, policy analysis, and many other fields. Discussions of risk range from the airily philosophical to the hyper-technical, from the broadest-brush histories to the most fine-grained investigations, from the most public speeches to the most private conversations. Anyone foolish enough to try to take in this huge vista in anything close to its full scope had better have a lot of help.

Fortunately, I have had many able guides in surveying this vast landscape, starting with the countless people who spoke with me about their own experiences with risk as I was writing this book. As I collected these stories (not all of which, I realized with a heavy heart, could make it into print), I was constantly amazed by and grateful for the willingness of people to speak with me about their own often-painful strains. I was also struck by how infrequently we as a society hear the quiet cries of middle-class Americans reeling under the weight of the Great Risk Shift. For these Americans,

I hope that I have added a sharp cry to the soft chorus of despair sweeping America today.

Another invaluable source of guidance was my professional colleagues, whose generosity was a heartening reminder to me that the pursuit of knowledge is, at its best, a cooperative activity. So many fine thinkers have shared their work and their insights that I cannot possibly list them all here, but I would be remiss if I did not thank the many participants in workshops, seminars, and private conversations who set me on new paths—or set me straight. I want to give special thanks to George Akerlof, Lily Batchelder, Richard Burkhauser, Nicholas Eberstadt, Sandy Jencks, Ron Kilgard, Jeffrey Liebman, Dean Lillard, and Mark Rank for offering helpful guidance or providing me with specific evidence from their own analyses.

Another group of academics also deserves special thanks: the participants in the Social Science Research Council's project on the "Privatization of Risk," which I have been fortunate enough to chair. The founding members of the project—Graciela Chichilnisky, Dalton Conley, Peter Diamond, Melissa Jacoby, William Janeway, Paul Krugman, Leslie McCall, David Moss, Katherine Newman, Robert Shiller, and Elizabeth Warren—represent as close to an all-star team of experts on risk as one could possibly imagine, and each of them has had considerable influence on my thinking. I am particularly grateful to Craig Calhoun, president of the Social Science Research Council, for seeing the important social-science issues posed by recent changes in American risk management and for bringing together such a wonderful group to address these issues.

I have also been fortunate to have the assistance of a stellar group of researchers. Pride of place must go to Nigar Nargis, who started helping me with this project when she was a graduate student at Cornell and continued through her current post at the University of Waterloo in Canada. An expert on the arcane complexities of the Panel Study of Income Dynamics, Nigar has been not just an invaluable assistant but also a friend, and I treasure her friendship as well as her assistance.

Along with Nigar, two graduate students at Yale—Sandy Henderson and Nicole Kazee—bore the brunt of the final rush to finish the manuscript, while Marlon Castillo, Zahreen Ghaznavi, Hans Christian Siller, and Alexandra Suich helped carry the book up to that point. Zachary Lawrence provided fact-checking and editing assistance. Annie Harper helped out even while she was living in England and then Pakistan, but somehow she still had a sharp eye for the tragedies and ironies of the American experience.

Writing this book would not have been possible were it not for the generous support of Yale University. Thanks to a Junior Faculty Fellowship, I enjoyed a year of leave to work on the book. Don Green, who heads Yale's Institution for Social and Policy Studies, and Alan Gerber, who runs the Center for the Study of American Politics, both placed research funds at my disposal. And everyone in the Department of Political Science—with their support and their example—helped bring this project to fruition.

The New America Foundation in Washington, DC, has also supported my work, beginning when I was a graduate student in the late 1990s. I feel fortunate to remain connected to an institution so engaged with public debate and so willing to consider issues from so many angles. The Foundation gives public intellectualism a good name.

Eight thinkers who give public intellectualism a good name also gave my manuscript a close and conscientous reading, and I want to thank deeply Anne Alstott, Jonathan Cohn, John Langbein, Michael Graetz, Jerry Mashaw, Paul Pierson, Gene Sperling, and Elizabeth Warren. Honesty compels me to admit that they saved me from many errors, but they of course bear no responsibility for any that remain.

This book would not have come into being were it not for the faith and hard work of everyone at Oxford University Press, who believed in this book even when it was just a hazy gleam in my eye. My amazing editor, Dedi Felman, has been involved in every aspect of this book, and her gentle but insistent questions and skillful but sharp editorial pen have pressed me to produce a book that I hope lives up to her intelligent, exacting standards. Joellyn Ausanka managed the production of the manuscript with ample skill and charm even when I was running behind. Christian Purdy (known to grateful authors simply as "Purdy") has managed publicity for the book with true indefatigability. My agent, Sydelle Kramer, deserves a special thanks. She didn't just help me figure out what I wanted to do with this book and guide me as I went; she also taught me almost everything I know about the world of publishing. I could not wish for a better guide.

My greatest debt, as always, goes to my family. My wife, Oona Hathaway, has been my best friend and my most trusted guide for more than seventeen years now—nearly half my life. So it is understandable why I can't fathom a world in which she isn't there helping me and teaching me and lifting me up. She has shaped who I am in the deepest sense, and she and my two children, Ava and Owen, make my life whole.

Finally, I dedicate this book to my parents, who taught me the value of both love and learning—and who shared with me their own simple conviction that injustice faced by any of us is injustice faced by all of us.

Notes

INTRODUCTION

1. Jacob S. Hacker, "Call It the Family Risk Factor," *New York Times*, January 11, 2004, sec. 4, 15. These estimates, like the other calculations based on the Panel Study of Income Dynamics (PSID) that appear in chapter 1, were carried out in cooperation with Dr. Nigar Nargis, assistant professor at the University of Dhaka in Bangladesh, currently a postdoctoral fellow of the Strategic Training Program of Tobacco Research at the Canadian Institute of Health Research at the University of Waterloo in Canada. The estimates in figure 1 use family income, adjusted for family size, for families with heads twenty-five to sixty-one years of age. Further description of the PSID analyses are contained in chapter 1. More information on the PSID is available on the study's excellent website: http://psidonline.isr.umich.edu.
2. For a thoughtful analysis of the ways in which advocates of public insurance constructed a link between natural and economic disasters, see Michele L. Landis, "Fate, Responsibility, and 'Natural' Disaster Relief; Narrating the American Welfare State," *Law & Society Review* 33:2 (1999): 257–318.
3. Franklin D. Roosevelt, "Second Inaugural Address," *Inaugural Addresses of the Presidents* (Washington, DC: U.S. GPO, 1989).
4. Jacob S. Hacker, *The Divided Welfare State: The Battle over Public and Private Social Benefits in the United States* (New York: Cambridge University Press, 2002), 14–15.

CHAPTER 1

1. Joel Friedman, Isaac Shapiro, and Robert Greenstein, "Recent Tax and Income Trends Among High Income Tax Payers" (Washington, DC: Center on Budget and Policy Priorities, 2006), available online at www.cbpp.org/4-10-06tax5.htm.

2. Data courtesy of Elizabeth Warren, Harvard Law School. The number of filings was inflated in 2005 by the rush of filings before the bankruptcy bill took effect. The number in 2004, however, still exceeded 1.56 million.

3. Elizabeth Warren, "Financial Collapse and Class Status: Who Goes Bankrupt?" *Osgoode Hall Law Journal* 41, no. 1 (2003).

4. Calculated from Peter J. Elmer and Steven A. Seelig, "The Rising Long-Term Trend of Single-Family Mortgage Foreclosure Rates" (Federal Deposit Insurance Corporation Working Paper 98-2, n.d.), available online at www.fdic.gov/bank/analytical/working/98-2.pdf.

5. Christian E. Weller, *Middle-Class Turmoil: High Risks Reflect Middle-Class Anxieties* (Washington, DC: Center for American Progress, December 2005), 3.

6. Suzette Hackney, "Families Fight for Their Homes," *Detroit Free Press,* October 15, 2005.

7. Joe Baker, "Foreclosures Chilling Many US Housing Markets," *Rock River Times*, March 22–28, 2006, available online at www.rockrivertimes.com/index.pl?cmd=viewstory&id=12746&cat=2.

8. *One In Three: Non-Elderly Americans Without Health Insurance, 2002–2003* (Washington, DC: Families USA Foundation, 2004), available online at www.familiesusa.org/issues/uninsured/about-the-uninsured.

9. *The Newshour with Jim Lehrer*, "Coping without Health Insurance," November 28, 2005, available online at www.pbs.org/newshour/bb/health/july-dec05/insurance_11-28.html.

10. John H. Langbein, "Understanding the Death of the Private Pension Plan in the United States" (unpublished manuscript, Yale Law School, April 2006).

11. Edward Wolff, *Retirement Insecurity* (Washington, DC: Economic Policy Institute, 2002), excerpt available online at www.epinet.org/content.cfm/books_retirement_intro.

12. Hackney, "Families Fight for Their Homes."

13. Stephen Moore and Lincoln Anderson, "The Great American Dream Machine," *Wall Street Journal*, December 21, 2005, A18; Gregg Easterbrook, *The Progress Paradox: How Life Gets Better While People Feel Worse* (New York: Random House, 2003).

14. "Fact Sheet: Economic Growth Continues—Unemployment Falls Below 5 Percent," White House News Release, January 6, 2006, available online at www.whitehouse.gov/news/releases/2006/01/20060106.html.

15. Mark Gongloff, "The Afternoon Report: The Miracle Continues," *Wall Street Journal Online*, December 6, 2005.
16. Exit poll results are at www.cnn.com/ELECTION/2004/pages/results/states/US/P/00/epolls.0.html.
17. Ray C. Fair, "A Vote Equation and the 2004 Election," Yale University, October 2004, available online at http://fairmodel.econ.yale.edu/vote2004/vot1004.htm.
18. Frank Newport, "Republicans All Alone in Viewing the Economy as Good," Gallup Poll News Service, March 21, 2006.
19. Robert J. Samuelson, "Presidential Prosperity Games," *Washington Post,* December 21, 2005, A31.
20. Noel Sheppard, "According to the Media, Most Economic News is Bad," Free Market Project, November 7, 2005, available online at www.freemarketproject.org/news/2005/news20051107.asp; John D. McKinnon, "Bush Plugs Economy, Hinting at Thrust of 2006 Campaign," *Wall Street Journal*, December 6, 2005, A4.
21. NBC News and *Wall Street Journal* Poll, March 15, 2004, available via the Roper public opinion database (http://roperweb.ropercenter.uconn.edu/iPoll) as USNBCWSJ.04MAR.R31.
22. Other polls showed even higher concern: In response to a 1995 *New York Times* survey, 53 percent of Americans said their own job was insecure, nearly 83 percent said it was hard to find a good job in their community, and 48 percent feared that they would lose their own job *and* that it would be hard to find a good job in their area. The survey, "Economic Insecurity," is available via the Roper public opinion database (http://roperweb.ropercenter.uconn.edu/iPOLL) as USNYT95-012. The same basic pattern appears in public responses to the Gallup Poll, which has been asking a standard question about economic conditions since 1992. The share of Americans describing the economy as "only fair" or "poor" was extremely high in the early 1990s (peaking at 90 percent in 1992) and did not fall below a majority until late 1997. It remained low in 1998, 1999, and 2000, bottoming out at 25 percent in 2000, before shooting back up to its current high levels of 60–80 percent in 2001. This pattern matches up almost perfectly with the trends in pre-tax income volatility discussed later in this chapter. Indeed, between the beginning of 1992 (when Gallup Poll data begin) and the end of 2002 (when the income volatility data end), the correlation between negative public appraisals of the economy and income volatility is greater than 70 percent. Gallup Poll data available online at http://poll.gallup.com. The question wording is as follows: "How would you rate economic conditions in this country today—as excellent, good, only fair, or poor?"
23. This is the core theme of Ulrich Beck, *Risk Society: Towards a New Modernity*, trans. Mark Ritter (London: Sage, 1992).
24. Calculated from Congressional Budget Office (CBO), *Historical Effective Federal Tax Rates: 1979–2003* (Washington, DC: CBO, December 2005).

25. Like all the other figures reported in this chapter, these numbers are adjusted for inflation and exclude both questionable data—mainly, people who report zero or negative incomes—and people younger than twenty-five and older than sixty-one, so as to leave out college students and retirees. Unless otherwise noted, they also include all sources of cash income (including alimony) and account for government taxes and benefits.

26. See, for example, Andrew J. Rettenmaier and Donald R. Deere, "Climbing the Economic Ladder" (Washington, DC: The National Center for Policy Analysis, 2003), 17–18. Though the overall tone of the report is cheerful, a closer look at the data tells a less sunny story. While in a given year almost half of people in the middle three quintiles are likely to move to a different quintile, they are more likely to move to the quartile below the one they're in than the one above. Those in the bottom quartile, who by definition cannot fall to a lower quartile, are much less likely to move. Only 31 percent are likely to change quartiles, and most of these move up by only a single quartile.

27. "Ever Higher, Ever Harder to Ascend," *Economist,* December 29, 2004, available online at www.economist.com/world/na/displayStory.cfm?story_id=3518560.

28. Alan B. Krueger, "The Apple Falls Close to the Tree, Even in the Land of Opportunity," *New York Times*, November 14, 2002, C2.

29. Daniel Kahneman and Amos Tversky, "Prospect Theory: An Analysis of Decisions Under Risk," *Econometrica* 47, no. 2 (1979).

30. Willem Adema and Maxime Ladaique, "Net Social Expenditures, 2005 Edition," OECD Social Employment and Migration Working Paper No. 29 (Paris: Organization for Economic Cooperation and Development, 2005), table 6 ("gross social expenditure"), available online at www.oecd.org/dataoecd/56/2/35632106.pdf.

31. George Washington University Battleground 2006 Survey, March 24, 2005.

32. International Labor Office, Economic Security for a Better World (Washington, DC: Brookings, 2004).

33. For a description of the model used to calculate over-time income variance, see Robert A. Moffitt and Peter Gottschalk, "Trends in the Transitory Variance of Earnings in the United States," *Economic Journal* 112 (March 2002): 68–73. Data on taxes and government benefits are from the Cross-National Equivalent File, Cornell University, available online at www.human.cornell.edu/che/PAM/Research/Centers-Programs/German-Panel/Cross-National-Equivalent-File_CNEF.cfm. In these analyses, family income variables are adjusted for family size by dividing by the square root of family size—a common equivalence scale, reflecting the lesser costs per person of maintaining a larger family.

34. Not surprisingly, volatility is also higher for lower-income Americans. See Lily Batchelder, "Taxing the Poor: Income Averaging Reconsidered," *Harvard Journal on Legislation* 40 (2003): 395–452.

35. This is not to say that there are no relationships; people with higher incomes do seem less worried about the risk of economic loss than

people with lower incomes, and people who have experienced substantial upward mobility are less worried about risk than those who have experienced flat or falling incomes.

36. Elmer and Seelig, "The Rising Long-Term Trend of Single-Family Mortgage Foreclosure Rates," 31.

37. What's more, all these results are based on analyses that transform income so that it is what statisticians call "mean-independent." This is just a fancy way of saying that the level of a family's income doesn't directly affect the measure of volatility. Take two families—each of whose income drops by 20 percent between two years. If family one has twice the income as family two, that 20 percent drop is going to be twice as large in dollar terms, even though the two families are experiencing exactly the same size change relative to their prior income. Using mean-independent measures fixes that, making it possible to compare volatility across people with different income levels and across years with different average income levels. All these analyses also use inflation-adjusted dollars, so year-to-year changes in the inflation rate don't show up as instability either.

38. Katherine S. Newman, *Falling from Grace: The Experience of Downward Mobility in the American Middle Class* (New York: Free Press, 1988).

39. Median drops in family income are estimated by looking at changes in post-tax family income over a two-year period among families experiencing income drops. As in the other PSID analyses, the sample is restricted to families with heads aged twenty-five to sixty-one with positive income. The table shows the median drops from 1969 to 2002.

Years	Median Drop in Family Income
1969–1971	27%
1970–1972	29%
1971–1973	29%
1972–1974	29%
1973–1975	27%
1974–1976	29%
1975–1977	29%
1976–1978	27%
1977–1979	26%
1978–1980	26%
1979–1981	26%
1980–1982	28%
1981–1983	30%
1982–1984	30%
1983–1985	28%
1984–1986	28%
1985–1987	31%
1986–1988	28%
1987–1989	25%

1988–1990	25%
1989–1991	27%
1990–1992	30%
1991–1993	39%
1992–1994	37%
1993–1995	35%
1994–1996	38%
1996–1998	44%
1998–2000	37%
2000–2002	38%

40. A logistic regression was used to estimate the average probability that an individual experiences at least a 50 percent drop in family-size-adjusted income over a two-year interval. The analysis controls for the demographic and social characteristics of individuals, as well as individuals' permanent family income levels (measured as the five-year moving average of family income). It also includes variables that account for different types of risks that may contribute to income drops, including unemployment, retirement, disability, illness, divorce, marriage, and the birth or adoption of children. A time-trend variable in the model captures any consistent change in the probability of income loss over time that cannot be accounted for by the other variables in the model. To predict the probability of income loss for each year for an "average" individual simply requires using the coefficients of the model to calculate the probability of an income drop of 50 percent or greater for an individual possessing the mean values on each of the variables. The rising trend shown in figure 1.4 is robust to the inclusion of individual fixed effects—that is, controlling for individual-specific attributes that are invariant over time but that may be correlated with the likelihood of an income drop.

41. U. S. Department of Health and Human Services 2006 Poverty Guidelines, available online at http://aspe.hhs.gov/poverty/06poverty.shtml.

42. Mark Rank, *One Nation, Underprivileged: Why American Poverty Affects Us All* (New York: Oxford University Press, 2004), 94.

43. Lee Rainwater and Timothy M. Smeeding, *Poor Kids in a Rich Country: America's Children in Comparative Perspective* (New York: Russell Sage Foundation, 2003), 52, 58.

44. Rank, *One Nation, Underprivileged*, 94.

45. Daniel Sandoval, Thomas A. Hirschl, and Mark R. Rank, "The Increase of Poverty Risk and Income Insecurity in the U.S. Since the 1970's" (paper presented at the American Sociological Association Annual Meeting, San Francisco, CA, August 14–17, 2004).

CHAPTER 2

1. Richard L. Kaplan, "Who's Afraid of Personal Responsibility?" *McGeorge Law Review* 36 (2005): 535.

2. Department of the Treasury, "Health Savings Accounts Frequently Asked Questions," available online at www.treasury.gov/offices/public-affairs/hsa/faq_basics.shtml.

3. According to America's Health Insurance Plans (AHIP), a health insurance trade group, 3.2 million people were covered by HSAs in January 2006. AHIP Center for Policy and Research, "January 2006 Census Shows 3.2 Million People Covered by HSA Plans," March 9, 2006, available at www.ahipresearch.org/pdfs/HSAHDHPReportJanuary2006.pdf.

4. Julie Appleby, "Health Accounts Would Eat Up Savings," *USA Today,* February 6, 2006, 4A.

5. Cybele Weisser, "A Health Revolution in Slo-Mo," *Money* 34, no. 7 (July 2005): 28.

6. Lawrence Mishel, Jared Bernstein, and Sylvia Allegretto, *The State of Working America 2004/2005* (Ithaca: Cornell University Press, 2005), data available online at www.epinet.org/content.cfm/datazone_dznational.

7. Robert Pear, "Budget Accord Could Mean Payments by Medicaid Recipients," *New York Times,* December 20, 2005, A26.

8. White House Press Release, "President Signs Bankruptcy Abuse Prevention, Consumer Protection Act," April 20, 2005, available online at www.whitehouse.gov/news/releases/2005/04/20050420-5.html.

9. David Boaz, "Defining an Ownership Society," Cato Institute, www.cato.org/special/ownership_society/boaz.html.

10. Dick Armey, *The Freedom Revolution: The New Republican House Majority Leader Tells Why Big Government Failed, Why Freedom Works, and How We Will Rebuild America* (New York: Regnery, 1995), 317; emphasis in original.

11. James O'Toole, "Health Savings Accounts Touted for Medical Expenses," *Pittsburgh Post-Gazette,* March 15, 2005, available online at www.post-gazette.com/pg/05074/471576.stm.

12. Allan B. Hubbard, "The Health of a Nation," *New York Times,* April 3, 2006, A17.

13. Ronald Brownstein, "Governors on Divergent Paths to Control Health Costs," *Los Angeles Times,* March 14, 2006, A19.

14. Peter H. Wehner, "Some Thoughts on Social Security," January 3, 2005, available online at www.talkingpointsmemo.com/archives/week_2005_01_02.php#004348.

15. Edwin E. Witte, *The Development of the Social Security Act* (Madison: University of Wisconsin Press, 1962), 21.

16. Ibid., 96.

17. Jacob S. Hacker, *The Divided Welfare State* (New York: Cambridge University Press, 2002); Robert Lieberman, *Shifting the Color Line: Race and the American Welfare State* (Cambridge, MA: Harvard University Press, 1998); Paul Starr, *The Social Transformation of*

American Medicine (New York: Basic Books, 1982); Bartholomew H. Sparrow, *From the Outside In* (Princeton: Princeton University Press, 1996).

18. Roy Lubove, *The Struggle for Social Security* (Cambridge, MA: Harvard University Press, 1968), 175.
19. David Moss, *When All Else Fails: Government as the Ultimate Risk Manager* (Cambridge, MA: Harvard University Press), chaps. 3–5.
20. "Text of Roosevelt Speech on Social Security," *New York Times*, August 16, 1938, 6.
21. Ibid.
22. Franklin D. Roosevelt, "Message to Congress on Social Security," January 17, 1935, available at www.ssa.gov/history/fdrstmts.html.
23. Michael K. Brown, *Race, Money, and the American Welfare State* (Ithaca: Cornell University Press, 1999); Colin Gordon, *Dead on Arrival: The Politics of Health Care in Twentieth-Century America* (Princeton: Princeton University Press, 2003); Hacker, *Divided Welfare State*; Jennifer Klein, *For All These Rights: Business, Labor, and the Shaping of America's Public-Private Welfare State* (Princeton: Princeton University Press, 2003).
24. Thomas Hopkinson Elliot, interview, *Social Security Administration Project*, pt. 3, no. 154, tape recorded in 1965 (New York: Columbia University Oral History Collection, 1976), 51–52. Elliot was the key Roosevelt lawyer charged with working out an acceptable compromise regarding the opt-out proposal after the Social Security Act passed.
25. Hacker, *Divided Welfare State*, 214.
26. Fredric R. Heidinger, *The Social Role of Blue Cross as a Device for Financing the Costs of Hospital Care: An Evaluation* (Iowa City: Graduate Program in Hospital and Health Administration, University of Iowa, 1966), 20–21.
27. Gordon, *Dead on Arrival,* 76.
28. Jacoby, *Modern Manors*, 57.
29. Marion B. Folsom, *Social Administration Project*, part 3, no. 158, tape recorded in 1965 (New York: Columbia University Oral History Collection, 1976).
30. Hacker, *Divided Welfare State*, 142.
31. Tom Baker, "On the Genealogy of Moral Hazard," *Texas Law Review* 75, no. 2 (1996).
32. Kenneth J. Arrow, "Uncertainty and the Welfare Economics of Medical Care," *American Economic Review* 53 (1963): 941–73.
33. Ibid., 961.
34. John Nyman, University of Minnesota health economist, quoted in Malcolm Gladwell, "The Moral-Hazard Myth," *New Yorker*, August 29, 2005, available online at www.newyorker.com/fact/content/articles/050829fa_fact.
35. Mark V. Pauly, "The Economics of Moral Hazard: Comment" *American Economic Review* 58, no. 1 (June 1968): 531–37.

36. See, for example, Martin S. Feldstein, "An Econometric Model of the Medicare System," *Quarterly Journal of Economics* 85, no. 1 (February 1971); "The Welfare Loss of Excess Health Insurance," *Journal of Political Economy* 8, no. 2 (March–April 1973); "Economics of the New Unemployment," *Public Interest* 33 (Fall 1973); "Social Security and Private Savings: Reply to Barro," *Journal of Political Economy* 90, no. 3 (June 1982).

37. This is a core theme of Mark A. Smith, *Turning Right in America: Rhetoric and Economics in the Conservative Ascendancy* (Princeton, NJ: Princeton University Press, forthcoming).

38. Ronald Reagan, "First Inaugural Address," Ronald Reagan Presidential Foundation and Library, available online at http://www.reaganfoundation.org/reagan/speeches/first.asp.

39. George L. Priest, "Rethinking the New Deal: The Role of the Government as an Insurer," *AEI Bradley Lecture Series*, February 12, 1996, available online at www.aei.org/publications/pubID.18105,filter.all/pub_detail.asp.

40. Charles Murray, *Losing Ground: American Social Policy, 1950–1980* (New York: Basic Books, 1994), 212.

41. Quoted in Baker, "On the Genealogy of Moral Hazard," 238.

42. The term is from Stuart Butler and Peter Germanis's blueprint for privatizing Social Security (discussed in chapter 5), "Achieving a 'Leninist' Strategy," *Cato Journal* 3, no. 2 (Fall 1993): 547–56.

43. Stuart Butler, *Privatizing Federal Spending: A Strategy to Reduce the Deficit* (New York: Universe Books, 1985). See also the perceptive analysis of Steve Teles and Martha Derthick, "From Third Rail to Presidential Commitment—And Back? The Conservative Campaign for Social Security Privatization and The Limits of Long-Term Political Strategy" (paper prepared for Conference on Conservatives and American Political Development, Institution for Social and Policy Studies, Yale University, February 24, 2006).

44. Interview with Stuart Butler, Vice President for Domestic and Economic Policy, The Heritage Foundation, May 11, 2006.

45. James K. Glassman, "A Nation of Citizen Investors," *American Enterprise*, March 2005, available online at www.taemag.com/issues/issueID.169/toc.asp.

46. Grover Norquist, "Ownership Can Be Revolutionary," *American Enterprise*, March 2005, available online at www.taemag.com/issues/issueID.169/toc.asp.

47. Grover Norquist, "The Democratic Party is Toast," *Washington Monthly*, September 2004, available online at www.washingtonmonthly.com/features/2004/0409.norquist.html.

48. Americans are "operational liberals" and "philosophical conservatives," public opinion analysts Lloyd Free and Hadley Cantril famously argued in their *The Political Beliefs of Americans* (New Brunswick, NJ: Rutgers University Press, 1967). Americans are

skeptical of government in the abstract, yet they embrace specific public programs of social protection for workers with genuine enthusiasm. For more recent assessments, which reach the same basic conclusion, see Fay Lomax Cook and Edith J. Barrett, *Support for the American Welfare State* (New York: Columbia University Press, 1992); and Stanley Feldman and John Zaller, "The Political Culture of Ambivalence: Ideological Responses to the Welfare State," *American Journal of Political Science* 36, no. 1 (February 1992): 268–307.

49. University of Minnesota, Office of Human Resources, "Medical Plan Description," University of Minnesota, available online at www1.umn.edu/ohr/benefits/medical/descriptions.html.

50. Amy Goldstein, "Uncertain Cure: Early Reaction to Health Savings Account is Two-Sided," *Washington Post*, March 12, 2006, F1.

CHAPTER 3

1. Timothy Egan, "No Degree, and No Way Back to the Middle," *New York Times*, May 24, 2005, available online at www.nytimes.com/2005/05/24/national/class/BLUECOLLAR-FINAL.html.

2. Jonathan Krim and Griff Witte, "Average-Wage Earners Fall Behind—New Job Market Makes More Demands but Fewer Promises," *Washington Post*, December 31, 2004, available online at http://washingtonpost.com/wp-dyn/articles/A37628-2004Dec30.html.

3. Egan, "No Degree, and No Way Back to the Middle."

4. Ann Huff Stevens, "The More Things Change, The More They Stay the Same: Trends in Long-term Employment in the United States, 1969-2002," NBER Working Paper 11878 (Cambridge, MA: National Bureau of Economic Research, 2005), available online at www.nber.org/papers/w11878.pdf.

5. Ian Dew-Becker and Robert J. Gordon, "Where Did the Productivity Growth Go? Inflation Dynamics and the Distribution of Income," NBER Working Paper No. 11842 (Cambridge, MA: National Bureau of Economic Research, December 2005), available online at www.nber.org/papers/w11842.pdf.

6. Diego Comin, Erica L. Groshen, and Bess Rabin, "Turbulent Firms, Turbulent Wages?" Federal Reserve Bank of New York Staff Reports no. 238, February 2006, 33, available online at www.ny.frb.org/research/staff_reports/sr238.html.

7. Gene Sperling, *The Pro-Growth Progressive: An Economic Strategy for Shared Prosperity* (New York: Simon and Schuster, 2005), 7.

8. Peter Cappelli, *The New Deal at Work: Managing the Market-Driven Workforce* (Cambridge, MA: Harvard Business School Press, 1999), 25–26.

9. Ibid., 2–3.

10. Peter Cappelli, "Examining the Incidence of Downsizing and Its Effects on Establishment Performance," NBER Working Paper 7742 (Cambridge, MA: National Bureau of Economic Research, June 2000), available online at www.nber.org/papers/w7742.

11. Henry S. Farber, "What Do We Know About Job Loss in the United States?" Federal Reserve Bank of Chicago, *Economic Perspectives* 2Q (2005): 13–27, available online at www.chicagofed.org/publications/ economicperspectives/ep_2qtr2005_part2_farber.pdf. These are difference-in-difference estimates of earnings loss that compare changes in displaced workers earnings with changes in the earnings of workers who are not displaced.

12. For a good recent analysis, see Robert G. Valletta, "Rising Unemployment Duration in the United States: Causes and Consequences," Federal Reserve Bank of San Francisco, May 2005, available online at www.frbsf.org/economics/economists/rvalletta/RV_duration_5-05.pdf.

13. Calculated from Bureau of Labor Statistics historical data, comparing 1969 and 2001—both business cycle peaks. Data available online at www.bls.gov/data/home.htm.

14. Stacey Schreft and Aarti Singh, "A Closer Look at Jobless Recoveries," *Federal Reserve Bank of Kansas City* 2Q (2003), available online at www.kc.frb.org/PUBLICAT/ECONREV/PDF/2q03schr.pdf; Andrew Stettner and Sylvia A. Allegretto, "The Rising Stakes of Job Loss: Stubborn Long-Term Joblessness Amid Falling Unemployment Rates," EPI & NELP Briefing Paper #162 (Washington, DC: Economic Policy Institute, May 2005), available online at www.epinet.org/content.cfm/ bp162.

15. Stettner and Allegretto, "Rising Stakes of Job Loss."

16. Two recent, powerful examinations of the economic situation of today's young Americans are Tamara Draut, *Strapped: Why America's 20- and 30-Somethings Can't Get Ahead* (New York: Doubleday, 2006), and Anya Kamanetz, *Generation Debt: Why Now is a Terrible Time to be Young* (New York: Riverhead Books, 2006).

17. Farber, "What Do We Know About Job Loss in the United States?" 24.

18. Stettner and Allegretto, "Rising Stakes of Job Loss."

19. Matt Murray, "After Long Boom, Workers Confront Downward Mobility," *Wall Street Journal*, August 13, 2003, available online at http:// online.wsj.com/article/SB106072264536741400.html.

20. Anna L. Berman, "Opting Out of Work: What's Behind the Decline in Labor Force Participation?" *Southwest Economy* 6 (November/December 2005), available online at www.dallasfed.org/research/swe/2005/ swe0506a.html.

21. Katharine Bradbury, "Additional Slack in the Economy: The Poor Recovery in Labor Force Participation During This Business Cycle," Federal Reserve Bank of Boston Public Policy Briefs, No. 05–02 (Boston, July 2005), available online at www.bos.frb.org/economic/ppb/ 2005/ppb052.pdf.

22. Sheldon Danziger, "Earnings by Education for Young Workers, 1975 and 2000," Network on Transitions to Adulthood Data Brief, Issue 17 (University of Pennsylvania, Philadelphia, November 2004), available online at www.transad.pop.upenn.edu/news/17.pdf.

23. Draut, *Strapped,* 84.

24. Leslie McCall, "Explaining Levels of Within-Group Inequality in U.S. Labor Markets, *Demography* 37:4 (2000): 415.

25. Sandy Baum and Marie O'Malley, "College on Credit: How Borrowers Perceive their Education Debt: Results of the 2002 National Student Loan Survey," *Nellie Mae: Research and Information*, February 6, 2003, www.nelliemae.com/library/research_10.html.

26. Draut, *Strapped*, 33; "Federal Student Loan Debt: 1993 to 2004," American Council on Education Issue Brief (Washington, DC, June 2005), available online at www.acenet.edu/AM/Template.cfm?Section= CPA&Template=/CM/ContentDisplay.cfm&ContentID=10777.

27. Graciela Chichilnisky and Olga Gorbachev, "Volatility in the Knowledge Economy," *Economic Theory* 24 (2004): 531–47.

28. W. Michael Cox and Richard Alm, *Myths of Rich and Poor: Why We're Better Off Than We Think* (New York: Basic, 2000), 201.

29. Ibid., 187.

30. U.S. Department of Labor, Bureau of Labor Statistics (BLS), "Computer Programmers," *Occupational Outlook Handbook, 2006-2007 Edition* (Washington, DC: BLS, 2006), available online at www.bls.gov/oco/ocos110.htm.

31. Stephanie Armour, "Workers Asked to Train Foreign Replacements," *USA Today*, April 6, 2004, available online at www.usatoday.com/money/workplace/2004-04-06-replace_x.htm.

32. Daniel W. Drezner, "The Outsourcing Bogeyman," *Foreign Affairs* 83 (May/June 2003), available online at www.foreignaffairs.org/20040501faessay83304-p10/daniel-w-drezner/the-outsourcing-bogeyman.html.

33. Stephen S. Cohen and J. Bradford DeLong, "Shaken and Stirred," *Atlantic Monthly* (January/February 2005), available online at www.theatlantic.com/doc/200501/cohen.

34. Educational qualifications from Bureau of Labor Statistics, "Occupational Outlook Handbook." Quote from Rachel Konrad, "Programming Jobs Losing Luster in U.S.," *ABC News Online*, June 19, 2005, available online at http://abcnews.go.com/Technology/wireStory?id=862041&CMP=OTC-RSSFeeds0312.

35. Daniel Bell, *The Coming of Post-Industrial Society: A Venture in Social Forecasting* (New York: Basic Books, 1973).

36. Paul Krugman, "Always Low Wages, Always," *New York Times*, May 13, 2005, 23.

37. Calculated from Bureau of Labor Statistics historical data, available online at www.bls.gov/data/home.htm. Congressional Budget Office, "What Accounts for the Decline in Manufacturing Employment?" Economic and Budget Issue Brief (Washington, DC: CBO, February 2004), available online at www.cbo.gov/showdoc.cfm?index=5078&sequence=0.

38. This is the core argument of Torben Iversen and Thomas Cusack, "The Causes of Welfare State Expansion: Deindustrialization or Globalization?" *World Politics* 52 (April 2000): 313–49.

39. Griff Witte, "As Income Gap Widens, Uncertainty Spreads: More U.S. Families Struggle to Stay on Track," *Washington Post*, September 20, 2004, A1, available online at www.washingtonpost.com/wp-dyn/articles/A34235-2004Sep19.html.

40. Lawrence Mishel, Jared Bernstein, and Sylvia Allegretto, *The State of Working America 2004-05* (Ithaca, NY: Cornell University Press, 2005), figure 3Z, available online at www.epinet.org/datazone/05/share_pt_ft_emp.xls; Bureau of Labor Statistics, "Contingent and Alternative Employment Arrangements, February 2005," July 27, 2005, available online at www.bls.gov/news.release/conemp.nr0.htm.

41. Chris Tilly, "Reasons for the Continuing Growth of Part-Time Employment," *Monthly Labor Review* 3 (March 1991): 10–18, available online at www.bls.gov/opub/mlr/1991/03/art2full.pdf.

42. Michael K. Lettau, "Compensation in Part-Time Jobs versus Full-Time Jobs: What if the Job is the Same?" Bureau of Labor Statistics Working Paper 260, December 1994, available online at www.bls.gov/ore/pdf/ec940080.pdf.

43. Tilly, "Reasons for the Continuing Growth of Part-Time Employment," 16.

44. Max Weber, *The Protestant Ethic and the Spirit of Capitalism*, trans. Talcott Parsons and Anthony Giddens (London: Unwin Hyman, 1930), available online at http://xroads.virginia.edu/~HYPER/WEBER/toc.html.

45. Jared Bernstein and Karen Kornbluh, "Running Faster to Stay in Place: The Growth of Family Work Hours and Incomes," New America Foundation Work and Family Program Research Paper, June 2005, available online at www.newamerica.net/Download_Docs/pdfs/Doc_File_2437_1.pdf.

46. Lee Price and Susan Vasavada, "Annual Unemployment Insurance Exhaustion Rate at Highest Level in 60 Years," Economic Policy Institute, September 22, 2004, available online at www.epinet.org/content.cfm?id=1900.

47. Paul Kersey and Tim Kane, "The Wrong Time to Extend Unemployment Insurance," Heritage Foundation Backgrounder #1754, May 4, 2004, available online at www.heritage.org/Research/Labor/bg1754.cfm.

48. Michael J. Graetz and Jerry L. Mashaw, *True Security: Rethinking American Social Insurance* (New Haven, CT: Yale University Press, 1999), 76.

49. United States General Accounting Office (GAO), *Unemployment Insurance: Role as Safety Net for Low-Wage Workers is Limited* (Washington, DC: GAO, December 2000).

CHAPTER 4

1. This is one of the profiles of indebted families contained in Tamara Draut and Javier Silva, *Borrowing to Make Ends Meet: The Growth of Credit Card Debt in the '90s* (New York: Demos, 2003), 15.

2. The story is told in Steven K. Wisensale, *Family Leave Policy: The Political Economy of Work and Family in America* (Armonk, NY: M. E. Sharpe, Inc., 2001).
3. Lois Wladis Hoffman, "The Effects of the Mother's Employment on the Family and the Child," available online at http://parenthood.library.wisc.edu/Hoffman/Hoffman.html.
4. Maria Cancian and Deborah Reed, "Changes in Married Couples' Intra-household Distribution of Work and Earnings" (paper prepared for presentation at the Population Association of America 2004 Annual Meeting, Boston, MA, March 2004).
5. US Census Bureau Historical Income Tables 2005, available online at www.census.gov/hhes/www/income/histinc/f07ar.html.
6. Jared Bernstein and Karen Kornbluh, "Running Faster to Stay in Place: The Growth of Family Work Hours and Incomes," New America Foundation Work and Family Program Research Paper, June 2005, available online at www.newamerica.net/Download_Docs/pdfs/Doc_File_2437_1.pdf.
7. The memorial is at http://griefnet.org/memorials/2001b/may1-902094727.html (visited January 29, 2006). I have edited it slightly to fix a small grammatical error.
8. In 1997, 2 percent of full-time employees were eligible to participate in a paid family leave program. Employee Benefits Research Institute (EBRI), "Leave of Absence Benefits Among Private-Sector Employers: Paid Holiday, Vacation, and Sick Leave," EBRI Fact Sheet, Washington, DC, July 2000, www.ebri.org/publications/facts/index.cfm?fa=0700fact1.
9. Janet C. Gornick, Marcia K. Meyers, and Katherine E. Ross, "Supporting the Employment of Mothers: Policy Variation Across Fourteen Welfare States," Luxembourg Income Study Working Paper #139 (Luxembourg: LIS, 1996), www.lisproject.org/publications/LISwps/139.pdf.
10. Jody Heyman, Alison Earle, Stephanie Simmons, Stephanie M. Breslow, and April Kuehnhoff, *The Work, Family, and Equity Index: Where Does the United States Stand Globally?* (Boston, MA: Project on Global Working Families, n.d.), www.hsph.harvard.edu/globalworkingfamilies/images/report.pdf. See also Jody Heyman, *The Widening Gap: Why America's Working Families Are in Jeopardy—and What Can Be Done About It* (New York: Basic Books, 2000).
11. The term is from Arlie Russell Hochschild, *The Time Bind: When Work Becomes Home and Home Becomes Work* (New York: Metropolitan Books, 1997),
12. Susan Dynarski and Jonathan Gruber, "Can Families Smooth Variable Earnings?" *Brookings Papers on Economic Activity* 1 (1997): 229–84.
13. Moreover, singles living alone and single parents have also become more common in recent decades—which might be thought to explain why the overall volatility of family incomes has increased. This

explanation, however, turns out not to be true. Change in the mix of American families does not by itself seem to be a major contributor to rising volatility. For example, if the only thing that had changed between the early 1970s and today was the balance between different family types, volatility would have risen by only 6 percent. Instead, income volatility has risen dramatically across all family types.

14. Data courtesy of the 2001 Consumer Bankruptcy Project run by Elizabeth Warren, Harvard Law School.

15. Elizabeth Warren and Amelia Warren Tyagi, *The Two-Income Trap: Why Middle-Class Mothers and Fathers Are Going Broke* (New York: Basic Books, 2003), 6–7.

16. Carlen Hempel, "Middle Class and Out of Work," *Boston Globe Magazine*, June 15, 2003.

17. "U.S. Savings Rate Hits Lowest Level since 1933," Associated Press, January 30, 2006.

18. Calculated from Federal Reserve Board, Survey of Consumer Finance, 2004, available online at www.federalreserve.gov/pub/oss/oss2/ scfindex.htm. All results are weighted.

19. Javier Silva, *A House of Cards: Refinancing the American Dream* (New York: Demos, 2005), 10.

20. Dynarski and Gruber, "Can Families Smooth Variable Earnings?"

21. Robert Haveman and Edward N. Wolff, "Who Are the Asset Poor? Levels, Trends, and Composition, 1983–1998," Discussion paper 1227–01 (Institute for Research on Poverty, 2001): table 7, available online at www.irp.wisc.edu/publications/dps/pdfs/dp122701.pdf.

22. Brian K. Bucks, Arthur B. Kennickell, and Kevin B. Moore, "Recent Changes in U.S. Family Finances: Evidence from the 2001 and 2004 Survey of Consumer Finances," *Federal Reserve Bulletin* 92 (February 2006): A1–A38.

23. Robert J. Samuelson, "Pressure of the American Dream," *Washington Post*, July 26, 2004, A11, available online at www.washingtonpost.com/ wp-dyn/articles/A14226-2004Jul25.html.

24. Cited in Elizabeth Warren and Amelia Warren Tyagi, "What's Hurting the Middle Class," *Boston Review*, September/October 2005, available online at www.bostonreview.net/BR30.5/warrentyagi.html.

25. Warren and Tyagi, *Two-Income Trap*.

26. Christian Weller, "The Middle Class Falls Back," *Challenge* 49, no. 1 (January/February 2006): 16–43.

27. Warren and Tyagi, "What's Hurting the Middle Class," 9.

28. Robert Shiller, *Irrational Exuberance,* 2nd ed. (Princeton, NJ: Princeton University Press, 2005).

29. Heather Boushey, "The Debt Explosion Among College Graduates," (Center for Economic and Policy Research, 2005), available online at www.cepr.net/publications/debt_college_grads.htm#_ftnref4; Sandy Baum, and Marie O'Malley, "College on Credit: How Borrowers

Perceive their Education Debt" (Nellie Mae Corporation, February 2003).

30. Draut and Silva, *Borrowing to Make Ends Meet*, 9, available online at www.demos.org/pubs/borrowing_to_make_ends_meet.pdf; Silva, *House of Cards*.

31. Calculated from Panel Study of Income Data Wealth Supplement, 1984 and 2003.

32. Tamara Draut and Javier Silva, *Generation Broke: The Growth of Debt Among Young Americans* (New York: Demos, October 2004), available online at www.demos.org/pubs/Generation_Broke.pdf.

33. Calculated from Panel Study of Income Data Wealth Supplement, 1984 and 2003.

34. Geoffrey Paulin and Brian Riordan, "Making It on Their Own: The Baby-Boom Meets Generation X," *Monthly Labor Review* 121, no. 2 (February 1998): 18, available online at www.bls.gov/opub/mlr/1998/02/art2full.pdf.

35. Anne L. Alstott, *No Exit: What Parents Owe Their Children and What Society Owes Parents* (New York: Oxford University Press, 2004).

36. Joan Blades and Kristin Rowe-Finkbeiner, *The Motherhood Manifesto: What American Moms Want—And What to Do About It* (New York: Nation Books, 2006); Warren and Tyagi, *Two-Income Trap*, 6.

37. On the amount of time parents spend with children, see Eugene Smolensky and Jennifer Appleton Gootman, *Working Families and Growing Kids* (Washington, DC: National Academies Press, 2003), 32–35. For a good recent review and extension of the time-use research, see Jerry A. Jacobs and Kathleen Gerson, *The Time Divide: Work, Family and Gender Inequality* (Cambridge, MA: Harvard University Press, 2004). The statistic on sleep comes not just from personal experience but also from Andrew Cherlin and Prem Krishnamurthy, "What Works for Mom," *New York Times*, May 9, 2004, sec. 4, 13.

38. Paul W. Newacheck et al., "An Epidemiologic Profile of Children With Special Health Care Needs," *Pediatrics* 102:1 (July 1998): 117–23.

39. Alstott, *No Exit*, 118; Anna Lukemeyer, Marcia K. Meyers, and Timothy Smeeding, "Expensive Children in Poor Families: Out-of-Pocket Expenditures for the Care of Disabled and Chronically Ill Children in Welfare Families," *Journal of Marriage and Family* 62, no. 2 (May 2000): 413.

40. Debby Feyerick, "Baby Boomers Feeling Strain of Caring for Older Parents," *CNN.com*, July 31, 1998, available online at www.cnn.com/HEALTH/9807/31/elder.care.

41. Richard W. Johnson and Joshua M. Wiener, *A Profile of Frail Older Americans and Their Caregivers* (Washington, DC: Urban Institute, February 2006), 64.

42. Feyerick, "Baby Boomers Feeling Strain."

43. Michelle J. Budig and Paula England, "The Wage Penalty for Mother-hood," *American Sociological Review* 66 (2001): 204–25; Deborah J. Anderson, Melissa Binder, and Kate Krause, "The Motherhood Wage

Penalty: Which Mothers Pay It and Why?" *American Economic Review* 92, no. 2 (May 2002): 354–58; Graciela Chichilinsky, "Catastrophic Risks: The Need for New Tools, Financial Instruments and Institutions" (paper prepared for Social Science Research Council Project on the Privatization of Risk, 2005), available online at http://privatizationofrisk.ssrc.org/Chichilnisky/.

44. Torben Iversen and Frances Rosenbluth, "The Political Economy of Gender: Explaining Cross-National Variation in the Gender Division of Labor and the Gender Voting Gap," *American Journal of Political Science* 50, no. 1 (January 2006): 1–19.

45. Centers for Disease Control, "Cohabitation, Divorce, Marriage, and Remarriage in the United States," *Vital and Health Statistics*, ser. 23, no. 22. Department of Health and Human Services, 2002, available online at www.cdc.gov/nchs/data/series/sr_23/sr23_022.pdf.

46. Pamela J. Smock, "The Economic Costs of Marital Disruption for Young Women Over the Past Two Decades," *Demography* 30 (1993): 353–71.

47. Karen C. Holden and Pamela J. Smock, "The Economic Costs of Marital Dissolution: Why Do Women Bear a Disproportionate Cost?" *Annual Review of Sociology* 17 (1991): 51–78.

48. David K. Shipler, *The Working Poor: Invisible in America* (New York: Knopf, 2004), 21–26.

49. Patricia A. McManus and Thomas A. DiPrete, "Losers and Winners: The Financial Consequences of Separation and Divorce for Men," *American Sociological Review* 66 (2001): 246–69.

50. There is some dispute about whether the costs of divorce for women have remained stable or fallen. A recent analysis suggest that the costs have declined, but it is not directly comparable to earlier estimates. Matthew McKeever and Nicholas H. Wolfinger, "Reexamining the Economic Costs of Marital Disruption for Women," *Social Science Quarterly* 82, no. 1 (March 2001): 202–17. Earlier studies suggested little change, at least through the 1980s. Smock, "The Economic Costs of Marital Disruption."

51. Lee Lillard and Linda Waite, "Marriage, Divorce, and the Work and Earning Careers of Spouses," University of Michigan Retirement Research Center, 2003, available online at www.mrrc.isr.umich.edu/publications/briefs/pdf/ib_003.pdf.

52. Warren and Tyagi, *Two-Income Trap*, 85.

CHAPTER 5

1. Associated Press, "United Flight 175 Victims at a Glance," *USA Today* (September 25, 2001), available online at www.usatoday.com/news/nation/2001/09/12/victim-capsule-flight175.htm.

2. Dale Russakoff, "Human Toll of a Pension Default," *Washington Post*, June 13, 2005, A1.

3. Alexei Barrionuevo, "Enron Prosecutors Have Another Key Witness, From Jail," *New York Times,* March 20, 2006, C1.

4. BBC News, "Regulators Probe Enron Stock Selloff," January 14, 2002, available at http://news.bbc.co.uk/1/hi/business/1758345.stm.

5. "Enron Ex-Workers Forlornly View Rubble," *New Hampshire Sunday News*, December 16, 2001, Business.

6. Pension Benefit Guarantee Corporation, "PBGC Announces Maximum Insurance Benefit for 2006," PBGC public affairs press release, December 12, 2005, available online at www.pbgc.gov/media/news-archive/2005/pr06-09.html.

7. Albert B. Crenshaw, "A 401(k) Post Mortem: After Enron, Emphasis on Company Stock Draws Scrutiny," *Washington Post,* December 16, 2001, H1.

8. John H. Langbein, "Understanding the Death of the Private Pension Plan in the United States" (unpublished manuscript, Yale Law School, April 2006).

9. Alicia H. Munnell and Annika Sunden, *Coming Up Short: The Challenge of 401(k) Plans* (Washington, DC: Brookings Institution, 2004), 75–77.

10. Edward A. Zelinsky, "The Defined Contribution Paradigm," *Yale Law Journal* (December 2004): 451–534.

11. Peter Wehner, "Memo on Social Security" (January 5, 2005), 1, available online at www.house.gov/etheridge/WhiteHouseMemo.pdf.

12. Eduardo Porter and Mary Williams Walsh, "Retirement Turns Into a Rest Stop as Benefits Dwindle," *New York Times*, February 9, 2005, available online at www.nytimes.com/2005/02/09/business/09retire.html.

13. Gallup Poll, "Gallup Poll Social Series: Economy and Personal Finance," 2003, question 17.

14. See AARP website, www.aarp.org.

15. Calculated from real stock-price data collated by Robert Shiller and available online at www.irrationalexuberance.com/ie_data.xls.

16. Jonathan Peterson, "Many Forced to Retire Early," *Los Angeles Times*, May 15, 2004, available online at www.latimes.com/business/la-fi-forcedout15May15,0,7334343.story?coll=la-home-headlines

17. Jon Elster, *Ulysses and the Sirens: Studies in Rationality and Irrationality* (New York: Cambridge University Press, 1979).

18. Although AT&T's plan is usually treated as the first formal pension, it was closer to a form of disability insurance, providing a minimal stipend to workers when they could no longer work, rather than providing a true retirement income. I am grateful to John Langbein for alerting me to this fact.

19. U.S. Senate Subcommittee on Labor, *Legislative History of the Employee Retirement Income Security Act of 1974* (Washington, DC: U.S. Government Printing Office, 1976), 4747, 4775.

20. Joint Committee on Taxation, *General Explanation of the Revenue Act of 1978*, 95th Cong., 1979, Joint Committee Print, 84.

21. Alan S. Blinder, "Why is Government in the Pensions Business?" in *Social Security and Private Pensions: Providing for Retirement in the Twenty-First Century*, ed. Susan M. Watcher (Lexington, MA: Lexington Books, 1988), 17–34; Steven Sass, *The Promise of Private Pensions: The First Hundred Years* (Cambridge, MA: Harvard University Press, 1997).

22. Hacker, *Divided Welfare State*, 154.

23. Hewitt Associates, *How Well Are Employees Saving and Investing in 401(k) Plans, 2005 Hewitt Universe Benchmarks* (Lincolnshire, IL: Hewitt Associates, 2005).

24. "Ten Questions with Ted Benna," *Journal of Financial Planning* (January 2003): 16, available online at www.fpanet.org/journal/ articles/2003_Issues/upload/13908_1.pdf.

25. Jason Zweig, "Look Back and Learn," *Money* 28, no. 4 (1999): 94–95.

26. Ibid., 551, 548, 551.

27. Assistant Labor Secretary David George Ball, quoted in Albert Crenshaw, "Pension Proposals Offer Workers Options, Control," *Washington Post*, March 10, 1991, H3.

28. "President Participates in Social Security Conversation in New York," news release, Office of the Press Secretary, White House, May 24, 2005, available online at www.whitehouse.gov/news/releases/2005/05/ 20050524-3.html.

29. Donald Lambro, "Is the 401(k) a GOP Secret Weapon?" *Human Events Online*, April 20, 2006, available online at www.humanevents online.com/article.php?id=14147.

30. All the figures in the previous two paragraphs come from Edward Wolff, *Retirement Insecurity* (Washington, DC: Economic Policy Institute, 2002), 1–2.

31. Employee Benefit Research Institute, "IRA and 401(k)-Type Plan Ownership," vol. 23, no. 6 (June 2002).

32. Peter Orszag, "Progressivity and Savings: Fixing the Nation's Upside-Down Incentives for Savings" (testimony before the House Committee on Education and the Workforce February 25, 2004), available online at www.brookings.edu/views/testimony/orszag/20040225.pdf.

33. Assistant Labor Secretary David George Ball, quoted in Crenshaw, "Pension Proposals Offer Workers Options," H3.

34. Brigitte C. Madrian and Dennis F. Shea, "The Power of Suggestion: Inertia in 401(k) Participation and Savings Behavior," *Quarterly Journal of Economics* 116, no. 4 (2006): 1159.

35. Leonard E. Burman, Norma B. Coe, and William G. Gale, "What Happens When You Show Them the Money: Lump Sum Distributions, Retirement Income Security and Public Policy" (prepared for Second Annual Joint Conference for the Retirement Research Consortium, 2000), available online at www.bc.edu/centers/crr/papers/SV-2%20Burman %20Coe%20Gale.pdf.

36. Gary Engelhardt, "Reasons for Job Change and the Disposition of Pre-Retirement Lump Sum Pension Distributions," available online at www-cpr.maxwell.syr.edu/faculty/engelhardt/econletters.pdf.

37. Wolff, "Is the Equalizing Effect of Retirement Wealth Wearing Off?" 51.

38. Munnell and Sunden, *Coming Up Short*, chap. 4.

39. Gary Burtless, "Risk and Returns of Stock Market Investments Held in Individual Retirement Accounts," Task Force on Social Security Reform, House Budget Committee, (May 11 1999), available online at www.brookings.edu/views/testimony/burtless/19990511.htm.

40. Olivia Mitchell, James Poterba, Mark Warshawsky, and Jeffrey Brown, "New Evidence on the Money's Worth of Individual Annuities," *American Economic Review* 89, no. 5 (1999): 1299–318.

41. Munnell and Sunden, *Coming up Short*, 143–51.

42. Craig Copeland, "Changes in Wealth for Americans Reaching or Just Past Normal Retirement Age," Employee Benefits Research Institute Issue Brief no. 277 (2005): 18.

43. Jeffrey R. Brown, "How Should We Insure Longevity Risk in Pensions and Social Security?" (Center for Retirement Research, an Issue in Brief 4, August 2000), available online at www.bc.edu/centers/crr/issues/ib_4.pdf.

44. Eduardo Porter, "When it Comes to Managing Retirement, Many People Simply Can't," *New York Times*, 18 March 2005, C3.

45. Wolff, *Retirement Insecurity*.

46. Congressional Budget Office (CBO), *Updated Long-Term Projections for Social Security* (Washington, DC: CBO, March 2005), available online at www.cbo.gov/ftpdocs/60xx/doc6064/03-03-LongTerm Projections.pdf.

47. Stuart Butler and Peter Germanis, "Achieving a 'Leninist' Strategy," *Cato Journal* 3, no. 2 (Fall 1983): 548.

48. Butler and Germanis, "Achieving a 'Leninist' Strategy," 552.

49. The articles are too numerous to list here, but see in particular Martin Feldstein, "Social Security, Induced Retirement and Aggregate Capital Accumulation," *Journal of Political Economy* 82, no. 5 (1974); and Feldstein, "Toward a Reform of Social Security," *Public Interest* 40 (Summer 1975). The finding in the first publication that Social Security greatly reduces private savings turned out to be the result of a programming error. Dean R. Leimer and Selig D. Lesnoy, "Social Security and Private Savings: New Time Series Evidence," *Journal of Political Economy* 90, no. 3 (June 1982): 606–29.

50. For a good compendium of the charges, one need look no further than the 2001 report of the President's Commission to Strengthen Social Security, available online at www.csss.gov/reports/Final_report.pdf. See also Michael Tanner, *Social Security and Its Discontents* (Washington, DC: Cato Institute, 2004).

51. In 1994, the advocacy group Third Millennium gained widespread
    attention with its claim that more eighteen- to twenty-year-olds
    believed that "UFOs exist" than that "Social Security will still exist"
    when Generation X retires. The poll on which the claim was based,
    however, was tailor-made to reach this misleading conclusion. In 1997,
    the Employee Benefit Research Institute, an independent research
    organization that forswears taking stands on policy issues, directly
    tested the Third Millennium claim and found that a large majority of
    young Americans believed more strongly that they would receive
    Social Security than that alien life exists. See Fay Lomax Cook and
    Lawrence R. Jacobs, "Americans' Attitudes Toward Social Security:
    Popular Claims Meet Hard Data," National Academy of Social Insur-
    ance, Social Security Brief, No. 10, March 2001, available online at
    www.nasi.org/usr_doc/ss_brief_10.pdf.
52. Butler and Germanis, "A 'Leninist' Strategy for Privatizing Social
    Security," 555.
53. Jason Furman and Robert Greenstein, "An Overview of Issues Raised
    by the Administration's Social Security Plan" (Washington, DC:
    Center on Budget and Policy Priorities, February 2005), 1, available
    online at www.cbpp.org/2-2-05socsec4.pdf.
54. Robert J. Shiller, "The Life-Cycle Personal Accounts Proposal for
    Social Security: An Evaluation," (unpublished manuscript, Yale
    University, March 2005), available online at www.irrational
    exuberance.com/shillersocsec.doc. The 50-50 portfolio is touted in the
    previously cited 2001 report of the President's Commission to Strengthen
    Social Security.
55. Peter J. Ferrara, *Social Security: The Inherent Contradiction* (Wash-
    ington, DC: Cato Institute, 1980).

CHAPTER 6

1. David U. Himmelstein, Elizabeth Warren, Deborah Thorne, and
   Steffie Woolhandler, "Illness And Injury As Contributors to Bankruptcy," *Health Affairs*, Web Exclusive, February 2, 2005, available
   online at http://content.healthaffairs.org/cgi/reprint/hlthaff.w5.
   63v1.pdf. The upper-bound estimate is based on the study's finding
   that 46 percent of bankruptcy filers cited illness or injury as a specific
   reason for bankruptcy and/or had medical bills exceeding $1,000. The
   lower-bound estimate limits the definition of medical bankruptcy just
   to filers who cited illness or injury.
2. John Leland, "When Even Health Insurance is No Safeguard," *New
   York Times*, October 23, 2005, A1.
3. Elizabeth Warren, "Sick and Broke," *Washington Post*, February 9,
   2005, A23, available online at www.washingtonpost.com/wp-dyn/
   articles/A9447-2005Feb8.html.
4. Families USA, "Have Health Insurance? Think You're Well Protected?
   Think Again," February 2005, available online at www.families
   usa.org/assets/pdfs/Health_Care_Think_Again.pdf.

5. Robert W. Seifert and Mark Rukavina, "Bankruptcy Is the Tip of a Medical-Debt Iceberg," *Health Affairs*, Web Exclusive, February 28, 2006, available online at http://content.healthaffairs.org/cgi/content/abstract/hlthaff.25.w89.

6. Carmen DeNavas-Walt, Bernadette D. Proctor, and Cheryl Hill Lee, "Income, Poverty, and Health Insurance Coverage in the United States: 2004," Current Population Reports (Washington, DC: U.S. Census Bureau, August 2005), 16, available online at www.census.gov/prod/2005pubs/p60-229.pdf.

7. Families USA, "One in Three: Non-Elderly Americans Without Health Insurance, 2002–2003 (2004)," 3, available online at www.families usa.org/assets/pdfs/82million_uninsured_report6fdc.pdf.

8. General Motors, "Letter to Stockholders: 2003 Annual Report" (General Motors Corporation, 2003), 3, available online at www.gm.com/company/investor_information/docs/fin_data/gm03ar/letter_3.html.

9. Leland, "When Even Health Insurance is No Safeguard."

10. Albert Crenshaw, "Workers' Family Coverage Reaches $10,880 Average; Small Employers Dropping Plans as Costs Rocket Another 9 Percent," *Washington Post*, September 15, 2005, D2, available online at www.washingtonpost.com/wp-dyn/content/article/2005/09/14/AR2005091400693.html; Milt Freudenheim, "Fewer Employers Totally Cover Health Premiums," *New York Times*, March 23, 2005, available online at http://cohealthinitiative.org/NYTfewer.htm.

11. Sara R. Collins, Karen Davis, Michelle M. Doty, Jennifer L. Kriss, and Alyssa L. Holmgren, "Gaps in Health Insurance: An All-American Problem," The Commonwealth Fund, Washington, DC, April 2006, available online at www.cmwf.org/usr_doc/Collins_gapshltins_920.pdf.

12. Steffie Woolhandler and David U. Himmelstein, "Paying For National Health Insurance—And Not Getting It," *Health Affairs* (July/August 2002): 88–98, available online at http://content.healthaffairs.org/cgi/reprint/21/4/88.

13. John Sheils and Paul Hogan, "The Cost of Tax-Exempt Health Benefits in 2004," *Health Affairs* Web Exclusive, February 25, 2004, available online at http://content.healthaffairs.org/cgi/content/abstract/hlthaff.w4.106v1.

14. Jacob S. Hacker, *The Divided Welfare State: The Battle over Public and Private Social Benefits in the United States* (New York: Cambridge University Press, 2002), 257.

15. George A. Akerlof, "The Market for Lemons: Quality Uncertainty and the Market Mechanism," *Quarterly Journal of Economics* 84, no. 3 (1970).

16. Technical Board on Economic Security, Minutes of the Meeting of the Executive Committee, September 27, 1934, Materials Related to the CES, "Committee Activities," SSAHA. I found this document thanks to the careful review of the CES materials by Jaap Kooijman, "Condition Critical: The Exclusion of a National Health Insurance Program from

the Social Security Act of 1935" (PhD diss., University of Amsterdam, 1994), 33–34.

17. Theodore R. Marmor, *The Politics of Medicare* (Chicago, IL: Aldine Publishing Co., 1973).

18. According to the AFL-CIO's point man for health insurance, Medicare was presented as "a public Blue Cross program. This was our pitch, our strategy: 'Now, we can get this through collective bargaining for our members up to retirement, but we can't do it for the older people.'" Nelson H. Cruikshank, interview, Social Security Administration Project, pt. 3, no. 151, tape-recorded November 18, 1965 (New York: Columbia University Oral History Collection, 1976), 200.

19. Paul Starr, *The Social Transformation of American Medicine* (New York: Basic Books, 1982).

20. Hacker, *Divided Welfare State*, 257.

21. DeNavas-Walt, Proctor, and Lee, "Income, Poverty, and Health Insurance Coverage," table C-1, 60.

22. Jacob S. Hacker, *The Road to Nowhere: The Genesis of President Clinton's Plan for Health Security* (Princeton, NJ: Princeton University Press, 1997), 128.

23. Starr, *Social Transformation*.

24. Dan Balz and Ronald Brownstein, *Storming the Gates: Protest Politics and the Republican Revival* (Boston, MA: Little, Brown, 1996).

25. Joseph Newhouse, *Free For All?: Lessons from the Rand Health Insurance Experiment* (Cambridge, MA: Harvard University Press, 1993).

26. Robert Dreyfuss and Peter H. Stone, "Medikill," *Mother Jones* (January/February 1996), available online at www.motherjones.com/news/feature/1996/01/medikill.html#start.

27. Jonathan Cohn, "Crash Course," *New Republic* 233, no. 19 (2005).

28. See, for example, John C. Goodman and Gerald Musgrave, *Patient Power: The Free Enterprise Alternative to Clinton's Health Plan* (Washington, DC: Cato Institute, 1994). For a more recent example, see R. Glenn Hubbard, John F. Cogan, and Daniel P. Kessler, *Healthy, Wealthy, and Wise: Five Steps to a Better Health Care System* (Washington, DC: AEI Press/Hoover Institution, 2005).

29. David Cutler and Richard Zeckhauser, "Adverse Selection in Health Insurance," in *Frontiers in Health Policy Research*, vol. 1, ed. A. Garber (Cambridge, MA: MIT Press, 1998), 1–31.

30. John C. Goodman, "Health Savings Accounts Will Revolutionize American Health Care," National Center for Policy Analysis, Brief Analysis no. 464 (January 15, 2004), available online at www.ncpa.org/pub/ba/ba464/.

31. Employee Benefit Research Institute, "Early Experience With High-Deductible and Consumer-Driven Health Plans: Findings From the EBRI/Commonwealth Fund Consumerism in Health Care Survey," Issue Brief no. 288 (December 2005), available online at www.ebri.org/publications/ib/index.cfm?fa=ibDisp&content_id=3606.

32. Cohn, "Crash Course"; Eric Dash, "Health Savings Accounts Attract Wall Street," *New York Times*, January 27, 2006.
33. Cybele Weisser, "A Health Revolution in Slo-Mo," *Money* 34, no. 7 (2005).
34. Dash, "Health Savings Accounts."
35. Milt Freudenheim, "Bush Health Savings Accounts Slow to Gain Acceptance," *New York Times*, October 13, 2004, C1.
36. Susan Chambers, "Reviewing and Revising Wal-Mart's Benefits Strategy," Supplemental Benefits Memorandum, Board of Directors Retreat FY06, Wal-Mart, Inc. (2005), available online at www.nytimes.com/packages/pdf/business/26walmart.pdf.
37. Ibid., 11.
38. Almost immediately after its creation, the key architect of the legislation in the Johnson administration started developing secret plans for extending Medicare to all children in the United States. Hacker, *Divided Welfare State,* 251.
39. Victoria Colliver, "Retiree Health Benefits Decline," *San Francisco Chronicle*, December 15, 2004, C1.
40. Jacob S. Hacker, "Privatizing Risk without Privatizing the Welfare State: The Hidden Politics of Social Policy Retrenchment in the United States," *American Political Science Review* 98, no. 2 (May 2004): 253.
41. Heather McGhee and Tamara Draut, *Retiring in the Red: The Growth of Debt among Older Americans*, 2nd ed. (New York: Demos, January 2004), available online at www.demos.org/pubs/Retiring_2ed.pdf.
42. Hacker, *Divided Welfare State*, 326.
43. Social Security Administration (SSA), *Income of the Aged Chartbook*, 2000 (Washington, DC: SSA, September 2004), available online at www.ssa.gov/policy/docs/chartbooks/income_aged/2002/index.html.
44. Henry J. Aaron and Robert D. Reischauer, "The Medicare Reform Debate: What is the Next Step?" *Health Affairs* 14, no 4 (1995). Proposals differ on how the level of this support would be determined; in most, it would be geared to some sort of average of private and Medicare premiums.
45. Families USA, "The Medicare Drug Program Fails to Reach Low-Income Seniors," Washington, DC, May 2006, available online at www.familiesusa.org/assets/pdfs/Medicare-Enrollment-report-May-2006.pdf.
46. See Jacob S. Hacker and Paul Pierson, *Off Center: The Republican Revolution and the Erosion of American Democracy* (New Haven, CT: Yale University Press, 2005), 85–93.
47. Marilyn Moon, "Restructuring Medicare's Cost-Sharing," The Commonwealth Fund (December 1996), available online at www.cmwf.org/Publications/Publications_show.htm?doc_id=221428.

48. Mark Merlis, "Opening the Federal Employees Health Benefits Program to Individual Purchasers," study conducted for the U.S. Department of Health and Human Services (July 31, 2001), 10–11, available online at www.markmerlis.com/FEHBP.pdf.

49. Adam Clymer, "Of Touching Third Rails and Tackling Medicare," *New York Times*, October 27, 1995, 21.

50. Presentation by Colleen Grogan at a conference on "Health Care in America," Northwestern University, January 2006.

51. Martha Shirk, with the assistance of Cathy Trost and Susan Schultz, *In Their Own Words: The Uninsured Talk about Living without Health Insurance* (Washington, DC: KFF, 2000), available online at www.kff.org/uninsured/2207-index.cfm.

52. Janet Currie, *The Invisible Safety Net: Protecting the Nation's Poor Children and Families* (Princeton, NJ: Princeton University Press, 2006), 60.

53. Currie, *Invisible Safety Net*, 45.

54. Ibid., 59–60.

CONCLUSION

1. The seminal work is Daniel Kahneman and Amos Tversky, "Prospect Theory: An Analysis of Decision Under Risk," *Econometrica* 47 (1979): 263–91. See also Daniel Kahneman, Paul Slovic, and Amos Tversky, *Judgment Under Uncertainty: Heuristics and Biases* (New York: Cambridge University Press, 1982); and Matthew Rabin and Richard H. Thaler, "Anomalies: Risk Aversion," *Journal of Economic Perspectives* 15 (2001): 219–32.

2. See, for example, Kevin J. Lansing, "Spendthrift Nation," *Federal Reserve Bank of San Francisco Economic Letter* 30 (November 2005), available online at www.frbsf.org/publications/economics/letter/2005/el2005-30.pdf.

3. Colin Camerer, Linda Babcock, George Loewenstein, and Richard Thaler, "Labor Supply of New York City Cabdrivers: One Day at a Time," *Quarterly Journal of Economics* (May 1997): 407–41.

4. This should not be confused with the question of whether college quality in general influences future earnings positively—the research clearly suggests it does. But there is only "weak evidence that alumni/ae from private institutions earn more than graduates from publicly controlled institutions." James Monks, "The Returns to Individual and College Characteristics: Evidence from the National Longitudinal Survey of Youth," *Economics of Education Review* 19, no. 3 (2000): 288.

5. Peter L. Bernstein, *Against the Gods: The Remarkable Story of Risk* (New York: Wiley, 1996).

6. Available online at www.nytimes.com/packages/html/national/20050515_CLASS_GRAPHIC/index_04.html.

7. The quote is from focus groups of middle-class families conducted by the Economic Policy Institute in Indianapolis and Atlanta in March

2005. I am grateful to Jared Bernstein for providing me with the Institute's interim report on these focus groups, which describes their main findings.

8. There is new evidence, for example, that economic instability, as distinct from low income, impairs childhood development, at least in lower-income families. See Ariel Kalil and Kathleen M. Ziol-Guest, "Lifetime Income Level, Stability, and Growth: Links to Children's Behavior, Achievement, and Health" (Harris School of Public Policy Studies, University of Chicago, May 2006).

9. Lloyd Free and Hadley Cantril, *The Political Beliefs of Americans* (New Brunswick, NJ: Rutgers University Press, 1967).

10. CBS News, "President Presses Economic Plan," February 7, 2003, available online at www.cbsnews.com/stories/2003/02/07/politics/main539829.shtml.

11. See, for example, Lake Snell Perry Mermin, "National Survey," June 2005, available online at www.ourfuture.org/docUploads/lake_poll_july2005.pdf.

12. Mary Williams Walsh, "Major Changes Raise Concerns on Pension Bill," *New York Times*, March 19, 2006, 1.

13. Daron Acemoglu, and Robert Shimer, "Productivity Gains from Unemployment Insurance," NBER Working Paper no. 7352 (Cambridge, MA, September 1999).

14. For a recent review, see Lori G. Kletzer, *Job Loss from Imports: Measuring the Costs* (Washington, DC: Institute for International Economics, 2001).

15. National Partnership for Women and Families, *Expecting Better: A State-by-State Analysis of Parental Leave Programs* (Washington, DC: National Partnership for Women and Families, 2005), 9.

16. Quoted in Tamara Draut, *Strapped: Why America's Twenty- and Thirty-Somethings Can't Get Ahead* (New York: Doubleday, 2005), 156.

17. National Partnership for Women & Families, *Expecting Better*, 9.

18. Draut, *Strapped*, 157.

19. Karen Kornbluh, "The Joy of 'Flex,'" *Washington Monthly*, December 2000, available online at www.washingtonmonthly.com/features/2005/0512.kornbluh.html.

20. Peter R. Orszag, "Progressivity and Saving: Fixing the Nation's Upside-Down Incentives for Saving," Testimony Before the House Committee on Education and the Workforce, February 25, 2004, available online at www.brookings.edu/views/testimony/orszag/20040225.htm.

21. See *Medicare Tomorrow: The Report of the Century Foundation Task Force on Medicare Reform* (New York: Century Foundation Press, 2001).

22. Jacob S. Hacker and Mark Schlesinger, "Good Medicine," *American Prospect*, October 2, 2004.

23. A basic description of the plan is available online at www.kaisernet work.org/health_cast/uploaded_files/Jacob_Hacker_Presentation.pdf. Further details are available online at www.rwjf.org/files/research/ costCoverageHacker.pdf

24. I estimate that Universal Insurance—with six months of unemployment and temporary disability benefits, a year of survivors' benefits, three months of sickness and maternity benefits, and coverage of catastrophic health costs—costs between $35 and $55 billion a year, depending on how generously it replaces lost income and finances catastrophic expenses. This may seem a huge sum, but it is only a small fraction of what Social Security costs, and no more than is spent to subsidize 401(k)s each year—for comprehensive insurance protection against a wide range of risks.

25. In the initial proposal I have developed, the losses covered are unemployment, loss of wages due to sickness or childbirth, temporary disability, and the death of a spouse, as well as catastrophic health costs.

26. Because Universal Insurance is an income-protection program, it would not take into account so-called in-kind benefits, such as Medicaid and subsidized child care. Under the proposal, Universal Insurance benefits would also not be counted against eligibility for antipoverty programs (although they would be treated as taxable income for all beneficiaries at the end of the year). Nonetheless, many Americans would be prevented from falling into poverty by Universal Insurance—more than a third of those who experience the risks that the program covers end up in poverty as a result—and thus would not need to sign up for antipoverty benefits in the first place.

27. Indeed, if Universal Insurance were successful, it could incorporate "caregivers insurance" that provides modest assistance to people for whom providing family care—either purchasing it in the market, or taking time off to provide it themselves—represents a substantial share of their income. If caring for a family member—whether a sick kid or an ailing parent—seriously risks someone's income, government should step in to ease the blow. After all, it is far better that family members care for each other than that they feel they must shift this care to more expensive publicly financed institutions. It makes no sense that government does not support an aging man who cares for his wife with Alzheimer's at home, while it will pay for her care if he sends her to a nursing home.

28. Across states, for example, entrepreneurship is associated with more lenient bankruptcy laws. Across nations, private venture capital is associated with strong risk protections for investors. Wei Fan and Michelle White, "Personal Bankruptcy and the Level of Entrepreneurial Activity," *Journal of Law and Economics* 46 (October 2003): 543–67; John Armour and Douglas Cumming, "The Legal Road to Replicating Silicon Valley" (paper read at Babson Entrepreneurship Conference, at Glasgow, Scotland, 2004).

Index

entrepreneurship, 67, 179, 225n. 28
Erksa, Dennis, 79–80
Erksa, Sandy, 79
estate taxes, 185
Europe, 24, 32, 43

"falls from grace," 30–32, 193
families. *See also* children and child
    care
  and debt, 94–100
  and divorce, 30, 105–7, 215n. 50
  and economic risk, 8
  family leave, 89–90, 183–84,
      212n. 8
  incomes of, 2–3, 3–5, 21–23, 30,
      88–89, 90–94, 96–97, 100,
      107–8, 181, 202–3n. 36, 203–
      4n. 38, 304n. 39
  and risk shift, 87–90, 107–8
  women in the workforce, 177,
      181
  work-family conflict, 183
Family and Medical Leave Act
    (1993), 89–90, 183–84
Farber, Henry, 70
Federal Employees Health Benefit
    Program, 158
Federal Reserve Bank of Boston, 73
fee-for-service care, 188
Feldstein, Martin, 49–51, 130
feminism, 89
Ferrara, Peter, 134
Fidelity Investments, 93
financial markets, 126. *See also*
    stock market
flexibility in the workforce, 82
Folsom, Marion, 45–46, 47
forced savings, 112–13
foreclosures. *See also* bankruptcy
  and children, 91
  and families, 94
  and layoffs, 61
  and medical expenses, 88, 137–
      38
  rates of, 13, 33

Fortune 500, 66
401(k)s. *See also* defined-
    contribution plans
  borrowing against, 170
  cost of, 225n. 24
  described, 53–54
  and Enron, 112
  and families, 93
  origins of, 113, 118–21
  and risk pooling, 121–28
  shortcomings of, 185
  and Social Security, 121, 122,
      134
  virtues of, 171, 186
  vs. pensions, 62
Franklin, Benjamin, 83
fraud, 47
Frazier, Kathleen, 155, 162
Free, Lloyd, 178

Gallup polls, 17, 101, 201n. 22
gambling, 26
Gates, Bill, 21
Geerling, Teresa, 61, 68, 71, 84, 167
gender
  and earnings gap, 105–7
  and education, 74
  and income volatility, 27
  and insecurity, 7
  and part-time employment, 81–
      82
  and raising children, 103, 104–5
  and unemployment, 73
  women in the workforce, 87, 88,
      177, 181
  and work hours, 83, 89
General Electric (GE), 66
General Motors (GM), 80, 138
Generation X, 99, 219n. 51
Gentry, Stephen, 77
geographic issues, 7, 78
Germany, 32
Gingrich, Newt, 150–51, 158
Glassman, James K., 52–53, 56
Global Crossing, 124
global economy, 6, 63–64

and public opinion, 129–30,
  219n. 51
and retirement stability, 128–34
threats to, 185
trends influencing, 36
vs. retirement accounts, 127
South Africa, 24
Southwest Airlines, 169
specific investment, 78–79
Sperling, Gene, 66
spot markets, 66
standard of living, 108
Stark, Pete, 189
states, 146, 161
stock market
  declines in, 5
  and families, 95
  and 401(k)s, 118, 121–22
  and retirement planning, 115,
    125–27
  and risk, 19
  and Social Security
    privatization, 131
stop-loss programs, 191
structural unemployment, 68–69,
  84
student loans, 75
subsidies, 43, 49, 54, 56–57
supplemental insurance, 154
surveys. *See* public opinion
Sweden, 24, 43
Sylvester, Linda, 104

taxation and tax policy
  and bankruptcy, 192
  and benefit restructuring, 54
  estate taxes, 185
  and 401(k)s, 119, 123, 125
  and income volatility, *2*, 27
  and insurance subsidies, 43, 44,
    49, 54, 56–57
  and market failures, 50–51
  and medical expenses, 140
  and Medical Savings Accounts,
    151
  payroll taxes, 185

and retirement planning, 171,
  184
and risk pooling, 179
and Social Security, 131–32, 185
tax cuts, 56
taxicab drivers, 67
technology, 3–4, 5, 11, 77
telecommunications, 75
terrorism, 5, 109
Texas, 161
Thatcher, Margaret, 55
Third Millennium, 219n. 51
time-use research, 102–3
Titusville, Florida, 147
transition costs, 131
Tversky, Amos, 25
two-income families, 90–94, 96–97,
  100, 107–8, 181
The Two-Income Trap (Warren and
  Tyagi), 96–97
Tyagi, Amelia Warren, 96–97

uncertainty. *See* insecurity
unemployment. *See also* layoffs and
  job loss
  cyclical, 68–69
  and the endowment effect, 26
  and gender, 73
  involuntary, 69–70
  long-term, 70–72, 83–84, 182
  as a market failure, 50–51
  rate, 18, 63, *70*, 71–72
  and recessions, 69
  shadow unemployment, 72
  structural unemployment, 68–
    69, 84
  temporary, 84
  and unemployment insurance,
    83–85, 182–84
uninsured population, x, 13–14,
  138, 139, 141
unions, 94, 117, 119, 166, 190
United Airlines, 109–10, 110–11
Universal 401(k)s, 186–87
universal health coverage, 161–63,
  187–90, 190–91